100 THINGS MARYLAND FANS SHOULD KNOW & DO BEFORE THEY DIE

Don Markus

TRIUMPH BOOKS

This book is available in quantity at special discounts for your group or organization. For further information, contact:

Triumph Books LLC
814 North Franklin Street
Chicago, Illinois 60610
(312) 337-0747
www.triumphbooks.com

Printed in U.S.A.
ISBN: 978-1-62937-268-6
Design by Patricia Frey
Photos courtesy of AP Images

For my two sons, Russell and Jordan,
who grew up hating Duke.

For my wife, Judy, who made the trip
to Atlanta to see grown men cry.

For all Maryland fans, who await
another trip to the promised land.

Contents

Foreword

Walking into Cole Field House in February of 1963 for the first time is something I will never forget. It was the Eastern Regionals and 14,000 people were packed in the stands. I was on my recruiting trip as a high school senior. Cole was a magnificent on-campus arena, as good as any in the country. I made my decision to attend the University of Maryland and play basketball that night. That started a 53-year relationship with Maryland basketball that is still ongoing.

I was fortunate to play for a sound, fundamental coach in Bud Millikan. If you were a point guard, you had to learn the total game and how to run a team. I was fortunate to have that background as a player to begin my coaching career.

In 1968, I left Maryland having been a very average player but having had the opportunity to compete against some of the best players and teams in the country. I was on my way to my first coaching job. I was taking the job as a junior varsity coach at Woodrow Wilson High School in Camden, New Jersey. My goal was to be a varsity head coach and be a career high school basketball coach. I would always be a fan of Maryland basketball.

The modern era of Maryland basketball started with the hiring of Lefty Driesell in 1970. Coming from Davidson, Lefty brought the swagger and confidence to compete in the Atlantic Coast Conference and put the program on a national level. Lefty brought excitement to Cole Field House. Lefty's early recruits, players like Jim O'Brien, Tom McMillen, and Len Elmore, set the stage for outstanding teams. The great Len Bias may have been the most talented player to play for Lefty. Both Bud Millikan and Lefty coached Maryland basketball for 17 years.

I became the basketball coach in 1989. I followed Bob Wade. We received serious sanctions from the NCAA and I needed help to get through the sanctions. It came from my players and assistants. We all bought in to being as good as we could be during this time. Billy Hahn, a former player and my top assistant, was a big help. Players like Tony Massenberg, Kevin Mclinton, and Cedric Lewis helped us to stay competitive during the sanction period. Being able to coach Walt Williams during that time was a highlight of my coaching career. We are lifetime friends.

Coming out of the sanctions, we only won two regular season ACC league games. But with Joe Smith and Keith Booth, both freshmen, we were able to get to the Sweet 16. That started a good run of Sweet 16s, but we were not able to crack the Final Four glass ceiling. Finally, in 2001, we broke through.

Beating No. 1–seed Stanford to get to the Final Four gave us confidence that we could win it all. But we lost a controversial game to eventual-champion Duke in our fourth game against them that season. We were able to regroup and win the national championship in 2002. Juan Dixon, Steve Blake, Byron Mouton, Lonnie Baxter, Chris Wilcox, Taj Holden, Drew Nicholas, Ryan Randle, Calvin McCall, and Mike Grinnon were a great NCAA tournament team. I had outstanding assistants in Jimmy Patsos, Dave Dickerson, and Maat Korvarik.

Greivis Vasquez was a special player who I coached from 2006 to 2010. He was an inspirational player who had many great games against the best teams. His greatest game may have been his last. In the NCAA tournament, we lost on a last-second shot. It is safe to say, though, that no Maryland basketball player ever had a better NCAA tournament game than Greivis that day.

Starting with Lefty Driesell, no one has covered Maryland basketball like Don Markus. In his book, *100 Things Maryland Fans Should Know & Do Before They Die*, Don shares his special insight with all Maryland basketball fans. His stories are part of the fabric of Maryland basketball.

The stories will continue as Mark Turgeon carries on the Maryland basketball tradition.

Don Markus' book brings back many memories for me. I am sure the book will do the same for you.

—Gary Williams

1 UCLA of the East

In the spring of 1969, Vince Lombardi was starting his first season coaching the Washington Redskins after coming out of a two-year retirement following his legendary career in Green Bay. Ted Williams was in his first season managing the Washington Senators, finally bored after nearly a decade of deep sea fishing following his retirement from the Boston Red Sox.

In a city torn apart by riots the previous year after the assassination of Dr. Martin Luther King and the mushrooming anti-war protests of Vietnam, sports fans in the nation's capital were counting on these two transcendent figures to lift the sagging fortunes of their hapless sports franchises. Then there was a third, not nearly as well-known as Lombardi or Williams.

Enter Charles "Lefty" Driesell.

That's how newly named Maryland athletic director Jim Kehoe pitched the idea to the 37-year-old Driesell of coming to coach the Terps.

"They came in and talked to me before the season was over and I told them, 'I have a chance to win the national championship, I'll talk to you after the season is over,'" recalled Driesell, who was then in his ninth season at little Davidson College in North Carolina.

Coincidently, and conveniently, Davidson's season ended in the NCAA tournament regional finals at Cole Field House, on a last-second shot by North Carolina star Charlie Scott, who according to Driesell had initially committed to playing for the Wildcats out of Laurinburg Institute, where he had been the school's valedictorian.

1

Kehoe, only a few months on the job, didn't want Driesell to leave town.

"Kehoe grabs me after the game and we started talking," Driesell said. "He said, 'We've got Vince Lombardi coaching the Redskins, we've got Ted Williams managing the Senators, and we need you to coach basketball. I thought, *That sounds pretty good.* Plus he was going to pay more money and do this and that."

The morning of Driesell's introductory press conference, he went to breakfast with Kehoe and Jay McMillen, who had finished his Maryland career the year before and was living in the area. McMillen compared the Maryland job to national power UCLA because it was a state school at the time made up mostly of commuters, its campus in close proximity to Washington.

"We were eating breakfast with coach Kehoe and Jay said, 'You could make this the UCLA of the East,' and I said, 'Yeah, we probably could if your brother came here,'" Driesell said. "I said, 'You've got to help me recruit him,' and he said he would. And that's one reason Tom came, to tell you the truth. More or less, it was a recruiting pitch to get Tom McMillen."

At the press conference that afternoon, Driesell boldly predicted that Maryland "had the potential to be the UCLA of the East Coast or I wouldn't be here."

Close to a half century later, Driesell said, "It was always my goal to have my team in the top 10, I said that at Davidson and they thought I was on drugs. That's me. I think I can take anybody right now [at age 83] and put 'em in the top 10. That's how cocky I am…. That's why my players were cocky, because they believed what I told 'em."

Driesell said that the line helped him recruit not only Tom McMillen, then considered the best high school player in the country, but Len Elmore and "all the other players I got the first couple of years."

Some believe that the line might have come back to burn Driesell.

"I don't care about that," Driesell said. "At Maryland, my goal was always to get in the top 10. I put a banner up in Cole Field House that I have a picture of, of every team that finished in the top 10. I had six teams ranked in the final top 10 and I had six banners up there in the rafters. To me, that's probably tougher than winning the national championship sometimes."

Of those six teams that finished in the top 10, three never even made it to the NCAA tournament, including the 1973–74 team that went 23–5 (with all five defeats to ranked teams) and saw its season end in a 103–100 overtime loss to North Carolina State in the ACC tournament championship, a game many considered the best ever played until the Duke-Kentucky classic in the 1992 NCAA tournament.

Driesell's teams won 348 games in 17 years at Maryland, and went to the NCAA tournament eight times, reaching the Elite Eight twice. During the course of his time in College Park, Driesell coached against North Carolina's Dean Smith for all of his tenure and against Duke's Mike Krzyzewski for his last six years ("and we beat Duke more than they beat us").

Only Smith won more ACC games during Driesell's time in the league.

"We were playing in the toughest league in the country, no question the ACC was the toughest league in the country," Driesell said. "Bobby Knight didn't have to win his league to get into the NCAA because the Big Ten didn't have a tournament then. UCLA didn't have a lot of competition out there. That was my goal, to put my team in the top 10."

2 Garyland

Gary Williams was a few months into his job at Ohio State when Lefty Driesell was fired in the fall of 1986. He had followed the tragic death of Maryland star Len Bias from a distance, as he was busy recruiting for the Buckeyes.

At 41, Williams was considered one of the up-and-coming stars in the business of coaching college basketball, having built his resume at American University in Washington, D.C., and later at Boston College in the early years of the Big East.

Some of his friends back East had told Williams that he would have been the perfect choice to replace Driesell, being an alumnus and having coached in the nation's capital.

But they also told him not to expect getting a call from the embattled chancellor, John Slaughter.

In the aftermath of Bias' death from a cocaine overdose that June, the entire athletic program was in upheaval. Popular athletic director Dick Dull, a cool Californian who once used Susan Anton to promote the Terps, had resigned amid the chaos.

Slaughter had consulted with several high-profile coaches, including basketball legend Dean Smith of North Carolina and John Thompson of Georgetown, about whom he should hire. Their answer: Bob Wade, a legend himself on the high school level at Dunbar in Baltimore.

"It was as if roosters were running the henhouse," said Marvin Perry, the president of the school's chief athletic fundraising arm, the Terrapin Club.

The phone call to Williams never came, at least not that fall.

"It would have been hard, but I would have had to do it," Williams said nearly 30 years later. "Maryland's my school."

It took three more years—a tumultuous stretch that saw Wade often overmatched on the sideline despite inheriting a lot of talent and using his recruiting connections with Nike impresario Sonny Vaccaro to get more—for Wade's reign of error to end amid NCAA violations.

This time, there was no doubt for the Terps or their former captain.

Gary Williams holds up the net after the Terps' 2002 NCAA final victory over Indiana. (John Bazemore)

Though the university went through the formality of naming a search committee to find Wade's successor, even one of the men brought in for an interview knew that Williams was going to be hired.

"He's the man," said George Raveling, a former Driesell assistant who by then was coaching Southern Cal.

At an emotional press conference, the first of several during what became a 22-season career in College Park that turned Williams from an up-and-comer to a Hall of Famer, the then–44-year-old teared up when talking about what pulled him from Columbus back to College Park.

Giving up a rising program that had just signed high school star Jimmy Jackson for one that was on the brink of NCAA probation, Williams inherited a talented team that included three future NBA players—Walt Williams, Jerrod Mustaf, and Tony Massenburg—but one that was relegated to the NIT after it was announced that the Terps would be put on three-year probation beginning the following season.

"To leave Ohio State, I think I can really say, honestly, that I would never have left there except for the University of Maryland," Williams said in an interview a few days before his Hall of Fame enshrinement in August of 2014. "I felt some responsibility [as an alumnus]. I knew they weren't in great shape, I didn't know how bad a shape they were in when I went back."

Told by then–athletic director Lew Perkins that the Terps would get a "slap on the wrist" by the NCAA, Williams watched as his ascending career plateaued and nearly derailed by what he and others believe were the toughest NCAA sanctions since the SMU football program was given the death penalty.

"We felt slighted, with that feeling that we were still paying the price for having that black cloud from the Len Bias tragedy hanging over us," said Massenburg.

The Terps had winning records his first two seasons, the second played without not only Mustaf, who became a first-round draft pick of the New York Knicks, and Massenburg, who had graduated and begun a long career in the NBA that culminated with him winning a ring with the San Antonio Spurs, but also a month without Walt Williams because of a broken leg.

Eventually, the probation caught up with the Terps. Williams recalled crying on the phone as Randolph Childress told him that he was going to Wake Forest (where he would be joined by relative unknown big man Tim Duncan) because of the sanctions that included two years out of postseason competition and one year off live television.

Other future college stars, including Lawrence Moten of Syracuse and Donyell Marshall of Connecticut, also passed up the Terps.

Even after coming off probation and recruiting local stars Duane Simpkins, Johnny Rhodes, and Exree Hipp, Maryland suffered through its worst season under Williams, going 12–16 in 1992–93. Those annual mentions of Williams as a candidate for this job or that—including Kansas after Larry Brown left—dried up.

"The doubts creep in as time goes by," he said, sitting in the basement of his home a few days before heading up to Springfield and the Naismith Hall of Fame, his voice choking with emotion. "So you're thinking, maybe you can't get this thing turned around."

The turnaround started the next year. After beating out Kentucky for Baltimore high school phenom Keith Booth, Williams' luck turned when a relatively unknown skinny center from Norfolk, Virginia,—Driesell's hometown—arrived. Two years later, and two Sweet 16 appearances later, Joe Smith was the No. 1 pick in the NBA draft.

Garyland was open for business.

3 Moses Malone Was Nearly a Terp

When Moses Malone died in the summer of 2015 of a heart attack at age 60, all of the obituaries talked about his Hall of Fame NBA career, highlighted by his now-famous "Fo, fo, and fo" comment that predated the championship run by the 1983 Philadelphia 76ers that was a game shy of the sweep their center had bluntly predicted.

There was also mention made of Malone's humble roots in Petersburg, Virginia, and how he was the first high school player to make the jump straight to professional basketball, in his case the Utah Stars of the old American Basketball Association, in the late summer and early fall of 1974. There was no mention made of how Malone had nearly become a Maryland Terp.

In reality, Lefty Driesell always considered Malone one of "my guys." After working nearly to exhaustion with the help of assistant coach Dave Pritchard to land the 6'11", 270-pound man-child, Driesell got a call from Malone one day after signing with Maryland. Malone said that a representative of the Stars was in the two-room house he and his mother shared.

"Moses' mother was making about $25 a week as an orderly. He said, 'He's got $10,000 on my coffee table, I've never seen a $10 bill,'" Driesell recalled a couple of months after Malone had passed away in 2015. "I told him, 'You get him out of your house and tell him if he ain't out of there in five minutes, [you're] calling the police.'"

After the man left, Driesell called Malone back and told him, "Moses, you're not signing for anything less than a million. So don't even talk to anybody for less than a million.' The guy from Utah calls me up one Sunday and says, "Coach, I've got a million-dollar contract here for Moses, is it okay if he signs it?' I said, 'He might sign it.'"

Malone spent the summer working a $7-an-hour construction job Driesell had arranged for him near College Park, and showed the kind of work ethic he displayed throughout his NBA career.

"His high school coach got mad at me because he had to wear safety shoes and a helmet. His coach said, 'Moses is going to get hurt,'" Driesell said. "I told his coach, 'I don't want him to get hurt more than you do.' The guy who hired him told him to meet him on his porch every day at 6:30 or 7:00 and [he'd] take [Moses] to work. He said, 'Moses was never late the whole summer.'"

As the summer went on, Driesell started to plan for the 1974–75 season, with Malone expected to take over inside from the recently graduated Len Elmore and Tom McMillen. The Stars were persistent, raising the offer at once to the million dollars Driesell had told Malone to negotiate for himself.

One day, the same representative showed up at Driesell's house.

"We go in the house, his name was Showalter or something like that, and I told him, 'This contract isn't worth more than $500,000,'" Driesell said. "He was guaranteed $500,000 and he would be given the rest if he made the team the next two years. I told him, 'Get out of here. He's not signing anything. I told you, he's not signing for anything less than a million.'"

A week later, the team rep called up Driesell again and said he had a million dollar guarantee from the team owner.

"I said, 'It's over my head,'" said Driesell. "If it is guaranteed, I told him to call Donald Dell, who was my agent."

A couple of days later, Dell called Driesell and asked him to meet him at a hotel by National Airport.

"I asked, 'What's up?' He said, 'Moses and his mother want to talk with you.' [Donald] said the Utah Stars had guaranteed him a million dollars. If he walks out of the hotel and gets hit by a car and can never play again, he will have a million dollars in his pocket. I told Donald that I wanted the Stars to pay him for every credit he takes toward a college degree. They put it in there that they would pay him $25,000 or $50,000 for every credit he passes toward a college degree."

The next year saw the NBA follow suit, drafting high school players Darryl Dawkins and Bill Willoughby.

"I told Donald, 'If Moses comes to Maryland and plays basketball I know he'll be first team All-American, he'll get $2 million from the NBA, because he'll have some bargaining power," Driesell said. "Donald said, 'Moses, I think you can probably do that.' [But] Moses said that his goal was to be the best high school player in the country by the end of his junior year and the first player to go straight to the pros from high school."

Malone said that his mother had him read the Bible every day and that "the Lord would punish me" if he turned down the chance.

"I told him, 'Moses, the Lord doesn't care if you come to Maryland for a year,'" said Driesell.

Malone signed with the Stars, who were on their last legs before folding, averaging 18 points and 14 rebounds as a rookie. Malone's 21-year career began in the ABA, but he made his reputation in the NBA, where he became a three-time league MVP, as well as being the MVP of the 1983 Finals, a 12-time all-star, and a member of the NBA's 50th anniversary team.

His picture also stayed in Maryland's press guide for the remainder of Driesell's career in College Park.

"If he'd gone two more days and not signed [with the Stars], he couldn't sign and he would've been at Maryland," Driesell said.

4 Cool Hand Luke

One of the most celebrated athletes ever to make his way through Maryland was John Lucas. He was not only the first freshman to start for Lefty Driesell—and the first ever to lead the ACC tournament in scoring—but he became an All-American in two sports in College Park.

When Driesell was recruiting the left-handed point guard out of Durham, North Carolina, his biggest competition did not come from North Carolina or Duke but from UCLA, which was recruiting Lucas to play tennis at the behest of former Bruins star Arthur Ashe.

Driesell first heard about this two-sport progeny from a close friend in Durham who knew Driesell from his days playing at Duke. Paul Williamson was the coach at East Durham Junior High School when Driesell was a student teacher there in the early 1950s.

"He just said, 'I think you ought to look at him; he's a great tennis player,'" Driesell said. "Arthur Ashe really wanted him to go to UCLA and that's where his sister wanted him to go to play tennis. Dean Smith said in the newspaper that he was a great tennis player and a good basketball player."

Driesell sent his assistant, George Raveling, down to scout Lucas and "he wasn't that impressed."

He called Williamson to tell him that he thought Maryland was going to pass, and "he told me if we don't take him I'll never speak to you again," Driesell said. "He was one of my best friends, I always asked him for advice."

So Driesell signed Lucas sight unseen. The first time Driesell ever saw Lucas play in person came during an East-West high school all-star game that spring in the Greensboro Coliseum.

"I think he scored 38 points, he might have had 40," Driesell said. "I was really happy."

When Lucas got on campus to join sophomores Tom McMillen and Len Elmore along with fellow freshman Mo Howard, the man everyone would soon be calling "Cool Hand Luke"—based on the Paul Newman movie—took over.

"He played a couple of scrimmages and he scored about 50 points," Driesell said. "I don't remember saying it, but he told me that I said, 'You're a point guard, you have to distribute the ball a little bit, don't worry about scoring so much.' He says, 'I could have averaged 50 if I wanted to.'"

Lucas averaged only 18.3 points over his career, but finished as the school's all-time leading scorer (now fifth) with 2,015 points and first in assists (now fifth) with 514. Lucas was the first Maryland player to be a three-time All-ACC player, a three-time All-American, and was the No. 1 selection in the 1976 NBA draft.

In the spring, Lucas was an All-American in tennis and went on to play briefly in the professional ranks in World Team Tennis. "Nobody would ever come to the tennis matches, but when he played, the place was filled up, standing-room only," Driesell said.

Driesell said that Lucas had a magnetic personality and "was a great leader," confident enough to go sit behind the coach's desk and plop his feet up and tell Driesell, "I'm going to be the head coach here someday." He also wrote on the blackboard in the locker room, "John Lucas, president of the United States."

Lucas helped recruit Moses Malone to Maryland.

Driesell recalled a story at Malone's memorial service in the fall of 2015 how after he had signed with the Terps out of Petersburg, Virginia, Lucas and some of his teammates jumped in a car and drove to play pickup with the big high school center.

"I kept telling him about Moses and I said he's a great player and John said he wasn't," Driesell said. "I told him, 'Put Steve Shephard, Mo Howard, and a couple of other guys [in a car] and drive down there and he'll scrimmage with ya. They drove to Petersburg and when they got back, Luke said, 'Hey coach, that guy's the truth.'"

One of Lucas' former teammates said that Lucas always strove to be the best at whatever he did. Unfortunately, after basketball and tennis, the teammate said, "He also wanted to be the best drug addict he could be."

Former All-American John Lucas II attends a 2016 game in College Park.
(Mark Goldman/Icon Sportswire)

Cocaine addiction curtailed Lucas' NBA career, as it did many other stars at the time. While he lasted 14 years, Lucas averaged only 10.7 points over his career, which started and ended in Houston, where he eventually settled and founded a drug rehab program geared toward helping rehabilitate athletes.

"I never talked to him about his drug addiction, but I prayed for him and I'm happy that he's out of it," Driesell said. "He's turned it in to something great, really."

5 This Bud's For You

When Bud Millikan showed up in College Park in the spring of 1950, the Maryland basketball program took a back seat to the school's national power football team and even to the boxing team.

"When Bud took over the program, there really was no program," said Gene Shue, who was a freshman on that team. "Boxing was more important than basketball. We had a terrific boxing team at the time and they would feature the boxing match [as the featured event] if we had a doubleheader."

Inheriting a program that had eight losing seasons in the previous 10 years under Flucie Stewart and Burt Shipley—including a 1–21 record in 1941 under Shipley—Millikan quickly turned the Terps around.

"He took over a group of players that didn't appear to be very good and he molded that group of players," Shue said. "He disciplined them and coached them and they wound up with something like a 15- or 16-win record. It was remarkable. He did a fabulous job."

Starting with a 16–11 record his first season, Millikan coached the Terps to winning records in each of his first seven years, culminating with the school's first ACC tournament title and NCAA tournament bid in 1958.

After Maryland went 10–13 the following season, the Terps turned it around briefly with two winning years but wound up being up and down for much of Millikan's last few years before he was fired after an 11–14 record in 1967.

Millikan, who had been an assistant under the legendary Hank Iba when the Cowboys won the national championship in 1944, went 243–182 in 17 seasons at Maryland.

"Bud has never gotten the recognition he deserved, in my opinion," Shue said. "He was a great defensive coach, he was a guy who ran really good offensive patterns. The players in our group, we had such incredible respect for Bud Millikan. He was not only an outstanding coach, but he had a great influence on our lives, the way we conducted ourselves."

While Shue was a prolific scorer under Millikan, another of Millikan's coaching disciples rarely did.

"If you were a guard for Millikan, if you took a shot, you'd better make it," said Gary Williams, who played for the Terps from 1963 through 1967. "You made it, you could take another one. But don't miss."

Williams can recall playing a game as a sophomore against Miami and Rick Barry, seeing Millikan out of the corner of his eye signal for another guard to come in as Williams launched a jump shot from the deep corner.

Did it go in?

"No," he said with a laugh. "I was out of the game. He would only play six [players] unless there was foul trouble. So if you went out of the game, you might be out for a long time."

But there was a night as a senior early in the season against South Carolina that Williams got to play most of the game because he made all eight shots he took, a record that stood for many years. He scored a career-high 18 points.

"We weren't very [good], we had Billy Jones, Peter Johnson, and me. We played basically a three-guard lineup with Rich Dresher and Jay McMillen [up front]," Williams recalled. "We were pretty small."

The Terps "played our asses off" and stayed with the Gamecocks right down to the end before Maryland lost 65–63. After losing 80–53 at South Carolina, Maryland matched up with the Gamecocks in the first round of the ACC tournament in Greensboro, North Carolina.

Apparently, Williams' record-setting night didn't mean much to Millikan.

"*The Diamondback* had written that maybe I was the MVP of the team that year, so now we're practicing to play South Carolina," Williams said. "We had lost both games.

"Millikan comes up to me in typical Bud fashion—very strict—and said, 'I'm going to make a change.' I asked him, 'What are you thinking about? I'm a senior. I'm 22.' He says, 'I'm going to play three big guys and I'm only going to have two guards.'"

When Millikan told Williams that he would be the odd man out, his reply came straight from the streets of South Jersey.

"I had nothing to lose and said, 'You got to be kidding,'" Williams said. "He said, 'We got to change it up.' I said, 'But their guards are really good.' He said, 'Yeah, but they're a little bigger than you, and Pete and Billy are bigger than you, [so] I think it will give us a better chance to win the game.'"

Williams figured he would be the first player off the bench.

With two minutes left and the game still close, Williams had not taken off his warmups when Millikan signaled for him to go to the scorer's table to check in. He first had something to tell Williams.

"It was like 53–51, two minutes left, and Frank McGuire is coaching South Carolina and there's no shot clock, and they're holding the ball," Williams said. "He grabs me and says, 'You've got

Thompson, I want you to take the ball off him.' He didn't know how to trap. He thought I could pick 'em clean. I played the last two minutes. That was the end of my career. It was a tough way to go out."

Williams wasn't the only one whose career at Maryland was over after the 57–54 defeat—at least as a player. A few days after the ACC tournament, Millikan was fired.

"We had a meeting, when the season was over, the season's over, he said he was fired," Williams said. "He was only in his forties."

Though their relationship was somewhat strained at the end, Williams credits Millikan for having a tremendous influence over his own career in coaching.

"Bud knew basketball," Williams said. "He was a good guy to play for if you were going to be a coach."

Williams' teams at all his coaching stops were known for their tenacious defense because of the influence Millikan had over him.

"I probably learned defense as well as anybody that got into coaching because he played for Henry Iba, the guy that got credited for starting man-to-man defense," Williams said. "It was a sagging man-to-man. You really learned how to slide, how to cover your man."

What Williams took from that last encounter with Millikan stayed with him for his entire career. Williams always had a tremendous loyalty to senior point guards, one in particular.

During the 1998–99 season, Williams stuck with Terrell Stokes at the point and played junior college transfer Steve Francis, an All-American, at shooting guard. Many criticized Williams for his loyalty, leading to a season-ending loss to St. John's in the Sweet 16.

"Terrell was a good player," Williams said. "People forget that we beat Illinois in Sacramento and we beat them to go to the Sweet 16. He was as smart as any guard I ever coached."

And, more importantly, he was a senior. That's something Williams hadn't forgotten for more than 30 years.

6 Not Your Average Joe

When Maryland opened preseason practice in the fall of 1993, there was finally some hope for the future of Gary Williams' program.

Despite a 12–16 record the previous season, which turned out to be the second straight (and last) losing mark in his 22 years with the Terps, freshmen Duane Simpkins, Johnny Rhodes, and Exree Hipp gained plenty of playing time.

The 1993 recruiting class had four players, the most important believed to be Keith Booth, a tough, 6'5" forward from Dunbar High in Baltimore considered among the top high school stars in the country. There was also a skinny, 6'10" center from Norfolk with the non-descript name of Joe Smith.

Assistant coach Art Perry had discovered Smith at Morey High when Perry was scouting another player, Ed Geth, who wound up going to North Carolina. Perry had also watched Smith play on the same AAU team as Allen Iverson.

"He didn't get the ball as much as if he had played with a normal guard," said Tom Konchalski, a New York–based recruiting analyst. "But unlike a lot of guards, Iverson would drive and finish, so there weren't that many opportunities."

Gary Williams recalled watching Iverson's team win the national AAU championship in Winston-Salem, North Carolina, beating a Charlotte team that included future Tar Heels Jerry Stackhouse and Jeff McInnis.

"When Joe would make a great defensive play, I would look around to see who was watching, but Iverson would take it up the floor and make a great drive, and most of the coaches looked at Iverson," Williams said.

The first inkling that Maryland had landed a future star came later that summer at the Boston Shootout. Already signed with the Terps, Smith was named the event's MVP, outplaying one of his teammates, Joey Beard, who was headed to Duke.

"When I went up to the Boston Shootout last spring, I knew the rest of us were in trouble," said Mike Brey, then a Duke assistant. "He was on the same team as Joey Beard, and you had no trouble telling who the better player was. But he wasn't just better than Joey. He was better than everybody else."

From the first day he arrived in the fall of 1993, Smith quickly showed he belonged.

"I knew he was quick and agile from that position, but I didn't know he could run the court or shoot like that until the first day of practice," said Williams, whose two previous teams at Maryland were on the NCAA probation he inherited from Bob Wade. "There was pretty good talent out there [but] Joe was the best the day he walked on the practice floor."

But even Williams didn't know how good Smith was going to be, nearly from the start. In the team's second exhibition game, a player who many thought was going to make an immediate impact as a rebounder and shot-blocker scored 38 points on 15 of 18 shooting.

When Williams was asked if he knew Smith could score like that, the Maryland coach warned, "Don't create a monster."

If Smith was still a secret when the season started, it got out quickly and to a rather large audience when the still relatively unknown freshman outplayed Georgetown's Othella Harrington in an opening-game upset by the unranked Terps of the 13th-ranked Hoyas on national television.

"I was so nervous going into that game, I didn't know what to expect," a 40-year-old Smith recalled before the teams played in 2015. "I knew that [Georgetown center] Othella Harrington had been the Rookie of the Year in the Big East. But once I got on the court for the opening tap and started to play, the nerves went away a little bit. It kind of worked out for us."

The nerves went away quickly. Williams, who was then in his fourth season as head coach in College Park, recalled one particular move that got the attention of Georgetown coach John Thompson.

"Joe's in front of the Georgetown bench and he's got the ball I'd say 25 feet from the basket, and they're out there playing pretty tough on the perimeter," Williams said. "Joe put the ball down with his left hand, took one dribble and a step, and went up and dunked it. I remember [Georgetown coach] John Thompson, he kind of looked down at our bench with this look like, *Who was that? What was that?*"

Smith finished with 26 points and nine rebounds to 16 points and 15 rebounds for Harrington. Maryland overcame a 14-point deficit in the second half to win in overtime.

"Othella was good," said Duane Simpkins, then a sophomore and Maryland's starting point guard who scored the game-winning basket, a runner in the lane over another Georgetown big man, Don Reid, with 3.5 seconds left in overtime. "But Joe was better."

Smith averaged 19.4 points, 10.7 rebounds, and 3.1 blocks as a freshman to lead the Terps back to the NCAA tournament for the first time since Williams had returned to his alma mater five years before. As a No. 10 seed, Maryland reached the Sweet 16 after beating St. Louis and then upsetting No. 2 seed Massachusetts, coached by John Calipari.

By the time his freshman year at Maryland ended, Smith had earned first-team All-ACC honors, helped the Terps reach the first of two straight Sweet 16s, and was an honorable mention All-American.

As a sophomore, Smith put up a career-high 40 points to beat Duke at Cameron Indoor Stadium. He wound up averaging 20.8 points, 10.6 rebounds, and 2.9 blocks, leading the 26–8 Terps to the Sweet 16, where they lost to Connecticut.

Touted as a Player of the Year candidate for his sophomore year, Smith wound up being a first-team All-American and the No. 1 overall pick in the NBA draft by the Golden State Warriors.

Asked if he regretted his decision to leave after his sophomore year given the way his 16-year NBA career turned out—after an impressive first two seasons with the Warriors, the player nicknamed "The Beast" never developed into more than a solid journeyman playing for a dozen teams—Smith said he missed out on two things.

"The only way I think about it is the fact that if I stayed, I think we had a chance to win the national championship," Smith said of a 1995–96 team that would have returned all five starters and added future NBA player Laron Profit. "I do regret not being able to enjoy college the way I wanted to be like other college students."

7 Old King Cole

From the outside, Cole Field House didn't look like anything special. Picture an airplane hangar smack dab in the middle of a college campus. Yet it didn't take long when you walked into the place—either from the street level and looking down to the court or from the back entrance, under the overhanging seats and looking up—to realize that you were walking into a time capsule.

Consider this: when it was opened in 1955, the William P. Cole Activities Field House sat 12,000 people and was the largest on-campus home court in the country. It grew by nearly 3,000 sets in the late 1960s when Lefty Driesell was hired to help the Terps compete with the schools on Tobacco Road. By the time it closed for men's basketball at the end of the 2001–02 season, Cole was considered a relic—a very hot one—from another time.

"They never worried about acoustics when they built places back then," Gary Williams said. "The way that roof was, the noise in Cole Field House just seemed to roll up the ceiling and down the other side. It magnified everything."

Gary Williams recalled walking into Cole for the first time as a high school student from South Jersey who was being recruited by Bud Millikan. It was for the 1963 NCAA regionals, the place was packed and Williams said he knew "that if they offered me a scholarship, I was coming to Maryland."

Nearly 50 years later, Williams reflected on that visit as the 2013–14 team was ready for a back-to-the-future moment of playing Maryland Madness at Cole.

"I had seen the Palestra in Philadelphia, which was 9,000 [capacity], but this was 14,000," Williams recalled. "I walked in from the street on the top level. It kind of took your breath away."

Lefty Driesell's first memories of Cole came five years later, when he brought his Davidson team up to the NCAA regionals from North Carolina. After advancing to the Sweet 16, Davidson wound up losing to the North Carolina Tar Heels on a last-second shot by Charlie Scott, a player Driesell had initially signed before losing him to the Tar Heels.

In between the visits from Maryland's two future iconic coaches was arguably the most historic game in NCAA basketball history. It came in 1966, when an all-black starting five from Texas Western upset an all-white starting five of No. 1 Kentucky. Miners coach Don Haskins told his four white players, including defensive specialist Jerry Armstrong, that he planned only to use his black players against the Wildcats.

It literally changed the face of college basketball.

"[Kentucky] Coach [Adolph] Rupp had made the comment before the game that five black players couldn't beat five white players," Texas Western center David "Big Daddy" Lattin recalled shortly before the 2006 movie *Glory Road* was released. "Somebody asked if that made us play harder. If you add to the fire and put gasoline on it, that will make it burn higher."

Years later, when another of Texas Western's players visited Cole for a game and went completely unnoticed by those in attendance, he smiled.

"My wife asked why I was smiling," recalled Nevil Shed. "I said, 'History was made here.'"

The 1966 title game between Texas Western and Kentucky might have been the most historic basketball game played at Cole—even bigger than the 1965 win by local high school power DeMatha over Power Memorial and Lew Alcindor to stop the New

Lefty Driesell announces his resignation at a press conference at the Cole Field House on October 29, 1986. (Bill Smith)

York City school's 71-game winning streak—but it wasn't the only historic event.

In 1972, Cole served as a site for a ping-pong match between the U.S. and China that was part of President Richard Nixon's ping-pong diplomacy strategy. Two years later, Elvis came for a concert and left the building after putting on two shows. The Grateful Dead played there in 1981, Bob Dylan in 1998.

By the time it closed, after Maryland's national championship season in 2002, Williams thought it was time. Williams joked the he would tell campers over the summer that the air-conditioning had broken, but wouldn't tell them it had been 10 years or more since it had been fixed. It was also not the healthiest environment given all the asbestos in the place.

"I always thought Cole was a difficult building to cool or to heat [especially] in game situations; that building always got hotter in big games," Williams said. "It was to our benefit because the other teams might not be used to that, but we were. We were in great physical condition because of that. Back then we were pressing all the time and playing in Cole Field House was certainly an advantage for us."

Fans weren't worried about risking their health for a couple of hours of happiness.

"Fans at Cole Field House always thought they were a part of the game," Williams said. "It was easy for people who didn't have what would be considered great seats to be yelling and screaming. In some of the bigger arenas now, you're pretty far away from the action. You might not be into the game as much as you would be in Cole Field House."

On the night the Terps officially closed it down with a 20-point win over Virginia, Williams went back and forth between tearing up and cracking jokes as the memories of Cole came flooding back. He admitted after the game that leaving Cole for the spanking-new

Comcast Center is "difficult, because obviously this place means a lot to me."

On his radio show that night, Williams shared a story about being asked what was "the happiest thing to happen to me in this building." It wasn't all the big wins—in particular the record six over No. 1 ranked teams—or of all the players he coached at Cole, from Walt Williams to Joe Smith and Keith Booth to Steve Francis and Juan Dixon and Lonny Baxter.

"The happiest thing was up there in Section 2 when I passed two final exams," he said with his trademark smirk. "I was happy to get out of here."

Was It the Bob Wade Era or Error?

In recalling the history of Maryland basketball, most tend to skip from Lefty Driesell straight to Gary Williams, and then from Williams to Mark Turgeon. It's almost as if the three years Bob Wade coached the Terps never existed.

A surprise choice by chancellor John B. Slaughter, Wade was hired the day after Driesell was forced to resign in late October of 1986, four months after the cocaine-intoxication death of Maryland superstar Len Bias.

In introducing Wade, Slaughter made reference to the "dearth of happy events" since the day Bias died.

"Today represents a major change in our future," Slaughter said. "It's a time when we are in a celebratory mood, a time when we could identify with a person who we've already developed a great sense of confidence and friendship."

At the time, Wade was a well-respected high school coach in Baltimore who had turned Dunbar into a national power with the likes of players such as Reggie Williams, Muggsy Bogues, and Reggie Lewis.

The day of the announcement, reports that Maryland had hired a high school coach fueled rumors that DeMatha coach Morgan Wootten, an alum, would be headed down the street to College Park.

Not only was Wootten never interviewed, Wade was the only coach Slaughter ever considered.

One of Driesell's assistants, Ron Bradley, was told of the decision only an hour before the announcement was made at a downtown Baltimore hotel. Gary Williams, then in his first season at Ohio State, was never called or consulted.

Bradley, who remained on Wade's staff for his entire tenure, said he was "mildly surprised" by the decision to hire a high school coach. Driesell told a friend that night, "I'm totally shocked and amazed by the decision. I feel bad for my assistants."

Slaughter consulted with a number of high-profile Division I coaches—including John Thompson at nearby Georgetown, who, like Wade, had come straight from the high school level, as well as North Carolina's Dean Smith—leading a former booster club president to comment, "It's like consulting the rooster on who should run the henhouse."

Wade's tenure started and ended badly, with a brief interlude of mild success in his second year.

Under restrictions by the university to delay the start of practice and the season after it was disclosed that several players, including Bias, were academically deficient, the Terps struggled to a 9–17 record his first season and didn't win a single ACC game.

Things turned around in the middle year, when freshman Brian Williams (later Bison Dele) helped the Terps to an NCAA tournament bid. But after the 18–13 season ended with a loss to

Kentucky in the second round, Williams joined five other players who had left the program under Wade.

Maryland never recovered. Despite the addition of two talented freshmen and future NBA first-round draft picks, Walt Williams and Jerrod Mustaf, the Terps regressed and finished 9–20, including 1–13 in the ACC. The pressure to fire Wade mounted as the NCAA moved in to investigate a number of infractions.

The irony is that the Terps pulled off one of the biggest upsets in ACC tournament history in what turned out to be Wade's last game, beating top-seeded North Carolina State at the Omni in Atlanta. Wade, suffering from high blood pressure, had to be hospitalized after collapsing in the locker room.

The other irony is that a coach hired to clean up what administrators believed was a loose ship under Driesell's leadership was left to his own devices by assistants he never trusted and a new athletic director, Lew Perkins, who believed that Wade would eventually commit a fireable offense.

Wade did, having his only trusted aide, a former Baltimore high school coach named Woody Williams, drive former Terp Rudy Archer to classes at Prince George's Community College after Archer had been kicked out of Maryland for cheating. Wade didn't realize—or care—that Archer was considered a recruitable athlete and the ride was considered an improper benefit.

The words of Charles Sturtz, a longtime campus administrator who found himself in the middle of the athletic department's mess following Bias' death, eventually came back to haunt Slaughter's choice to replace Driesell.

"You know the chancellor wants to continue with a tradition of a strong athletic program in the Division I category and we intend to do that with a balance that reflects more academic interests than was the case in the past," Sturtz said. "We believe our choice represents the proper balance between the athletic accomplishments and the academic responsibilities."

Wade, who was the first African American men's basketball coach in the ACC, knew that his tenure would not be long if he couldn't keep the program in the steady, upward trajectory.

Even during his most successful season—an 18–13 overall record and a second-round exit in the NCAA tournament—Wade said he would not be fully accepted at Maryland.

"I'm not the people's choice," he said.

Things changed dramatically for Wade when Williams left after one year to transfer to Arizona. Though Wade said the 6'10" center wanted to play closer to his California home, Williams and his mother, Patricia Phillips, said at the time that he didn't like playing for Wade.

Williams became a lottery pick playing for the Wildcats, while things unraveled quickly for Wade in College Park.

"I control my own destiny," Wade said before the 1988–89 season began. "Dr. Slaughter gave me and my family an opportunity, it's up to me to show I'm worthy. Whatever decision is made, I have not done anything wrong. I have worked very hard."

Part of Wade's problems at Maryland stemmed from the fact that he trusted very few people outside his wife, Carolyn, and Woody Williams, a fellow high school coach he brought with him to be his director of operations.

"I've always been aware that this is a risky business, even if you make it you can't rest on your past accomplishments," he said. "There are always people out to discredit you, people who will smile at you one minute and stab you in the back the next. There's a lack of loyalty in this business."

Wade said that after Williams' departure, "We have to go on."

He didn't go on for long.

Booth Opens Doors to Baltimore

As Keith Booth progressed through his high school career at fabled Dunbar in Baltimore, the promising forward heard many times that he shouldn't stay home to play his college ball at Maryland. There was bad blood between the city's basketball powerbrokers and the state's flagship program.

What started when former Dunbar star Ernie Graham left College Park without a degree or much of an NBA future in 1981 and continued when Dunbar's coach, Bob Wade, was hired and fired at Maryland within three years, essentially ended when Booth chose to play for Gary Williams and the Terps in 1992.

"I was definitely aware of it, it was around, you'd hear it through the neighborhood, my family had pressure and they'd hear from people at their jobs," Booth recalled. "For me, growing up a big Len Bias fan, I wanted to play at Maryland."

Booth met Bias during the spring after his senior year in College Park, a couple of months before the Maryland star's death from a cocaine overdose in June of 1986. It was an autograph signing at a sub shop in East Baltimore. At the time, Booth was a promising 12-year-old who had just started making a name for himself.

"I told him, 'I'm going to go to Maryland one day and try to break all your records,'" Booth said. "Keith Gatlin was with him and years later, he remembered that story. When the opportunity presented itself and I went through the process, and I saw everything Maryland had to offer.

"From a basketball standpoint, it wasn't a lot because they had just come off probation. I got to know Coach Williams and I had been down to school several times to watch Walt Williams. It was a situation that I definitely saw myself succeeding in. In my heart, it was the best place for me to be."

Though he was overshadowed his first two years by Joe Smith, Booth became one of the most respected and beloved Terps in memory. His preseason introduction—even when he became an assistant coach long after he had graduated—was followed by a prolonged "Boooooooooooooooooooooooooooooothhhh."

Booth broke one of Bias' records as a senior, a school-record 576 free throws made, shattering the mark of 460. Booth also had the record for free throws attempted (824, 106 more than Lonny Baxter). The 6–5 forward is also ninth in scoring (1,776) and sixth in rebounding (916) and steals (193).

What Booth is most proud of is not that he never missed a game—starting all 126 he played, a record that lasted until it was broken by Steve Blake's 136 and later surpassed by both Juan Dixon and Jake Layman, who share the record of 141—but the fact that he never missed a single practice in four years in College Park.

"I take more pride in that I never missed a practice," said Booth, now an assistant coach at Loyola University in his hometown. "That's hard to do. You practice way more than you play games. You can tweak an ankle here or there, you can get sick.

"The guys I played with—Joe Smith, Laron Profit, Obinna Ekezie, Sarunas Jasikevicius—all played in the NBA and other guys like Rodney Elliott had long careers in Europe. They pushed me to get better and they helped me get better. I wanted to be out there."

Booth was certainly the big name in his recruiting class after being recruited by powers such as Kentucky, but he and a group of sophomores led by McDonald's All-American Duane Simpkins quickly became overshadowed by the out-of-nowhere Joe Smith.

It never seemed to bother Booth.

"Joe and I were roommates from Day 1, and I knew going in and watching Joe at the high school level that he was a very good player," Booth said. "For me, at every level, I had never had people around me from coaches to family members telling me 'You're the man' going in. I was surrounded by people that told me that every level is different and I had to prove myself at the college level like I did at the high school level."

If anything, Smith's remarkably swift ascension into being one of the best players in the ACC as a freshman and the Naismith Award winner as a sophomore (before becoming the No. 1 player taken in the 1995 NBA Draft) "took some of that pressure off me early," Booth said. "Joe really let me fit into my role at the college level and put me in position to play professional basketball as well. That was the mentality back then. It was never how fast I could get to the NBA."

Eventually, it became Booth's team after Smith left following their sophomore year and Simpkins, Johnny Rhodes and Exree Hipp left after Booth's junior year. As a senior on a team that finished a respectable 21–11 (9–7 in the ACC), Booth averaged a career-high 19.5 points, including a school-record 213 free throws (breaking Bias' record by four) that represented more than a third of his points.

Though his pro career was short-lived after being drafted in the first round by the defending NBA champions Chicago Bulls—an undersized power forward in college, Booth never developed a reliable enough perimeter game to sustain himself in the pros— Booth has found his niche as a college assistant, first for six years at Maryland under Williams and now at Loyola.

"The goal for me is to become a head coach," he said. "I've been brought up the right way, I've been taught the game the right way. I've been fortunate to play for great coaches at every level. In high school I played for Pete Pompey, who was national coach of the year. In college, I played for a Hall of Famer in Gary Williams. Even prior to high school, I grew up with the tutelage of Bucky Lee, who coached every great player who ever came through the city. I enjoy teaching this game and I'm going to teach it the right way."

10 We're Off to See the Wizard

Walt Williams was a skinny 6'8", 175-pound guard who grew up near the Maryland campus when he arrived in the fall of 1988, a few months after the Terps made the NCAA tournament for the first and only time in Bob Wade's three-year tenure.

He wasn't "the Wizard" then, a nickname Wade bestowed on him during their one season together. He came to College Park mostly because he idolized the late Len Bias, who had died of a cocaine overdose two years before. He wore his socks high and fancied his game after Magic Johnson and George Gervin.

In fact, just like Joe Smith a few years later—a player who also wore high socks because of Walt Williams—the future Maryland star was the No. 2 man in his own recruiting class behind Jerrod Mustaf, a McDonald's all-America from Catholic League power DeMatha High.

Williams played at a public school, Crossland, in Prince George's County.

While Mustaf certainly lived up to his billing by averaging 14.3 points, Williams averaged about half of that, around the same number that Bias did as a freshman. After Wade was fired following that season in which the Terps went 9–20, Williams knew he was going to play a prominent role for Gary Williams.

But after averaging 12.7 points as a sophomore, the 20-year-old rising junior had a decision when the Terps were put on NCAA probation for what would be the remainder of his college career. While Mustaf quickly decided to turn pro after leading Maryland in scoring, Williams thought about whether he wanted to transfer.

Several schools, including reigning NCAA champion UNLV and perennial Big East power St. John's, came after Williams.

Many friends and family members told Williams that he should consider it.

"The only thing that made me think *Maybe I should think about [leaving] or at least consider other options* was because of what other people were saying about what we were going to go through," Williams recalled. "Being able to transfer and play right away, all of those things, people were putting in my head [and saying] 'This is a great opportunity here.'"

Having bonded with his namesake, Williams didn't give it any serious thought.

"When everybody was telling me about the information, it made me think about it a little bit but I didn't want to beat myself up or consume myself with those thoughts or whatever," he said. "I just let it all come to me naturally and I wanted to get it out of my mind. Every morning when I woke up, I wanted to be a Terp. It was just a natural process for me."

With 20 additional pounds and a promise from his new coach that he could be a point guard, Walt Williams blossomed into one of the best players in Maryland history.

With Mustaf struggling in the NBA and center Tony Massenburg starting a long career with a short stint in Europe after being cut by the San Antonio Spurs as a second-round pick, Williams averaged 18.7 points and more than five rebounds and five assists despite missing 11 games with a broken leg.

Fully recovered for his senior year, Williams put together one of the most memorable seasons by a Terp. Playing with Syracuse-transfer Matt Roe, some far-from-blue-chip freshmen, junior college transfers, and former walk-ons, Williams kept a 14–15 Maryland team competitive by averaging a school-record 26.8 points a game.

"We did lose a lot in terms of being able to recruit and bring top 10 talent in, it just seemed to fall on my shoulders in terms of me carrying the load," Williams said, "It was tough times, man. I told myself, 'I can get this done.' I was projected to be a first-round pick after my junior year but I decided to come back because I knew I could be a lottery pick."

"We're off to the see the Wizard," became the go-to line for many Maryland fans as well as one sportswriter covering the team whose kids thought he was talking about Dorothy, Toto, and the Wicked Witch of the West.

While he didn't exactly conjure up comparisons to Magic despite being of a similar height, Williams' performance was good enough to make him a lottery pick in the 1991 NBA Draft. He was taken seventh overall by the Sacramento Kings and went on to have a solid 11-year career.

More importantly, Williams caught the attention of a high school player in Virginia named Joe Smith, who arrived two years after "the Wizard" had taken his act to the NBA. Gary Williams attributes his ability to return the program to prominence and eventually win a national title to his last namesake.

"Just the type of person he was kept us relevant," Gary Williams said in the summer of 2014, on the eve of his induction into the Naismith Hall of Fame. "It really worked out for me, coaching-wise, because it gave me a reason to make Maryland as good as anyone else. That was always the goal after that."

Williams never regretted staying, though he did think about what kind of team the Terps might have had if the NCAA hadn't come down so hard on the school.

"I knew Jerrod left because of the probation, but I always thought, *What if we played together a little longer?* We would have been an NCAA tourney team," he said. "You talk about myself, Matt Roe, 6'8", and 6'6" guards, then Mustaf at 6'11", tremendous scorer, I think we would have tore the tournament up. It could have been a whole different outcome for myself."

Williams never attended an NCAA tournament game until 2016, when he finally gave in to a longstanding invitation to attend as a member of the team's radio broadcasts.

Even when the Terps made their previous three trips to the NCAA tournament under Gary Williams in 2009 and 2010—the latter ending with a heartbreaking last-second loss to Michigan State, in Spokane—as well as last season under Mark Turgeon, Walt Williams remained back in Maryland.

"Subliminally, maybe I just didn't want to go," he said.

In watching the Terps make their first Sweet 16 since 2003, Williams admitted that it did make him think about his decision more than a quarter century ago.

"Absolutely, man, I did," he said. "I really didn't give any thought about what the atmosphere would be like out there in the NCAA tournament or whatever. I was just going to go out there and do my job. But man, when I was out there, it was just a different environment. So much electricity out there. I was like, 'Man, I wish I could have played in these conditions.' Watching it on TV is a different perspective than actually being there. Of course I thought, *Would my career been different if I had the opportunity to play on a stage like that?*"

11 Maryland's First Big Shue Deal

Believe it not, one of Maryland's first big stars nearly didn't make it to College Park.

Coming out of Towson Catholic High in Baltimore in 1950, Gene Shue was one of the best players in the state—"if not best player," according to Shue—when he started looking for a college team.

Shue first tried nearby Loyola, which in the early 1950s was the best program in the area. He knew one of the team's players, Mike

Zedalis, and asked him to find out about tryouts. Shue never heard back from the coach, Lefty Reitz.

"There was no interest," Shue said.

Shue then drove down to Washington to visit Georgetown because his cousin went to the school, but was "absolutely pathetic" in the tryout. Still, Hoyas coach Buddy O'Grady invited Shue back for a second tryout.

"I played a little bit better, but not all that good," said Shue. "I didn't get the scholarship. The guy who got the scholarship was a guy named Lou Gigante, who was a very good college player. One of his relatives [Vincent 'Chin' Gigante] was a crime figure in New York. Lou became a priest."

Next up was College Park, where a new coach named Bud Millikan was still putting the team together late in the summer of 1950. A Towson attorney named Howard Jennifer wrote a letter on Shue's behalf to the university and that was forwarded to Millikan, who invited Shue for a tryout.

Unlike his trip to Georgetown, Shue put on quite a shooting exhibition at Ritchie Coliseum.

"I had the best day I ever had in my life," Shue said. "I absolutely could not miss a shot."

Not that Millikan seemed that impressed.

"This is the kind of guy Bud was," recalled Shue. "After the workout was over, he said, 'We're still deciding who we're going to bring in. We liked what you did.' There was no 'Wow! You've got a scholarship.' It was not like that at all. It was like, 'Yeah, we'll probably take you.'"

Good thing. Shue went on to become one of the most prolific scorers in school history. When he graduated in 1954, Shue's 1,384 points in three varsity seasons was the most by a Terp, as was the 41 points he scored against Washington & Lee as a junior, despite playing in Millikan's methodical offense.

"We would pass the ball like 15 or 20 times," Shue recalled. "When we get together, some of my old teammates said, 'Nobody was allowed to shoot, except for you, you could shoot every time you got it. We had a helluva lot of fun, we won a lot of games.'"

Maryland went 51–24 in Shue's three varsity seasons, including a then-school-record 23 wins his senior year.

Two games that stand out to Shue more than 60 years later are two losses: a three-point defeat at West Virginia his sophomore year and a double-overtime loss to Wake Forest in the old Southern Conference tournament as a junior. The Terps lost to the Demon Deacons 64–56, with Shue scoring 40.

The game in Morgantown was particularly memorable.

"They had the highest scoring team in the country," Shue said. "Our whole defense was geared up to stop Mark Workman. He was about a 6'10", 6'11" center, a tremendous offensive player. We didn't have a lot of height on the team. Coach decided to [guard him with] Ralph Grecco, who was about 6'4"."

Long before Dean Smith popularized the four corners at North Carolina, Millikan used a version of it against West Virginia.

"The first half was about 19–13 at halftime, and I think we were winning," Shue recalled. "At halftime, I'll never forget, one or two West Virginia fans burst into our locker room and start yelling and screaming, 'You're holding the ball!' It was like a weird scene. We were holding the ball and we were loudly booed."

It nearly worked.

"The score ended up something like 39–33 [actually 39–36], and Mark Workman wound up getting around 30 points," Shue said.

Part of Shue's scholarship at Maryland involved him cleaning two floors of the dormitory in which lived.

"That was kind of pathetic," he said.

By his senior year, Shue had a better job—cleaning the floor at the old Ritchie Coliseum before practice—and even started getting the $16 monthly laundry money stipend the football players received.

Picked third overall in the 1954 NBA draft by the Philadelphia Warriors, Shue played a total of six games with the Warriors before being traded to the New York Knicks.

A five-time All-Star who scored a career-high 45 in the Boston Garden against the Celtics, Shue wound up playing for three other teams for a total of 11 years before retiring with his hometown Baltimore Bullets in 1964.

Shue wound up starting his coaching career in Baltimore two years later. He coached nearly a quarter of a century in the NBA, taking the Philadelphia 76ers to the Finals in 1977, four years after the team set a record for futility with 73 losses.

"I've had a charmed life," Shue told the *Baltimore Sun* in 2009. "I've been blessed. To be able to dribble a basketball all my life was an incredible privilege."

12 Tom McMillen's Dilemma

The summer of 1970 was winding down and Tom McMillen's decision about where he would play college basketball was not getting any easier.

The 6'11" center, already a cover boy on *Sports Illustrated* during his senior year of high school in Mansfield, Pennsylvania, had verbally committed to North Carolina, where his brother Paul was a student.

His mother had hoped that the youngest of her three sons would become a Virginia Cavalier. His father had wanted him to stay close to home and go to Maryland, where older brother Jay had played.

As the days ticked down before McMillen had to enroll—somewhere—he found himself on an Olympic development team tour in Europe with two Tar Heels, Steve Previs and Dennis Wuycik. "I got very deep into Carolina," McMillen said.

When he returned to the U.S., his mother told him that his father, Charles, a physician, was in the hospital and in the beginning stages of an illness that would kill him within the next few years.

"I felt that some of the pressures I had put the family under hadn't been helpful," McMillen recalled. "I had to rethink the whole thing, so I went down to Maryland for another visit."

The night before McMillen said he had to make a decision, Cavaliers coach Bill Gibson showed up at the family's door, ready to play a marathon game of bridge that would last into the early morning hours the next day. Gibson had been part of a regular bridge group with the McMillens when he coached at Mansfield State.

"I'm packing and he's sitting there with a plane down the road waiting to take me back to Virginia," McMillen said. "I called my brother Jay, who was in dental school in Baltimore, and said, 'You'd better get up here.' He got to the house about one in the morning and Bill Gibson was still playing cards with my parents."

McMillen went to bed and got up the next morning having decided to become a Terp.

While Lefty Driesell, then in his third year as Maryland's coach, believed it was his persuasive personality that convinced McMillen, it had more to do with his father's fragile health.

"There were a lot of reasons why I wanted to go play for [Carolina], but the real core reason I went to Maryland was my dad was ill and I wanted him to watch me play," McMillen said. "That's kind of how it went down and I'm glad I did because he saw all my [home] games before he passed."

North Carolina fans seemed to accept McMillen's decision.

"When I went down for the first game my sophomore year, my brother was still there and the whole thing was to kill me with kindness," McMillen said. "They didn't boo me or anything. It was a very classy thing to do. Dean did it that way. One of the hardest things I had to do was tell him I wasn't coming to Carolina."

To this day, longtime Tar Heel fans don't give him a hard time for passing up coming to Chapel Hill, "and I appreciate that," McMillen said.

13 Maryland's Greatest Athlete

Most Maryland fans assume that Renaldo "Skeets" Nehemiah is the school's greatest athlete, given that he excelled as both a track star and later had the skills to play in the National Football League.

As far as their time in College Park, no Maryland athlete contributed more as a Terp than Louis "Bozey" Berger.

Berger played three sports—basketball, baseball, and football—and earned a total of eight varsity letters during a career that spanned from 1929 through 1933.

A Baltimore native who grew up in Northern Virginia, Berger came to Maryland on a football scholarship mainly because the Terps did not give money to play basketball in those days.

In a 1980 profile for the *Baltimore Sun* written by Kent Baker, the author of *Maryland: Red, White and Amen*, before Berger's 70th birthday, the retired Air Force colonel talked about how money played a factor in his decision to become a Terp.

"I told Ship [basketball coach Burt Shipley] and [assistant coach] Jack Faber I didn't have much money," said Berger, who was working for the telephone company after graduating from McKinley Tech. "I had about $100."

Berger wound up living at the coach's house for a while and turned out to be a pretty productive house guest, given what he did on the court for the Terps.

The 6'2", 185-pound Berger led the Old Liners (this was before the nickname Terrapins took hold) to the old Southern Conference championship in 1931, with Berger eventually being named twice to the Helms' All-American team. Berger was a unanimous pick in 1932 along with a Purdue star named John Wooden. He also won the school's citizenship award that year.

"That boy was an All-American gentleman too," Sacha Spector said after sponsoring Berger for the Helms Foundation Athletic Court Hall of Fame in 1961.

While the Wooden fellow made a name for himself in basketball, Berger opted for baseball. He signed with the Cleveland Indians after graduating with a degree in economics from Maryland, played one game for the Indians that summer before going back to the minors and working his way back to the big leagues in 1937.

Berger split six seasons in the big leagues among 10 teams and gained a reputation as solid utility infielder who was better in the field than at the plate. He retired from baseball after being called to duty in 1941 as a military police officer at Fort Myer, where, according to the *Sun*, his father had been stationed for years.

He spent 20 years in the military before retiring in 1981 and served all over the world, including China and what was then called Palestine (now Israel), and "was known more for security in the Air Force than for baseball," Berger told the *Sun*. When talking about working at places such as the Pentagon and Andrews Air Force base, "That's batting over .300."

14 What Was the Best Recruiting Class In Maryland History?

Lefty Driesell built his reputation on recruiting, starting with his famous "We Want You" ad in the *Washington Post*. Bob Wade tried, but top recruit Brian Williams left after one season and suddenly things deteriorated. Gary Williams took three-star recruits and turned them into blue-chip players. And Mark Turgeon got Melo Trimble and Diamond Stone in successive classes.

While the best recruiter in Maryland history remains Driesell, the best recruiting class is up for discussion.

Here are the top five:

1970–71: It's hard to distinguish between a few of Driesell's early classes, but his second class in College Park brought in Tom McMillen, who along with Bill Walton was considered the best high school player in the country, and Len Elmore, as well as Jap Trimble and Rich Porac. Though Trimble and Porac were quickly recruited over when Driesell brought in John Lucas and Mo Howard, they certainly played their roles in the rise of the Terps.

1972–73: There's a case to be made that Lucas and Howard were the best backcourt in Maryland history—or at least a close second to Juan Dixon and Steve Blake—but there was more to this class than the two flashy guards. Tom Roy and Owen Brown saw their roles increase with the departure of McMillen and Elmore and were big part of a 24–5 team as seniors that had six players average in double figures.

1977–78: After a bit of a lull in recruiting, Driesell hit the jackpot when he brought in New York–sensation Albert King as well as Ernie Graham and Greg Manning. With the addition the following year of Buck Williams after a 15–13 season as freshmen, they became the nucleus of a team that won 64 games the next

Buck Williams joined the 1977–78 recruiting class to form a dynamic young nucleus.

three seasons. King left as the school's all-time leading scorer (now fourth), Williams is still the all-time field goal percentage leader, and Graham's 44 points against N.C. State is still a school record.

1992–93: After losing several top recruits because of the NCAA probation he inherited from Wade, Williams finally got the class he needed to turn around the scandal-ridden program. Point guard Duane Simpkins proved to be the big prize, because fellow local stars Johnny Rhodes and Exree Hipp quickly followed. Though the Terps finished 12–16 their freshman year, the arrival of Joe Smith and Keith Booth the next season put Maryland back into the NCAA tournament.

1993–94: What McMillen and Elmore were to Driesell's success at Maryland, Smith and Booth were for Williams. Part of a five-player class that also included Mario Lucas, Nick Bosnic, and Matt Kovaric, Smith led the Terps on the first of back-to-back Sweet 16 trips before turning pro as the No. 1 overall pick after his sophomore year. Booth was considered one of the hardest-working players in Maryland history and reopened the recruiting doors to Baltimore.

In Maryland's case, Lefty Driesell's ability to get Tom McMillen and Len Elmore in his second class and Brad Davis and Steve Sheppard with his third led to the Terps quickly ascending the national rankings in the mid-1970s.

Later on, he got Ernie Graham, Albert King, and Greg Manning one year, then followed it up with Buck Williams, Reggie Jackson, and Dutch Morley.

Bob Wade was able to use his summer all-star connections to land Jerrod Mustaf and Walt Williams during his first season after replacing Driesell, then snagged Brian Williams the next year. Unfortunately for Wade, Brian Williams transferred out to Arizona after one season and the former Dunbar coach didn't make it past his third year before getting fired.

Gary Williams had to wait out a couple of years of empty classes because of his inherited NCAA probation before getting three three-year starters in Duane Simpkins, Johnny Rhodes, and Exree Hip in one class and following it up with Joe Smith and Keith Booth. That group reached two Sweet 16s, and Williams wound up using his next group—led by Juan Dixon—to get to two straight Final Fours and win a national championship in 2002.

Mark Turgeon's recruiting has been a little more piecemeal: inheriting a patchwork roster from Williams that included Alex Len, Terrell Stoglin, and Pe'Shon Howard, as well as recruit Nick Faust. After Len left for the NBA in 2013, Stoglin was suspended from the program, and Howard transferred, five players—including Faust—left after the 2013–14 season.

Two five-star recruits, Melo Trimble in 2014 and Diamond Stone in 2015, became the centerpieces that led to back-to-back NCAA tournament appearances in 2015 and 2016. After four players, including Stone, left to pursue professional careers in 2016, the Terps brought in four-star recruits Kevin Huerter, Justin Jackson, and Anthony Cowan, Jr., as well as three-star recruit Micah Thomas and Joshua Tomaic of the Canary Islands.

15 Terps Win at Dean Dome

When the Maryland team travelled down to Chapel Hill, North Carolina, on February 20, 1986, most didn't expect the Terps to beat the No. 1 ranked Tar Heels for many reasons—one in particular.

The Dean Dome.

The Dean E. Smith Activities Center was a little more than a month old. The Tar Heels had christened the building with a victory over No. 2 Duke weeks before and everything from the décor to the expanse was more than a little intimidating.

"It was state-of-the-art, massive, everything in that facility was sky blue—the soda machines were sky blue, the towels as well," recalled Jeff Baxter, then a senior and Maryland's starting shooting guard. "Coach [Lefty Driesell] told us they had done that to psych us out. We were really pumped up to play in there."

Keith Gatlin, then a junior and the starting point guard, recalled how the Smith Center was "more like a basketball museum than an actual arena," in part because the big-money boosters sat quietly courtside and the rowdy students were several rows up.

North Carolina was 25–1 at the time, while the Terps had only recently started to recover from an 11–10 start, including losing their first six games in the ACC. As the first-year beat writer for Maryland, I suggested in print that the Terps might not even make the NIT.

"It wasn't that we were playing really bad, there were good teams back then," said Gatlin, now a successful high school coach in High Point, North Carolina. "The mood [of the team] was good, better than expected because we were 15-point underdogs and Carolina was ranked No. 1 in the country. We felt that we could compete with them."

Double-digit underdogs coming into the game, the Terps fell behind by nine points midway through the second half before the team's star player, Len Bias, led a comeback that included the 6'8" forward scoring six points in 29 seconds, highlighted by a steal and reverse dunk off an inbound pass that followed his hitting a jump shot to help force overtime.

In overtime, Bias made a block of a runner by North Carolina guard Kenny Smith that kept the Terps in front for good. Maryland's 77–72 victory was the first in program history over a

No.1–ranked team, and North Carolina's first loss in a building that had already been nicknamed "The Dean Dome."

Driesell scoffed when asked that night whether it was the biggest win of his career.

"Nah, they're all big. I won't even remember this tomorrow," Driesell said.

Before the Terps played at North Carolina in the 2015 ACC–Big Ten Challenge, Driesell was reminded of what he had said.

"That was a lie," he said with a laugh.

In fact, he had told his players, "When you come back here with your grandchildren, you can talk about the night we gave North Carolina the first loss in [its] building."

Though Bias had put on other memorable performances, the 35-point outburst against the Tar Heels that night might have been the most important of his college career. It came in his first ACC game back after serving a one-game suspension for violating curfew.

"The whole world saw how great a basketball player he was that night," Gatlin said of Bias, who made 13 of 24 field-goal attempts and all nine of his free throws.

North Carolina coach Roy Williams, then an assistant to the legendary Dean Smith, recalled before the 2015 game how "unbelievable" Bias played.

"Every jump shot he made, he looked like he was four feet off the ground," Williams said.

"They double- and triple-teamed him, and he just dominated their front line," said Derrick Lewis, then a sophomore and Maryland's starting center. "They couldn't stop him."

My own memories of that night are clear as well. Accustomed to sitting courtside to cover games, the media sat on the mezzanine level in what eventually become skyboxes. Given the 9:00 PM start and all the TV timeouts, making deadline was as tense as the game itself.

When I finally got my story in to the *Baltimore Sun* and made my way down to the floor and over to the locker room, both Driesell and the legendary coach after whom the building was named had long since concluded their respective postgame press conferences.

As I made my way into the Maryland locker room, Driesell was waiting for me, ready to pounce.

"Where were ya?" he growled.

"I had transmission problems," I said sheepishly.

"What, you drive a car in here?" Driesell said.

He had one more question.

"Think we make the NIT now?"

16 The Origins of Midnight Madness

Long before it became a national event on the college basketball landscape, more than a decade before other high-profile programs popularized it and the 12:01 practices on October 15 each year officially had a name, the first "Midnight Madness" was held at Maryland.

It wasn't called "Midnight Madness" back then, in the fall of 1971, when Lefty Driesell, a cigar in his mouth and a stopwatch in his hand, brought his third Maryland team to the track surrounding Byrd Stadium to time the players in the one-mile run.

Driesell didn't look at it as an historical event, just a way to get his team ready for what turned out a breakthrough season for the Terps.

"It was a motivational thing more than anything else," he said years later. "I knew we were gonna have a pretty good team. I told the players, 'Look, we're gonna start the first practice this year ahead of anybody in the country, and we're gonna be playing in the last game for the national championship."

According to Len Elmore, then a sophomore, the midnight run had more to do with "we're going to be the first team to practice, nobody is ever going to outwork us." Driesell told his players that they had to finish the mile in six minutes or less in order to start practicing.

With car headlights illuminating part of the track, Elmore said that most of the juniors and seniors took a shortcut across the field

Gary Williams pumps his fist to the Midnight Madness crowd on Saturday, October 16, 1999, at Cole Field House. (Nick Wass)

in order make their time. Elmore, trying to impress his coach, "was stupid enough not to do it and I didn't make my mile so I had to do it later on."

Coming off a 14–12 season in his second year, Driesell's boast of Maryland becoming "the UCLA of the East" had started to pick up steam with the arrival of a sophomore class than included Elmore and *Sports Illustrated* cover boy Tom McMillen from a freshman team that had finished unbeaten.

The Terps would win a national championship that season— just not the one Driesell was talking about. Finishing 27–5 after losing to North Carolina in the ACC semifinals, Maryland swept four games at Madison Square Garden to win the 1972 NIT.

This time, Driesell had changed the format to having his players finish a one-and-a-half-mile run in 10 minutes. The modern-day event started to take shape in the fall of 1973.

Welcoming in a freshman class that included John Lucas and Mo Howard, it was Howard who convinced Driesell to move the bulk of Midnight Madness inside Cole Field House for a preseason practice and scrimmage.

Asked what inspired him to make such a suggestion, Howard said, "Just being an impetuous freshman more than anything. We had a pretty good team that year and I thought it would be a great time for our students and our fans to see what was in store."

Howard said that the roster was stocked with several high school All-Americans, including two players, McMillen and Tom Roy, who had their high school uniforms retired by the Naismith Basketball Hall of Fame.

"We had the equivalent of nine or 10 McDonald's All-Americans," Howard said. "When I went there, we had [pickup games] and I sat on the sideline, wondering to myself, *Did I make a mistake coming here?* Elmore, McMillen, [Jim] O'Brien, Howard White, Owen Brown, Tom Roy, Lucas."

A crowd of around 8,000 reportedly showed up.

"It was jam-packed, people just wanted to get a glimpse of the new freshmen, it was fun," Elmore recalled.

Ironically, Driesell considered ending Midnight Madness before it really began when Howard fractured his ankle after trying a windmill dunk in warmups and missed a month of practice.

"He let us dunk because that's when dunking was banned [in games]," Howard said. "Poor Mo.... That's what I get for running my big mouth I guess."

Elmore said that nobody could predict what Driesell had started.

"We thought there'd be some copycats, obviously," Elmore said. "To think that the idea of being the first team in the nation to practice and nobody is going to outwork you evolved into this where television grabbed hold of it and make it a cult thing, nobody thought that would happen," Elmore said.

It took a few years to catch on, but by the early 1980s, Kentucky was selling out Rupp Arena and Kansas, after the arrival of Larry Brown, brought it to Phog Allen Field House. By the fall of 1993, ESPN joined in. In 1994, televising the event at Cincinnati, a student named Corey Clouse won free tuition from ESPN after sinking a half-court shot.

While many schools have continued to hold their first practice right after midnight, school officials in College Park changed the schedule a few years ago—and the name to Maryland Madness—in order to cut down on student drinking late into the night.

"The only wish I have is that they still played it at midnight," Driesell lamented when he and Gary Williams returned in 2013 when the event was held at Cole Field House.

It's not really the only wish.

Truth is, Driesell was a good salesman, but not as good a businessman as he could have been. Driesell should have "tried to patent" the name when he held the event for the first time.

"Every time I see one of these car dealerships or department stores announcing some kind of Midnight Madness sale, I think about all the money I could have made," Driesell said.

17 The Promoter

If Lefty Driesell was the showman who put Maryland basketball on the proverbial map, Russ Potts was the Sherpa with a similar down-home twang who provided the new coach an invisible compass to help navigate this uncharted territory.

Potts, who had graduated with a journalism degree from Maryland in 1964 and worked as a sports editor for several years in his hometown of Winchester, Virginia, returned as the nation's first director of sports marketing at a university in the summer of 1970.

Driesell had been there a year and had already started to raise interest in the floundering program, displaying his own salesmanship as a first-class recruiter by bringing the likes of Jim O'Brien to College Park with the famous "We Want You" ad in the *Washington Post*.

But it was Potts who helped Driesell's Terps become must-see TV.

Potts recalled a conversation he had with first-year athletic director Jim Kehoe, the school's track coach, after being hired. It centered around getting the football games on radio.

"The first day, I asked to see the file on our network and he said, 'There is no file because there is no network,'" Potts said.

After spending the first month driving north to Delaware and New Jersey and south to Virginia handing out Maryland hats,

T-shirts, and pennants at a variety of radio stations, Potts said, "We had 17 stations when we kicked it off for the first game. And we built it to 55 stations. Last I looked, they have six."

Potts then created the first prime-time television package for the men's basketball team, including the game that saw the Terps beat South Carolina on a last-second shot by O'Brien. It was slow going the first season, with only four or five games on television.

With the addition of Tom McMillen and Len Elmore for the start of the 1971–72 season, the Terps became nationally ranked and stations that were previously hesitant to preempt their regularly scheduled programming began putting Maryland on during weeknights.

"We beat *Happy Days* head to head; we killed 'em," Potts recalled. "We were the No. 1 ranked television show in the Washington area. Pretty soon, these players and Lefty could walk in anywhere, they were instant celebrities. We were the only team in the country doing this. Indiana copied us later."

As the basketball program gained stature, Potts had another brainstorm: playing games on Super Bowl Sunday.

With ACC rival North Carolina State scheduled to visit Cole Field House on January 14, 1973—the same day the unbeaten Miami Dolphins would play the Washington Redskins in the Super Bowl, as it turned out—Potts went to Driesell and Kehoe to tell him of his idea.

"They thought I was crazy. They said, 'Everyone will be so engrossed in the Super Bowl, nobody will watch,'" Potts recalled. "I said, 'Absolutely not, it'll be a great lead-in and we'll have the whole nation watching us.'"

With ACC syndicator C.D. Chesley clearing markets for a nationwide telecast, Potts said, "We got huge numbers. You couldn't have written a script any better. The only downside is that we got beat.... It lasted for a few years and then NBC had the rights to both college basketball and the Super Bowl and had a game."

The No. 2 Terps would lose to the No. 3 Wolfpack 87–85 on a last-second bomb by star guard David Thompson, who also led No. 3 N.C. State to an 80–74 win in Raleigh on Super Bowl Sunday the following season.

"David Thompson was the hero in both games," Potts recalled. "The game at Cole Field House he hit a shot at the buzzer, a 30-footer. I was right behind the Maryland bench and Lefty said to the team, 'Whatever you do, deny Thompson the ball. Make one of the other four guys beat us.'"

Potts, who had helped formulate the idea for Midnight Madness a couple of years before, later put together the first women's nationally televised game between the Lady Terps and perennial powerhouse Immaculata.

But one of the biggest money makers was the annual men's basketball banquet, held in a hotel ballroom in nearby Lanham that was big enough to accommodate 1,000 fans.

The highlight of the evening was usually a guest speaker, starting with Bill Russell and later including Oscar Robertson, Al McGuire, Red Auerbach, Adoph Rupp, and John Wooden.

The biggest name by far to speak at the banquet was heavyweight champion Muhammad Ali.

"The way I got him, I had booked the ballroom a year in advance and the Sheraton in Lanham comes to me with a representative of Muhammad Ali and said, 'You've got to give up the ballroom, there's going to be a heavyweight championship fight at the Capital Center and we're going to have sparring in the ballroom.'"

Potts turned them down—twice.

"The third time they come, 'What would it take for you to give up the ballroom and I said, 'If you get Muhammad Ali to the banquet as a speaker, I'll give up the ballroom,'" Potts said. "What blew my mind was the way those players looked at Muhammad Ali like he was God Almighty. They were totally awestruck."

Ali came with a guest whom he introduced to Potts.

"He said, 'I want you to meet my friend, Rubin "Hurricane" Carter,' who was out on appeal for murder one," Potts said. "I'm sitting next to the president of the university and he asked, 'Who is the gentleman with Mr. Ali?' I said, 'I really don't know who that is.' I didn't go back to sit in that seat until the damn banquet started. I said, 'This is going to get me fired.' Talk about finessing it."

Potts would buy a gift for the guest speaker and he gave Ali a clock with the time of several world capitals on it.

"At the end of the banquet, Lefty gets up to give him the clock and Muhammad Ali looks at him, laughs and said, 'Lefty, I like your class and I like your style, but your gift is so cheap that you won't see me for a while,' and the place goes crazy," Potts said.

18 Turgeon the Surgeon

In grade school in Topeka, Kansas, kids used to tease Mark Turgeon about his size and his last name. While his friends called and still call him "Turg," those who wanted to get under his skin would turn the "g" into a "d" and add a few choice pronouns to the package.

That changed as Turgeon grew into one of the area's best youth basketball players. Despite being a head shorter than most of his friends, Turgeon's tenacity and shooting touch helped attract attention throughout the state.

When he was "about nine or 10" and still so small that most figured he'd have trouble reaching the rim on a free throw, Turgeon won a state foul shooting contest by making 24 of 25 shots.

"Missed the first one," the Maryland coach recalled during the 2015–16 season.

After Turgeon's fifth-grade team lost a chance to go to a national YMCA tournament because he missed the front end of a one-and-one, he went to the court behind his family's home and shot free throws for hours.

"He was up the next day shooting about 500 free throws on our court," recalled Bob Turgeon, who coached his son's team.

Bob Turgeon can still feel the vibration of the basketball shaking the walls of the house as his younger son watched an instructional tape made by NBA star Pete Maravich over and over again "and then doing these Maravich deals."

By the time he reached his junior year at Hayden High, Turgeon's game was well-documented in game accounts of the *Wichita Eagle*. But it was one game in particular—against a previously unbeaten team from Kansas City—that launched the nickname he carried for years.

After Turgeon led Hayden to an upset—en route to the first of back-to-back state titles—the opposing coach called the 5'9" but still scrawny point guard "Turgeon the Surgeon" for the way he "carved up" his team's defense.

"It kind of stuck with me from there, right through college," Turgeon said of the nickname.

That was the University of Kansas, where Turgeon went in the fall of 1982.

His father, who had come to know longtime Jayhawks coach Ted Owens after selling him a couple of cars and sending his sons to Lawrence for summer camp, convinced one of new coach Larry Brown's assistants to give Turgeon a one-year, make-good scholarship.

The opportunity to play came when Cedric Hunter was ruled ineligible.

Turgeon's first game as a college basketball player was against the famed "Phi Slamma Jamma" team at Houston. It was 1983 and the Cougars were in the midst of going to the Final Four three straight years—and never winning—with the likes of Akeem Olajuwon and Clyde Drexler.

"I was real naïve," Turgeon said. "I was the third point guard to go in the game. I was so pissed at Coach [Larry] Brown. Here I was this little skinny kid playing the team that had lost in the national championship game [to North Carolina State].

"I was little and [Houston point guard] Alvin Franklin kind of started laughing at me and it really pissed me off. Because it made

Gary Williams, left, and Lefty Driesell, right, pose for a picture with Mark Turgeon during Maryland Madness on Friday, October 18, 2013. (Nick Wass)

me mad, I actually played well. And we got hammered pretty good. I learned the highest level of basketball right out of the gate and where we had to go."

By his junior year, Turgeon had helped the Danny Manning–led Jayhawks to the 1986 Final Four, where Kansas lost to Duke in the semifinals. Turgeon stayed on as a graduate assistant on the "Danny and the Miracles" team that won the title two years later.

Turgeon got his first taste of college coaching when he coached the school's junior varsity teams.

"That was a great experience for me, because I also travelled with the varsity," Turgeon said. "That was when I realized practice was important, but players being fresh mentally and physically was even more important. I'd be on the road [with the varsity] and come home and we hadn't practiced in two days and we'd play our tails off."

As a young coach there and later in his first Division I head coaching job at Jacksonville State in Alabama, Turgeon said, "I was pretty demanding, I probably wasn't a lot of fun to play for. I've learned over the years to dial it back. I realize the sun's going to come up. Kids are going to be kids, they're a little different than they were 20 years ago."

Boyhood friend Rob Reilly said that in many ways Turgeon is much like his own father, who, with Reilly's dad, founded the Capital City Youth Basketball League when their sons were small and later coached the AAU and summer league teams as they became more competitive.

"His dad was a really good coach, but moreso, he's a really good guy," Reilly said of the elder Turgeon, who lives in Lincoln, Nebraska, but has been a presence at Maryland games since his son took the job. "He cared about us, our success, what kind of men we were going to be. I see that in Mark. I see his dad in him."

Turgeon said a lot of what he did on the court in Topeka, and later in Lawrence, is still transferable to what he does with the Terps.

"Almost everything, to be honest with you," Turgeon said. "You are who you are and you hope your personality comes out on your teams. I like to think I was an attention-to-detail guy as a player. Had to be, was so little. I just think that everything I've learned from my mentors, plus my personality, comes out in my teams."

Having children of his own—sons Will and Leo, and daughter Ella—had a tremendous influence on Turgeon.

"I think that changed everything," Turgeon said. "I don't want anyone treating my kids [badly]. I try to treat each player with respect. I'm demanding still, but I do it in a different tone than when I first started."

If anything, Turgeon tries to take the pressure off his players and put it on himself. Admittedly, it doesn't always work.

"I've always been really hard on myself, it's one of the worst things I do," he said. "Because I critique myself so hard, I critique my team the same way. No one could ever put the pressure on me that I put on myself or my team, I said that when things were going well."

19 A Forgotten Rivalry, the Fight, and the Shot

When South Carolina left the ACC in 1971, the Gamecocks took with them the memories of a game earlier that season that summed up the heated rivalry with Maryland.

Though Frank McGuire's teams had won their share of battles with the Terps when Bud Millikan was Maryland's coach, things heated up in Lefty Driesell's second season in College Park.

The Gamecocks were ranked second, and the Terps had started to rebuild under the former Davidson coach, whose own relationship with McGuire started when Driesell played at Duke and McGuire coached at North Carolina.

In the first Maryland–South Carolina game in Columbia, South Carolina, played at the old Carolina Coliseum, Terps guard Howard White was on his way to setting an arena scoring record when Maryland forward Jay Flowers got in "some kind of tussle" under the basket with a South Carolina player.

"I think he was the one who started it, but all of a sudden, a big-time fight broke out," Driesell recalled. "People were coming out of the stands and hitting my players, and my players were hitting their players. I know Jack Neal, who was on my team, somebody was on top of him beating him up."

Driesell went over to rescue Neal when he found himself one of the combatants.

"John Ribock, he was the biggest guy on their team, he was about 6'9", 230 or 240, he comes up and slugs me in my mouth," Driesell said with a laugh. "Of course I started running or something. He kind of bloodied my lip, it wasn't that bad."

After the game, McGuire told the press that Driesell "must have been swinging and hit himself."

The game was called off with "five or six minutes" left with the Gamecocks ahead 96–70. When the Terps retreated to the visiting dressing room, one of Maryland's players, Darryl Brown, told Driesell that he thought his hand was broken.

"Darryl's holding his wrist. He said, 'I think I broke my hand, I knocked two guys cold,'" Driesell said. "I told the trainer to take him to the hospital to get it X-rayed. He did, and the trainer said there was no broken bones."

Maryland's game photographer had taken a 16-millimeter film of the game—and the fight. After Driesell got the film back two or three days later, "right in the film, clear as day, there's Darryl hiding underneath the bleachers. He didn't hit anyone."

A month later, when it was South Carolina's turn to play in College Park, McGuire told ACC commissioner Bob James that he was afraid to take his team up north and asked to cancel the game.

James assured McGuire that nothing was going to happen, even though Driesell vowed "to get even" with the Gamecocks when they played in College Park.

On the day of the game, hundreds of Maryland students lined up outside Cole Field House, many of them dressed like Roman soldiers, togas and all. After going to their seats—moved closer to the floor that season by Driesell—the students stood in stony silence as the Gamecocks warmed up.

"I think that spooked them," said Len Elmore, who was then an ineligible freshman sitting on the team's bench.

After Maryland hit the game's first basket and then got the ball back, Driesell ordered his point guard, Howard White, to "hold it" until McGuire pulled out of the 2–3 zone he always employed. The Terps took a 4–3 lead into their locker room at halftime.

"That's all he ever played, that 2–3 zone, his philosophy was that as long as the score was tied or he was ahead, he would never come out of that zone," Driesell said. "He wasn't coming out of his zone and everyone knew it."

Though McGuire pulled his team out of the zone to start the second half and eventually took a 30–25 lead, Driesell said his Terps "still held it a little bit" and wound up winning the game 31–30 on a last-second 30-foot shot by Jim O'Brien, giving the Terps their first signature win under Driesell.

"The crowd went crazy, they stormed the court and tore one of the baskets down. They climbed up on top of the basket, and the whole thing came down," Driesell said.

As the years went on, the fight was still talked about among older Maryland fans. South Carolina fans, too. Driesell said that he got an invitation to speak at a function run by his former assistant, Joe Harrington, who had moved to South Carolina.

"They wanted me to talk about The Fight," Driesell said. "It's a famous thing down there."

20 Bilas Remembers Bias

Nearly 30 years later, Jay Bilas has vivid recollections of the night Len Bias scored a career-high 41 points at Duke's Cameron Indoor Stadium. It was a performance Blue Devils coach Mike Krzyzewski has called "the best ever by an opposing player" at Duke.

Though it would not get nearly the attention of Bias' 35-point game at North Carolina later that season—handing the Tar Heels and legendary coach Dean Smith their first loss in the newly christened Dean Dome—Bilas said that it showed how unstoppable Bias was as a Terp.

"We won by a pretty big number [80–68], but we couldn't stop him," Bilas recalled in the fall of 2015. "We would go back to the huddle, guys were saying, 'What do we do?' We tried everything. I remember coming back to one huddle, guys were going, 'I'm trying to foul him, but I can't foul him.' We didn't have anybody to guard him, nobody else did in the league."

Bias scored Maryland's first 10 points of the game and finished 14 of 20 from the field, while hitting all 13 of his free throws to finish three points shy of Ernie Graham's school record of 44, which still stands. What made the performance even more remarkable is that the Terps played without point guard Keith Gatlin, who sat out the game with an illness.

Ultimately, a Duke team led by the backcourt of Johnny Dawkins, who scored 26 points himself that night, and later

Len Bias wears a Boston Celtics hat after being selected as the No. 2 overall pick in the NBA draft on June 17, 1986. Two days later, Bias was dead.

reached its first Final Four under Krzyzewski was too much for the Terps, who had yet to win in the ACC that year but ultimately reached the NCAA tournament.

Krzyzewski used four different players on Bias but opted not to go to a box-and-one that other ACC teams had employed with some success.

"What difference does it make?" Krzyzewski said during one timeout.

Bilas said that the Blue Devils were not totally shocked by what Bias did that night, considering that as a rising but still relatively unknown sophomore two years before, Bias had scored 26 points in the 1984 ACC tournament final that had given the Terps their first tournament championship since 1958.

The following year, Bilas said that he and his teammates were watching tape of that game in preparation of a game against the Terps.

"Something happened where there was a turnover and I wound up being back [on defense], a shot went up from the top of the key area, and I had to either block out either a trail big guy coming down the lane or turn and get Bias who was in the corner," Bilas recalled.

Bilas figured that a shot taken from the top of the key was going to bounce back toward the key if it missed, so he chose to box out one of Maryland's big men following for a rebound. He ignored Bias, which turned out to be a bad move.

"I thought, *It's not going to bounce sideways*," Bilas recalled. "I go block out the trail big, and Bias dunked the crap out of it. It was a highlight dunk, and Coach K stopped the tape and said, 'I don't care about angles, next time just block out Bias.'"

Bilas said that during his four years at Duke, the three best opposing players were Michael Jordan, Ralph Sampson, and Bias.

"Aside from Dawkins, who was my teammate, they were the three players who were head and shoulders above everyone else," Bilas said.

Bilas said around the 20th anniversary of Bias' death that he might have been Jordan's rival in the NBA had he lived.

"When we were in college, he was Superman," Bilas said. "He had everything you'd want in a player. He was a tremendous athlete, great body. Bias could really shoot it. As good a shooter as Jordan became later in his career, he still wasn't the shooter Bias was."

21 Greivis Vasquez, Gary's Alter Ego

Of all the players he coached in College Park, the one whose passion and personality came the closest to matching that of Gary Williams was probably Juan Dixon. But Greivis Vasquez would be a close second.

When Vasquez showed up at Maryland in the fall of 2006, he was something of an unknown. Eric Hayes, the quiet point guard from Northern Virginia, was supposed to be the second coming of Steve Blake.

Vasquez?

He was mostly known for being one of Kevin Durant's teammates at nearby Montrose Christian, a 6'6" combo guard from Caracas, Venezuela, who many thought was too slow and too streaky to be an effective player in the ACC.

Even though Hayes would become the first freshman to start at point guard in his first game since Blake did it in 1999, Vasquez introduced himself—and his trademark shimmy—during an early season game at Illinois as a freshman.

Coming off the bench, Vasquez scored 15 of his 17 points in the second half as the Terps upset the No. 23 Illini at Assembly

Hall. Vasquez not only showed his potential as a player, but as a player who spoke his mind.

"I'm not afraid, I'm ready for this," Vasquez said after the Terps stopped Illinois' 51-game non-conference home winning streak. "I'm from Venezuela and I didn't come here just to sit on the bench. I came here to play."

Vasquez didn't sit on the bench for long. He eventually took over the starting point guard job from Hayes, who became a solid—and much quieter—counterpart to Vasquez in the backcourt as a three-point specialist.

Vasquez became a full-fledged star.

Though not as fundamentally sound as Blake and certainly not as explosive an athlete as Steve Francis, Vasquez made his mark on the program, finishing his four-year career with his name firmly entrenched in the record books both at Maryland and in the ACC.

Only Dixon scored more points than Vasquez (2,171). Only Blake had more assists than Vasquez (772), who as a senior won the Bob Cousy Award given to the nation's best point guard. No one attempted more three-pointers (699).

In leading the Terps to a share of the ACC regular season title with Duke in 2009–2010—helping beat the Blue Devils with a running bank shot down the lane—the 6'6" guard was named the ACC Player of the Year. He finished his career with 2,171 points, 772 assists, 647 rebounds, and 191 steals.

Williams recalled a conversation he had with Vasquez at the start of his college career.

"He told me that he wanted to play in the NBA," Williams said early in Vasquez's pro career. "I told him, 'You've got the size, you see the court really well, you can shoot fairly well. It's just a matter of getting better every year.' He just took that to heart and went with it. Greivis got better every year."

It was typically after hitting one of those three-pointers in clutch situations that Vasquez would shake his shoulders and hips and, as he would say with his South American accent, "chimmy." Infuriating to many early in his career—even to Maryland fans and members of the local media that mistook Vasquez's emotion for ego—Vasquez became one of the most popular and respected players ever to wear the red and white (or yellow and black).

What Vasquez did in his final game at Maryland, against Michigan State in the NCAA tournament, is still talked about and might have been what pushed him into becoming a late first-round draft choice of the Memphis Grizzlies in what has become a solid NBA career.

With Maryland trailing by as many as 16 points in the second half, Vasquez carried the Terps into the lead before a last-second 3-pointer—by Spartans guard Korie Lucious after the inbound pass went into his hands when a teammate ducked—provided Williams with what might have been the toughest defeat of his career outside of the Final Four loss to Duke in 2001.

Vasquez scored 11 points in the last two minutes, with a runner giving the Terps an 82–80 lead with 31 seconds to play.

"To watch Greivis play the way he did in that game, I thought he deserved to play another game," Williams recalled as the two schools were set to renew their rivalry when Maryland joined the Big Ten in 2014.

Said Michigan State coach Tom Izzo, "We got lucky in the end. It was a tough loss because [Williams] had that great point guard, Vasquez, and they had a special relationship like I had with [Mateen] Cleaves."

22 The Biggest Shots in Maryland History

It's often difficult to determine or define the biggest shot in the history of the program—unless it was to win a national championship.

The most memorable, and the most replayed, is Drew Nicholas' three-pointer at the buzzer in Nashville in the opening round of the 2003 NCAA tournament to hold off UNC-Wilmington's upset bid when the Terps were defending national champions, though that was hardly the same team after the graduation of 2002 Final Four MOP Juan Dixon as well as two-time regional MVP Lonny Baxter and sophomore phenom Chris Wilcox.

Steve Blake, a senior on that team, might have outdone Nicholas in the Sweet 16 a week later. In nearly the exact same scenario, this time against Michigan State, Blake had an even better look but missed a straightaway three-pointer after Paul Davis had put the Spartans ahead with back-to-back baskets. Blake did have one big shot in his career: a clutch three-pointer to beat Connecticut in the Elite Eight matchup in Syracuse en route to the national championship.

Another possibility were two shots in the overtime period of the 1986 win over No. 1 North Carolina.

The steal and over-the-head reverse dunk by the team's superstar, the late Len Bias, might be second only to Nicholas running up the carpet and seemingly out of the arena. But Maryland's win over the Tar Heels, the first ever in the brand-new Dean Dome, also featured the ultimate trick play: point guard Keith Gatlin bouncing the inbound pass off the back of Kenny Smith's leg, stepping in bounds, and sealing the upset.

Then there were a pair of shots by another Maryland point guard, Duane Simpkins. The first was when Simpkins was a sophomore, playing in the season opener against Georgetown in 1993 at USAir Arena. His runner in the lane over Don Reid gave the unranked Terps a one-point win in a game even more famous for the coming-out party of unknown freshman Joe Smith. The second came when Simpkins missed another last-second job the following season at Duke, and Smith was there to clean up the boards to cap his career-high 40-point performance.

Those with longer memories can go back to Jim O'Brien's 30-footer to beat South Carolina at Cole Field House in 1971 in what was seen as a revenge game after the teams brawled in Columbia a few weeks before. Another big shot is when Adrian Branch's long jumper took down Virginia.

Ultimately, the biggest shot in the history of the Maryland program could be a shot that went against the Terps in the 2010 NCAA tournament. It was taken by Michigan State's Korie Lucious, who received a long inbound pass after one of his Spartan teammates ducked. The shot ruined what had been a spectacular comeback by the Terps, who trailed by as many as 16 points, and an even more remarkable performance by Greivis Vasquez in what turned out to be his final game at Maryland.

103–100

The 1974 Atlantic Coast Conference tournament concluded with fourth-ranked Maryland losing in overtime 103–100 to top-ranked North Carolina State in a matchup television analyst Billy Packer deemed at the time as "the greatest college basketball game ever played."

There were a number of story lines Lefty Driesell still talks about decades later in regard to the 1974 game.

The year before, Maryland and North Carolina State met in the title game at the Greensboro Coliseum. Since the Terps knew they were heading to the NCAA tournament with the Wolfpack on probation, Driesell was considering not playing his starters.

"In those days, the ACC was one of the only big conferences to have a tournament, so teams like Indiana and UCLA were at home resting," Driesell said.

An interesting sidebar to the 1974 game: after South Carolina left the ACC, leaving the league with only seven teams, the league's regular season champion received a first-round bye. That year it was the Wolfpack.

"That's the excuse I always use: that was our third game, that was their second," Driesell said. "It was a factor, especially in an overtime game. I've always thought that."

"The pressure going in, it was all she wrote. Because if we don't win, we go home," Elmore said. "We pretty much knew we weren't going to play in the NIT because we had already won that [two years before]. We already climbed that mountain."

Still, Driesell knew how talented the Wolfpack were. While Maryland might have had more overall talent with Tom McMillen, Len Elmore, John Lucas, and Mo Howard, N.C. State had a transcendent player in David Thompson and one of the most underrated big men ever to play in the ACC in 7'4" Tom Burleson.

"One of the things that made David Thompson so good was that Norman [Sloan] ran a very simple offense, I can almost remember it," Driesell said. "Burleson would post up on the left-hand side of the lane, and you had to get some help on him. David Thompson was on the right side."

Elmore said that the fourth-ranked Terps went in "pretty confident" after beating Duke by 19 points in the quarterfinals and No. 6 North Carolina by 20—the largest loss ever by the Tar Heels in an ACC tournament at that point—in the semifinals. Maryland had lost both of the regular season matchups with the Wolfpack, each by six points.

"We know they [North Carolina State] have an extra day's rest," Elmore said. "We jumped out to a quick lead, but we did run out of gas."

Elmore said that the problem was the fact that Driesell rarely played his bench and barely rested his starters and a couple of reserves even in the rout of the Tar Heels. After the Wolfpack erased an early Maryland lead, "it was just nip and tuck," Elmore recalled.

It came down to the final seconds of regulation with the Terps down a point.

"The reason I didn't take the shot was because Tom Burleson was playing like a madman," Howard recalled. "I was a little reluctant because I thought he might have a chance to block the shot."

Howard said that Elmore has mentioned many times over the past four decades the fact that Howard should have shot what many considered a fairly uncontested 15-footer.

"I say, my man didn't score 38 points on me," Howard said with a laugh. "I've listened to this over the years. I don't necessarily hold that—because I didn't take the shot—it lost the game for us. It shouldn't have come down to a single shot.

"I'm sorry that this is all Lenny remembers after all these years."

Driesell can still see Thompson flying in from the free throw line to take a lob from North Carolina's pint-sized point guard, Monte Towe, or driving to the basket and elevating above everyone else.

"He would go back down and get an alley-oop," Driesell said. "He couldn't dunk it [since the dunk was still disallowed in college basketball], but he might as well have dunked it. Or he'd drive it. He was tough to stop. We'd try to put pressure on Monte Towe and we did a good job. The offense was very simple and good. He didn't have a lot of plays like we have now."

The 7'4" Burleson, who was miffed after Elmore's selection as first-team All-ACC prevented him from becoming the first player in league history to be selected three straight years, wound up with 38 points.

"He was pretty good," Driesell said of Burleson.

After the game, Driesell walked onto the N.C. State team bus and congratulated the Wolfpack and their coach, Norm Sloan. Driesell told the victors that he hoped they would go on to win the national championship.

Some believe that it was Driesell's toughest defeat at Maryland.

"Probably," he said. "But every time you lose it feels bad."

24 John Gilchrist's Rise and Fall

Few players in Maryland history have had the kind of careers in College Park as John Gilchrist.

Not too many had his talent, either.

Unfortunately for Gilchrist, his sometimes preternatural ability was often overshadowed by his own instability and immaturity.

"Unpredictable," Gilchrist called it years later.

Most remember Gilchrist, then a sophomore, leading the Terps to their last ACC tournament title in 2004.

After averaging 15.4 points and five assists, Gilchrist was voted third-team all-league, in large part because Maryland was just a 16–11 team that finished 7–9 in the ACC.

In Greensboro, North Carolina, during the ACC tournament, Gilchrist could have been voted all-world.

After his perfect three-point shooting (4 of 4) and clinching free throw helped Maryland beat Wake Forest in the opening round, Gilchrist went on a tear, scoring 23 of his game-high 30 points to lead the Terps back from a 19-point deficit to No. 2 seeded North Carolina State.

Then came the win over Duke in the finals. While many recall walk-on Mike Grinnon's free throw shooting to put away the top-seeded Blue Devils in overtime, Gilchrist hit a big shot toward the end of regulation and scored 26 in the victory.

"In recent years, [I] think it's pretty safe to say I don't think anyone was any more dominating than John was [in an ACC tournament]," Gary Williams said in an interview for a 2014 story about Gilchrist in the *Baltimore Sun*.

Some thought Gilchrist could have been an NBA lottery pick had he come out after the 2003–04 season, which ended with a 72–70 loss to Syracuse in the second round of the NCAA tournament. That Gilchrist scored just seven points and fouled out didn't play into his decision to stay in college.

"At that point, I was just a kid playing ball," he said. "I viewed the world totally different than I do now, how I carry myself, things of that nature. The maturity of handling fame and money, I think it would have been a concern for me.… Even my mom didn't think I could have handled it."

Though Gilchrist had displayed erratic behavior throughout his first two years in College Park—even getting into a fight with Steve Blake at practice as a freshman—he became even more unsteady as a junior.

Problems started the summer before his junior year, when the team took a trip to Italy and Gilchrist began challenging Williams at every chance.

"He just didn't want to do anything that anybody else did," Williams said. "He wanted to be [treated] different. That was a part of his personality. John needed the attention all the time. He had his own ideas about how the game was to be played."

Plagued by injuries for most of the season, Gilchrist basically quit on the team at halftime of an opening-round loss to Clemson in the ACC tournament in Washington, D.C., claiming he hurt his wrist.

The Terps went to the NIT, and Gilchrist stayed home.

He never played for Maryland again.

"It's been an uphill battle ever since," he said in a 2014 interview with the *Baltimore Sun*.

After going undrafted, Gilchrist began a professional career overseas in Israel. He played there for four of the next five seasons, wound up in Australia, and suffered what appeared to be a career-ending knee injury in 2010. He ended up in Kosovo and Hungary before another wrist injury—this one apparently for real—ended his career in 2013.

Gilchrist said it took him only a few months playing in Israel to realize that he had made a mistake leaving after his junior year. He apologized to Williams and former assistant Dave Dickerson in a long, emotional email he sent them in 2005.

"I just basically poured my guts out to them," Gilchrist said. "I told them that 'I appreciated the tough love y'all gave me. At the time being in the immature mind-set that I was in, I felt like I was being blamed for things unfairly. I came to understand that it's not just about what you do as a player, it's how you affect the whole team…. At the time it was me, me, me.'"

Gilchrist was starting to feel pressure off the court after his daughter was born that summer.

Williams eventually forgave his former star, who finally returned to College Park in the winter of 2016 to resume his studies. He hoped to graduate in the fall.

"We all grow up at different times, and I think John saw some things that he really appreciated and he wasn't a part of them. I wish there was a button I could have pushed [while Gilchrist was at Maryland] that could make him realize the same things he realized when he got to Israel," Dickerson said.

25 Others Who Left Early and How They Fared

There have been a number of Maryland players who left before their eligibility was up—to mixed results. Some, like Buck Williams, went on to have long and prosperous NBA careers. Others, like Jordan Williams, made a significant error in judgment.

After the 2015–16 season, Maryland had more than one player leave off the same team for the first time in school history, with freshman center Diamond Stone and junior forward Robert Carter opting to forego their remaining eligibility.

From best to worst, this is how it worked for some notable Terps.

Buck Williams: After being taken third overall in the 1981 draft after his junior year, Williams had a 17-year career split mostly between the New Jersey Nets and Portland Trail Blazers. He is only one of seven players in NBA history to amass more than 16,000 points and 13,000 rebounds. He left marks on both franchises, as the Nets' all-time scorer and Trail Blazers' all-time field goal percentage leader.

Brad Davis: One of the first to leave early for the Terps after freshmen were allowed to play, Davis was picked No. 15 overall by the Los Angeles Lakers in 1977. It took three years and three more teams for Davis to get his NBA career solidified, but he wound up with the expansion Dallas Mavericks in 1980 and played there 12 years, becoming the first Mav to have his jersey retired.

Steve Francis drives and scores in the second half of a game in College Park on December 7, 1998. (Nick Wass)

Joe Smith: The Naismith Award winner as a sophomore, the once relatively unknown 6'10" center was the No. 1 pick overall in the 1995 draft by the Golden State Warriors. Smith lived up to that status his first couple of years. A trade to Philadelphia midway through his third year was the first of many stops in what became a 16-year career that saw Smith average just under 11 points overall.

Steve Francis: Selected second overall by the Vancouver Grizzlies in 1999 after spending only one season in College Park, "Stevie Franchise" forced a trade to Houston, where he won the NBA's Rookie of the Year in 2000 and earned the first two of his three straight (2002–04) All-Star selections. After gaining similar stature in Orlando, Francis' career was derailed by injuries after nine years.

Chris Wilcox: After playing sparingly as a freshman on Maryland's first Final Four team in 2000–01, the athletic 6'9" forward started as a sophomore and averaged a solid 12 points and 7.1 rebounds. While he showed enough in the shadows of Juan Dixon and Lonny Baxter to get drafted eighth overall by the Los Angeles Clippers after the Terps won the title, Wilcox was a journeyman for most of his 13-year NBA career that was cut short by a heart condition at 31.

Brian Williams: One of the top freshmen in the ACC in 1987–88, Williams transferred to Arizona after saying that he couldn't get along with Bob Wade. He wound up going 10th overall in the NBA draft to Orlando in 1991. He had a solid career and earned a ring with the Chicago Bulls in 1997 before retiring suddenly at age 30 despite having five years left on a $36 million contract. Williams, who changed his name to Bison Dele, died under mysterious circumstances in 2002.

Alex Len: Nobody could blame Len for leaving after his sophomore year to become the No. 5 overall pick in the 2013 NBA draft. While his career with the Phoenix Suns got off to a slow start after Len underwent surgery twice before his first season to correct a foot injury suffered in College Park, the 7'1" center from the Ukraine finally started to show progress in 2015–16 by averaging 9.0 points and 7.6 rebounds.

Jerrod Mustaf: Coming in along with Walt Williams in the fall of 1988, Mustaf was clearly the more talented of the two players, leading the Terps in scoring (18.5) his sophomore year. Though many, including Gary Williams, advised Mustaf to stay through his junior year, Mustaf was picked 17th overall by the New York Knicks. He was out of the league within five years.

Terrell Stoglin: As a sophomore, Stoglin led the ACC in scoring during Mark Turgeon's first season, but he was suspended for a year by the athletic department that spring for violating student-athlete conduct code. Rather than staying at Maryland or transferring to another school and sit out, Stoglin applied for early eligibility and went undrafted. He has played in seven European countries.

Danny Miller: Very few players leave a Final Four team as a non-starter, but that's exactly what Miller did following Maryland's first trip to the NCAA semifinals in 2001. Recruited as a scorer, Miller was forced to be more of a role player than he wanted and wound up at Notre Dame. He ended up scoring 13.9 points his senior year—a year after the Terps won the national championship.

Jordan Williams: Not as highly touted coming in as James Padgett, Williams proved to be a double-double machine in his two years as a Terp, breaking Len Elmore's school record with 13 straight as a sophomore. As was the case with Mustaf, Williams was advised to stay another year, in part because of an impending NBA lockout. He was drafted 36th overall by the New Jersey Nets and barely saw the court there or in Atlanta, where he was traded, in two seasons.

26 A Wild Weekend in Atlanta

Most Maryland fans think happy thoughts when the city of Atlanta is mentioned. It is, of course, the place where the Terps won the 2002 national championship by beating Kansas and Indiana at the Georgia Dome.

Dave Dickerson was there in his role as an assistant coach under Gary Williams. As Williams talked that night in the locker room about how far the program had come under his watch, Dickerson was asked for his perspective.

"Most people have no idea," he said.

It was in the same city, in a different arena, where Dickerson's college career as a Terp had ended some 13 years before after a crazy 36-hour period during the ACC tournament.

Coming in as the No. 8 seed after finishing dead last and winning just one conference game during the regular season, the Terps were given no shot to beat top seed North Carolina State in a quarterfinal round game.

No bottom seed had ever upset a No. 1 seed in the history of the tournament before or since. Third-year coach Bob Wade, who had replaced Lefty Driesell, was under fire for possible NCAA violations and a second losing record in three years.

"There was some desperation from the coaches and players going into the tournament," recalled Dickerson, then a senior. "We wanted to play in the NCAA tournament and we thought if we could just get past that first game, we could do it. Coach Wade did an unbelievable job of preparing us."

As he had done often during the season, Wade had installed a new offense right before the tournament.

"It was called 'Trips,' I think," said Dickerson. "We had some very smart players on the team and we came out and beat the best team in the ACC. They were loaded with talent, and we beat them from start to finish. After that game, we felt we had played our best complete game of the year and we thought anything can happen."

What happened in the aftermath of Maryland's upset was equally shocking.

As Dickerson was getting attention from trainer Bill Saylor after his shoulder had popped out of place during the game—a common occurrence for the 6'6" forward—he noticed some commotion as Saylor was called away to attend to Wade, who appeared to be having a heart attack.

Tony Massenburg, then a redshirt junior, ran out of the locker room with fear in his eyes, calling for a doctor or for someone to call 911. Massenburg had been a freshman when Maryland star Len Bias had collapsed in his dorm suite following the 1986 draft and died from a cocaine-induced seizure.

"I can remember it like it was yesterday," Dickerson said. "I was in the training room with our trainer. I saw Coach Wade having chest pains. The attention quickly went from me to him. That was a very difficult weekend in that you go from beating the top to seeing your head coach looked like he was having a heart attack."

After being treated in the locker room, Wade was wheeled out on a stretcher and taken to Grady Memorial Hospital, where he was diagnosed with hypertension. It was not surprising given that he suffered from high blood pressure and his job at the time was in jeopardy.

Wade, a former high school coaching legend at Dunbar High in Baltimore, never coached another game at Maryland. He stayed in the hospital as the Terps lost the next day to North Carolina with assistant coaches Oliver Purnell and Ron Bradley—both future Division I head coaches—took charge.

"The most difficult part of that was the few hours after the [North Carolina State] game," Dickerson said. "When we got confirmation that he [Wade] was okay, how do we switch to prepare for another basketball game? It was very difficult. Carolina was as talented a team as there was in college basketball."

Even though the Tar Heels "had kicked our butts twice" during the regular season, the Terps thought their Cinderella run would continue.

"Can we keep the magic going?" Dickerson said. "The fact that we had beaten the best team in the ACC that year, could we be the Cinderella team of college basketball? Everything took its toll—the fact that we had to expend so much energy to beat N.C. State, what happened to Coach Wade afterward. It was too much to overcome."

The Terps were blown out. It barely registered for Dickerson, fellow seniors John Johnson and Greg Nared, as well as Massenburg.

"We were numb to a lot of things that were happening to our careers," Dickerson said. "The one thing we resigned ourselves to was that we were going to stick it out and believe in the university and we were going to graduate and go out and represent the university the best we could. That was the calming force for us."

Dickerson never put on his class ring until he returned to become an assistant coach at Maryland nearly a decade later.

"For me to go back and coach there for nine years and for us to accomplish the things we did validated why I came to the university," Dickerson said. "There was [initially] some resentment, some embarrassment, but as I got older and learned the nuances of coaching and how universities work and the ups and downs of that, I began to have an appreciation for the university."

27 Early Lessons for Gary

In referencing his coaching roots in what was an emotional induction speech to the Naismith Memorial Hall of Fame during the summer of 2014, Gary Williams spoke about the first and second head coaching jobs he ever had.

The first was in 1969 at Woodrow Wilson High School in Camden, New Jersey, not far from where Williams had grown up. In his second year at the school, the head coach quit and turned the job over to the 23-year-old Maryland grad.

The second was a couple of years later at Lafayette College in Easton, Pennsylvania, where Williams had followed former Maryland junior varsity coach Tom Davis.

"You think about key situations in your life and your career," Williams said that night in Springfield, Massachusetts. "Tom Davis was the only guy I knew who could get me into college coaching. If I had turned that down, I would have been happy. I would have been a high school coach, I never would have coached in college. I would never be here tonight."

Since Davis couldn't pay Williams to be an assistant basketball coach, Williams took over the soccer program for six years.

"You ask me how I did as a soccer coach," Williams said at the Hall of Fame ceremony. "Let me say this—the Soccer Hall of Fame hasn't called."

Reflecting about his early coaching career a couple of years later, Williams said that the high school job in South Jersey probably prepared him more for what he eventually did on the college level, but coaching soccer didn't hurt either, even though Williams admits that he had to read books and coaching manuals before practice.

"So when I got my first head coaching job at American [in 1981], I had experience running a team," Williams said.

And when Williams took Maryland to its second straight Final Four in 2002, he recalled the experience he had in winning a New Jersey state title and saw some interesting similarities. Just as he learned the game from Bud Millikan as a point guard in College Park, Williams also took what he gained from his predecessor at Woodrow Wilson.

"Art DiPietro was a great fundamental coach," Williams said.

It didn't hurt that the summer before his second year as Woodrow Wilson's coach, a 6'8" forward named Harold Sullinger moved to Camden from Columbus, Ohio, where decades later his nephew Jared became a star for the Ohio State Buckeyes.

With the addition of Sullinger, who wound up playing college ball at Iowa, Woodrow Wilson steamrolled the competition by some 28 points a game. Only one game was a nail-biter. Williams would keep telling his assistant, Stan Pawlak: "How is this happening? Is it really that easy?"

Williams was only a few years older than his players and the rest of the student body. As there was at many other high schools that were integrated in the 1960s, there had been tension at Wilson.

"He was like a big brother to us," Sullinger said in an interview with the *Baltimore Sun* in March of 2002, a few weeks before the Terps beat Indiana for the NCAA title.

Derek Brown, who played point guard on the team and would later became a women's head college coach at Coppin State as well as an assistant on the men's team that upset the Terps in Williams' first season, said that the young high school coach had a different temperament than later in his career.

"There was a lot of pressure on him," recalled Brown. "We were a real experienced team, so he didn't have to yell a lot. But you could tell he was nervous. He would always hold a piece of paper in his hand, and during timeouts it would be shaking."

Yet during halftime of Wilson's semifinal game of the 1970 New Jersey state championships, Williams showed a part of his personality that he would become known for as a college coach. In a game at Princeton's Jadwin Gymnasium, Wilson fell behind Elizabeth's Thomas Jefferson by 15 points.

"They had [future Notre Dame star] John Shumate and a bunch of other big guys," said Brown. "It was the first time we had ever heard Gary yell. The principal of the school was listening, and he asked Gary to apologize to the team later on."

Smith also threw a chair across the room during halftime—years before Bobby Knight perfected the art—and Jefferson scored the first 12 points of the second half, took a five-point lead by quarter's end, and won by 10 points as Sullinger dominated Shumate.

The next week Wilson beat East Orange by 11 points for the state championship. A brawl ensued and the team had to be escorted out by friends and family from Camden. "We had to come back later to cut the nets down," Brown recalled.

Williams spent one more year at Wilson and then joined Davis.

"I wasn't a very good coach, but I had very good players," said Williams, recalling his time at Wilson. "I think what that year gave me [was] the confidence to think I could be a good high school coach, and it also gave [me] the courage to take the next step."

One that ultimately led to the Hall of Fame.

28 The Best Players Whose Jerseys Don't Hang in College Park

There's only so much ceiling space at what started out as Comcast Center and is now called Xfinity Center to hang the jerseys of former Maryland greats.

A lot of the decision-making is subjective, and some of it is downright political. Are offensive stats the only ones that matter? Should a player's post-college life off the court be considered?

Everyone is going to differ in their opinions about whose jerseys should be honored—there are multiple numbers currently up there—and whose should not.

Here are five that should be considered:

Adrian Branch: Aside from Scott Van Pelt, there are few talking heads who bleed Terp red (and gold and black and white) more than A.B. It's pretty remarkable, considering how he's been snubbed by his former school.

The former guard, who was often overshadowed his last two years by an otherworldly talent named Len Bias, is the only player currently in the top 10 in scoring who has not been so honored. His 2,017 points were second only to Albert King when he left.

Another remarkable stat was that Branch committed just 86 turnovers in 4,179 minutes and 123 games, less than one a game. Branch was a part of three NCAA tournament teams, and along with Bias led the Terps to their only ACC tournament title under Lefty Driesell in 1984.

Derrick Lewis: When Maryland fans talk about the best defensive player in school history, most of the attention is focused on big men such as Len Elmore and Buck Williams, as well as guards such as Johnny Rhodes and Steve Blake.

Given that he played center for four years at 6'7", 195 pounds, Lewis is used to being overlooked. He remains—and will likely forever be—Maryland's all-time shot blocker. His 339 rejections are 83 ahead of the player in second place, Terence Morris.

Lewis was also more than a capable scorer, finishing 17th overall with 1,458 points, an 11.5 point average. He also was the school's third all-time leading rebounder with 948. Lewis was one of the unsung heroes on Bob Wade's only NCAA tournament team.

Terence Morris: Had Maryland won back-to-back national championships in 2001 and 2002, there is no doubt that Morris' jersey number would be up there with those belonging to Juan Dixon, Steve Blake, and Lonny Baxter.

Unfortunately for Morris, who played on the school's first Final Four team, the end of his career was largely overshadowed by the one-year sensation caused by Steve Francis and the ascension of Dixon as the school's most beloved figure.

Morris was the opposite of both as a player and a person. Yet there is no denying the impact he had both in helping the Terps become a national power and more than solid career stats that included 1,733 points (12th), 925 rebounds (fifth), and 256 blocked shots (second).

Byron Mouton: It's impossible to find Mouton's name in the Maryland record books since he only spent two seasons in College Park after transferring in as a junior after two years at Tulane. It's also impossible to ignore Mouton's role in Maryland's rise to the national championship.

Mouton was close to being a double-digit scorer as a junior (9.6) and averaged a solid 11.1 points as a senior. Considering that he transformed himself from a scorer at Tulane to a player who did a lot of the dirty work defensively for the Terps, Mouton was certainly appreciated by his teammates and coaches.

Gary Williams has said many times over the years that if not for Mouton, who took over as a starter when Danny Miller transferred following the 2001 run to the Final Four, Maryland would not have won its only title in school history the following year.

Dez Wells: It seems only fitting that Wells should be the first of Mark Turgeon's former players to have his jersey honored. Given that Wells changed his number from 32 to 44 as a senior to honor the memory of a former high school teammate, maybe he should have both hanging.

As much as Maryland rescued Wells after he was unlawfully expelled from Xavier after being falsely accused of rape as a freshman—he settled an out-of-court suit against the school and its president as a senior in College Park—the 6'5" guard helped keep the Terps on track.

Just as Walt Williams was a key figure in Maryland's rise under Williams by staying all four years, Wells will be remembered as a key figure for the Terps' rebirth under Turgeon, leading Maryland back to the NCAA tournament as a first-team all-Big Ten player his senior year.

29 Albert and Buck

Their college careers were tied together like so many other Maryland duos that played on the same team.

But unlike Tom McMillen and Len Elmore, John Lucas and Mo Howard, or Juan Dixon and Lonny Baxter, Albert King and Buck Williams never quite led their respective teams to the same level of sustained success while both individually are considered among the best to ever play in College Park.

In three seasons, King and Williams led the Terps to an average of 21 wins a season and two NCAA tournament appearances—a Sweet 16 loss to Georgetown and a 35-point second-round shellacking by eventual champion Indiana.

King, who arrived a year before Williams, left as the school's all-time leading scorer with 2,058 points and was named the ACC's Player of the Year as a junior. Williams, who played three seasons, left as the school's all-time field goal percentage leader and was twice All-ACC.

"I don't think there is one ounce of disappointment in the kind of player Albert became, the kind of player Buck became," said Greg Manning, who came in with King and Ernie Graham in the fall of 1977.

Neither King nor Williams seemed comfortable with stardom. After being compared to Julius Erving and Connie Hawkins coming out of high school in Brooklyn, New York, the reticent King admitted after an up-and-down freshman year that he could sense resentment from some of his teammates at the attention he was receiving.

It was a program in transition, with Brad Davis opting to leave early for the NBA and Brian Magid, a local player known as a great outside shooter, transferring to George Washington. James "Turkey" Tillman was kicked off the team during the season, in which the Terps finished 15–13.

"When we got there, as a 19-year-old coming out of high school, you're not aware of turmoil that's going on," Manning recalled. "You're happy to be there. You're worried about playing, you're worried about starting. The winning becomes a by-product of all that."

In an interview early in the season with Tony Kornheiser, then with the *New York Times*, King said, "It's different now. Before it used to be a game. Now it's more. I used to have fun and try to win. I miss high school a lot. I had a lot of friends there. In college, I get the feeling that if you don't win, they [fans] hate you."

Manning said he never felt any animosity directed at the burgeoning star.

"Albert probably could have scored 35 a game if he really wanted to," Manning said. "That wasn't who he was, that wasn't his personality. That's not a negative. Could Albert have scored more? Sure, but he was a great player."

Long before there was King James, there was King Albert. But unlike LeBron James or Kobe Bryant or even Michael Jordan, King was uncomfortable with the spotlight, going as far as to admit, "I don't want to be a star."

While his otherworldly talents often forced King into that role, he never seemed to possess the killer instinct that others—including his older brother Bernard—did. Even in nine NBA seasons, King was rarely his team's main scoring option and he eventually played his way back to the bench as injuries piled up.

Williams came to Maryland with a lot less hype.

In becoming the ACC's Rookie of the Year, Williams was once asked in an interview with a Baltimore newspaper why North Carolina's Dean Smith hadn't recruited him out of Rocky Mount, North Carolina, where as a high school senior he averaged 21 points and 20 rebounds.

"He came and watched me play a lot," Williams said of the legendary Smith.

Williams said that Smith suggested he go to junior college for a couple of years before coming to Chapel Hill. Partly, it was because the Tar Heels were so loaded with a team that featured Mike O'Koren and Al Wood. Williams admitted that it also might have had to do with his grades.

"To be truthful, I was a very lazy student in high school," Williams said. "I went to class, but I didn't realize the value of an education. I'm sure Smith heard I wasn't a very good student, and that was one of the question marks."

Smith's loss was Lefty Driesell's gain. Williams became known as one of the hardest-working players ever to come through Cole Field House—and one of the humblest. After averaging 10.8 rebounds and being named the ACC's top freshman, Williams said he could do better.

"It was disappointing because I set very big goals," Williams said after that season. "I'm not going to tell you what they were because I'm going to set them again this year. I put my goals in a

Bible and each day I look at them and read a few verses of scripture for spiritual uplifting."

After moving to center as a sophomore, Williams averaged more than 15 points and 10 rebounds. After helping the Terps hand Syracuse its first loss in the Carrier Dome, Driesell said that the 6'8", 215-pound Williams "got to playin' like a horse."

It was that combination of hard work and humility that served Williams well during a 17-year NBA career. Drafted along with King to the New Jersey Nets—Buck went No. 3 and Albert No. 10—Williams split most of his career between New Jersey and Portland.

Unlike King, who finished his career as a vagabond playing overseas in Europe and Israel, Williams left as one of the most respected. He was Rookie of the Year in 1982, was an NBA All-Star three times, and remains the Nets' all-time leading scorer and rebounder.

Manning recalled the lack of publicity surrounding Williams when he came in as a freshman.

"He was not a scorer, he was never a scorer. He was a guy that rebounded, set picks, ran the floor, and played great defense," Manning said. "He became a great leader. Obviously he played in the NBA for all those years and was never a scorer there. But that's not who he was."

30 From Walk-On to Captain

On a list of the most overachieving players in Maryland history, Vince Broadnax might be at the top.

On a list of Gary Williams' favorites in his 22-year career in College Park, Broadnax would probably find himself occupying a similar spot.

Broadnax went from a regular student playing intramurals as a freshman in the fall of 1989 to a walk-on under Bob Wade to a scholarship player under Williams as a junior to team co-captain with Walt Williams during their senior year.

During a period when the Terps were undergoing a transition from Wade to Gary Williams, going through a tumultuous three-year NCAA probation, playing more than half of Walt Williams' junior year while their star sat out with a broken leg, Broadnax showed more than anyone—including himself—could believe.

The highlight came during an upset of North Carolina State while Williams was sidelined.

Playing against a team that would include future ACC Player of the Year Rodney Monroe, future NCAA assist leader Chris Corchiani, and future NBA first-round pick Tom Gugliotta, Broadnax led the Terps to one of their biggest victories that season by scoring 24 points.

Cracked Gary Williams, "If Vince played in a pickup game upstairs in the auxiliary gym, I don't know if he'd score 24."

The outburst came during an eight-game stretch that season when Broadnax, known more as a defensive stopper despite a scrawny 6–3 build, scored in double figures five times. Most of his baskets came on a designed play that was a staple of Williams' Flex offense—a little curl-in shot from the lane.

Against the Wolfpack, Broadnax was not only the offensive star but the defensive stopper, holding Monroe, the ACC's leading scorer, to two field goals in the last 16 minutes.

Later that season against Georgia Tech, Broadnax made Yellow Jackets star Kenny Anderson rush a three-point shot into an air ball that helped preserve a 96–93 upset.

"I'd rather stop someone like that than score points myself," said Broadnax, who also scored 21 against Clemson and 18 against Duke that season. "I've come a long way. But you never forget where you came from."

Broadnax didn't have a single Division I scholarship offer out of Forestville High School in Prince George's County, Maryland.

Kevin McLinton, who took over the point guard spot as a sophomore when Williams got hurt and then started there as a senior after "The Wizard" graduated, said that Broadnax was symbolic of the team of overachievers who came to Maryland in Wade's last year and Williams' early years.

"He's kind of like this team, proving he can play on this level," McLinton said. "He's been an inspiration for a lot of guys on this team."

In Broadnax's case, it was inspiration fueled by perspiration. A defensive-minded, work-ethic coach like Gary Williams appreciated Broadnax for both. But Gary Williams didn't like to say that Broadnax was an overachiever, which he was.

"I don't think of it as overachieving because that implies a player doesn't have talent," Williams said. "It means you go after it a little harder. He's proven he's a good ballplayer. Period."

When Broadnax started getting some meaningful playing time as a junior, he was clearly afraid to shoot. In one 10-game stretch before Walt Williams broke his leg, Broadnax took all of 18 shots. That he made 12 didn't satisfy his father.

"My father asked me why I didn't take some more shots," said Broadnax, who led the Terps in field-goal percentage that season. "Now I take the shots if I'm open."

Gary Williams had players like Broadnax before and throughout his 22-year career—the last of the bunch of overachievers might have been Dave Neal—but none of them started as a walk-on.

After getting a scholarship, Broadnax was once asked if he minded being referred to as a former walk-on.

"You can look at it two ways," he said. "You were a nothing and look how far you've come. Or just like this team, you had talent all along and proved a lot of people wrong."

Cole Magic for the Miners

Willie Worsley spent nearly a lifetime going through the back doors of high school and college gyms, as well as pro basketball arenas as a player and coach.

When he entered Cole Field House through the front door on a frigid February day in 2016, along with four of his former Texas Western teammates, the sign in the lobby above what had once been a ticket window brought the significance of what they had accomplished 50 years ago back to life.

The sign noted that the 1966 NCAA men's Final Four had been played on the Maryland campus and that the little Texas school was there along with national powers Kentucky and Duke, as well as Utah.

What it didn't mention was in upsetting the heavily favored and top-ranked Wildcats, 72–65, the Miners became the first team to win a championship with five African American starters.

"Anyone who loved to be a part of history, anyone who loves to be talked about 50 years after the event, and if you don't understand that, look at the joy on our face and the love in our heart, thank you guys for keeping us alive for 50 years," Worsley, the team's feisty point guard, said later at an event to honor the team before Maryland hosted Wisconsin at Xfinity Center.

History has told us about Texas Western coach Don Haskins deciding to use only his African American players after hearing his Kentucky counterpart, the legendary Adolph Rupp, said that a team with black players was incapable of beating his Wildcats despite the fact that the Miners had lost only once.

History has told us that two first-half steals by Bobby Joe Hill off Kentucky star Pat Riley shook the confidence of Rupp's team and a thunderous follow dunk by David "Big Daddy" Lattin in the second half gave the Miners a 60–51 lead and a sense that the game was all but over.

As the former Texas Western players said, history didn't tell us the complete story.

History doesn't tell us how Haskins summoned only his African American players to a hotel room near the Maryland campus shared by Lattin and Hill, the team's star guard.

"Coach Haskins obviously had something else in mind," Lattin recalled. "He kind of looked around the room and said, 'It's up to you.' And he walked out of the room. Everybody looked at each other. We had no idea what he was talking about.

"We didn't know he was just going to play only the African American players. The other guys walked out, and Bobby looked at me, and I looked at Bobby, and he said, 'We're not going to lose this game.' I said, 'You're right.'"

Said Shed, "The attitude we had was that losing was not an option."

History didn't tell us about the look on Riley's face after Lattin's dunk.

"He was shocked," said Willie Cager, who is confined to a wheelchair after suffering a stroke several years ago.

History didn't tell us that NCAA officials at Cole Field House couldn't find a ladder for the Miners to stand on in order to cut down the nets. Or that the Texas Western players were as resourceful as they had been on the court, with "little Willie climbing on top of my head," Shed recalled.

Shed became emotional as he recalled how the 1966 Final Four marked the first time his father had ever seen him play in a basketball game. After the final horn sounded, Shed said he walked off the court looking for his father.

"I pointed to my father," said Shed, his voice choking. "That was my way of thanking my champion for all the hard work and the things that he went through to nourish me so I could have that chance to become an NCAA champion."

Considering that the 1966 NCAA tournament was a lot different—with the championship game on taped delay—many were unaware of what Texas Western had done. When Shed went back to his Bronx neighborhood in New York that summer wearing a sweatshirt that read TWC, people were perplexed.

"Nobody knew what TWC stood for. Texas Women's College? Teeny Weeny College?" Shed said with a laugh. "But it said '1966 NCAA champions.' That's what it showed."

It wasn't until years later, after his brief pro career ended quickly when he tore up a knee in training camp with the Boston Celtics that Shed began to understand the significance of the victory.

"I was coaching at the University of Wyoming and I had my ring on, and this football player came over and said, 'Bobby Joe Hill, Big Daddy Lattin, Nevil Shed,'" he recalled. "I said, 'Yeah, that's me.' He said, 'I just want to thank you for what you did some time ago. My father was a great football player and could not go to a big school. What you did, you opened the doors so that individuals such as myself could go—if qualified.'"

Lattin, who played two seasons in the NBA and four more in the old American Basketball Association, said that Texas Western's victory gave African American athletes a chance to play at major colleges—including Kentucky, where Rupp recruited his first black player four years later.

"When they let the athletes in, it made it possible for the other young African Americans as well. It helped open doors for everybody," Lattin said.

Interestingly, Lattin's grandson, Khadeem Lattin, was the starting center for Oklahoma in 2015–16 when the Sooners reached the Final Four.

"We don't talk about it a lot," Lattin said. "We talked about it a little when we watched the movie [*Glory Road*] a couple of times. We looked at the games we played, but he's so young."

Perhaps Lattin's grandson and others will learn more if they read his soon-to-be-published book, *Slam Dunk to Glory*. Depending on how much of Cole Field House is preserved when the school's new athletic performance center opens in 2017, others will learn about Texas Western as well.

As the group was about to leave Cole Field House for Xfinity Center, Shed looked around. Given that he had not been back in a half-century, he knew it would probably be for the last time.

"We were given the chance, and the eyes were opened," Shed said. "I remember in the movie [*Glory Road*] they asked if you ever thought colored guys could master basketball as we do. It's out there, and I guess you can say, 'Yes, we are legends.'"

32 Lefty Looks Back At 1974

Of all the ACC tournaments the Terps played in during Lefty Driesell's 17 seasons, 1974 and 1984—both played in Greensboro, North Carolina—are probably the most memorable.

The 1974 tournament concluded with third-ranked Maryland losing in overtime 103–100 to top-ranked North Carolina State in a game Billy Packer deemed at the time as "the greatest college basketball game ever played."

Driesell said that had the Terps beaten the Wolfpack, they would have likely faced defending champion UCLA in the championship game. N.C. State went instead and stopped the Bruins' streak of seven straight NCAA titles.

It would have been a rematch of the season opener at Pauley Pavilion.

"They had won something like 60 consecutive games, and we opened the season at UCLA," Driesell said.

Down a point in the waning seconds against the Bruins, Maryland fouled Richard Washington, who missed the front end of a one-and-one.

"We had the ball with about 12 seconds left. There was plenty of time. We ran what we called 'Special,' which was a pick-and-roll with Lucas and Elmore," Driesell said. "UCLA did a smart thing. They trapped John when we got the ball, and the ball went off his leg and out of bounds."

After losing to N.C. State in the ACC finals, Maryland athletic director Jim Kehoe got a call from the NIT, which the Terps had won two years earlier.

"Coach Kehoe came to me and said, 'The NIT's on the phone, they want to know if you want to play,'" Driesell recalled. "I told the guys on the team to vote. They all voted 'Don't play.' So we didn't play. I didn't even vote. If I voted, I would have probably voted to play."

When N.C. State beat UCLA in the NCAA finals, it triggered a national debate about opening the tournament field to include conference runner-ups such as the Terps.

"The next year, they said two teams can come and play," Driesell said. "When we won the NIT, we had better teams in the NIT than they had in the NCAA because a lot of smaller schools got into the NCAA. We beat Niagara in the final, and it was one of the most lopsided games in the NIT."

33 Top High School Signings

Here is a look at the top 10 signings in history for the Terps:

1. **Tom McMillen:** When he signed with Lefty Driesell in the summer of 1970, McMillen had already been on the cover of *Sports Illustrated* as the most celebrated high school player in the country. That Driesell, in his second year in College Park, beat out North Carolina's Dean Smith for the 6'11" McMillen became the start of a recruiting rivalry that began when Smith took Charlie Scott away from Driesell, then the coach at Davidson, the year before. When McMillen graduated, the future Congressman was the school's all-time scorer (1,807, still the most by a three-year player) and second to teammate Len Elmore in rebounding (859).

2. **Albert King:** Like McMillen, King was also considered the best high school player in the country and was a major figure in Rick Telander's book, *Heaven Is a Playground*, about basketball at Brooklyn's Foster Park. Just as McMillen had Elmore, Lucas, Mo Howard, and Brad Davis to lead the rise of the Terps under Driesell, King had Buck Williams, Ernie Graham, and Greg Manning to lead Maryland back into the national spotlight. Though the Terps never quite achieved as much as some thought the talent merited, King was the leading scorer (2,058, now fourth) in school history when he left in 1981 as the No. 10 overall pick of the first round by the New Jersey Nets.

3. **Diamond Stone:** Maryland was thought to be a long shot when Stone cut his list down to four schools, and most figured he would head to Connecticut, the defending national champion, if he didn't stay home to play at Wisconsin. The turnaround

in 2014–15 from a 17–15 record to 28–7 improved Mark Turgeon's chances, as did Melo Trimble's decision to stick around for his sophomore year, to help sway Stone to College Park. Stone came off the bench for the first half of what turned out to be his only season as a Terp, including the night he scored a freshman record 39 points against Penn State. He finished the season third in scoring, third in rebounding, and first in blocked shots in helping the Terps reach their first Sweet 16 in 13 years.

4. **John Lucas:** Though he is closely tied to all the others who led Maryland's rise under Driesell, Lucas would have had bigger numbers had he gone elsewhere. There's a story that Lucas basically scored at will in practice as a freshman until Driesell told him to share the ball with his teammates. As it was, he finished his career one year after McMillen and Elmore as the first player in history to score over 2,000 points (2015, now sixth) and as the school's all-time assist leader (514, now fifth). Along with King, Lucas still has the record for the most field goals made (862).

5. **Keith Booth:** While the former Dunbar star didn't put up the career numbers that might merit this kind of consideration—he is sixth in rebounding at 916 and ninth in scoring at 1,776—he was a key player as a freshman and sophomore on the back-to-back Sweet 16 teams led by recruiting classmate Joe Smith and kept the Terps competitive after Smith, a virtual unknown when he showed up in 1993, left as the No. 1 pick in the draft in 1995. Booth's signing also helped smooth some rocky relations between Maryland and the Baltimore high school community still upset over the firing of Bob Wade.

6. **Melo Trimble:** While Trimble exceeded the expectations of most who questioned whether he was overrated in high school, his signing was a major coup for Turgeon considering that he was Maryland's first McDonald's All-American since Mike

Jones in 2003. Aside from what he did on the court in 2015 leading the Terps in scoring (16.2) and becoming the first freshman point guard to be named first-team all-Big Ten since Eric Gordon in 2008, Trimble's best move might have been announcing that he was coming back since Stone said that played a big part in his decision to come to Maryland. A midseason hamstring injury curtailed his production and shooting as a sophomore.

7. **Steve Francis:** The most electrifying player in recent Maryland history would have been higher on this list had his signing created the buzz it did while he was still in high school. Admittedly, Francis was more a playground legend than a legitimate Division I prospect when he left Montgomery Blair High in Silver Spring for a two-year junior college journey that wound up at Allegany College in Cumberland. Still, there was excitement from the moment Francis arrived in the summer of 1998 until he left less than a year later as the No. 2 pick in the NBA draft after leading the 28–6 Terps to the Sweet 16 as their top scorer (17.0) as well as their assists leader (4.5). It's one of the reasons he's the only one-year player to have his jersey honored in the rafters.

8. **Johnny Rhodes:** Like Francis, Rhodes signed after leaving high school, spending a year at Maine Central Institute. Joining fellow freshmen Duane Simpkins and Exree Hipp, Rhodes was compared to John Lucas when he first arrived because he was left handed and wore the same jersey number (15). Rhodes wasn't quite Lucas, but when he left Maryland after helping the Terps to NCAA tournament appearances his last three seasons, he was (and remains) the school's all-time steals leader (344), sixth in scoring (1,743, now 10th), seventh in assists (437, now 10th), and 10th in rebounding (704, now 15). Like Lucas, his No. 15 hangs from the rafters as well.

9. **Brian Williams:** The year before Williams came out of high school in Los Angeles, Bob Wade thought he was on the verge of signing the top high school big man in the country, Alonzo Mourning. But the rumor at the time was that Nike executive Sonny Vaccaro, then the powerbroker in recruiting, had promised Mourning to John Thompson at Georgetown and told Wade he would get Williams the following year. Unfortunately for Wade, Williams only stayed a year at Maryland before transferring to Arizona, where he played two years before getting picked No. 10 in the 1991 NBA draft. Williams played eight years in the NBA, changed his name to Bison Dele, retired at age 30, and mysteriously disappeared with his girlfriend and the skipper of a catamaran they were sailing on with Dele's brother—the only person to survive—near Tahiti in 2002.

10. **Moses Malone:** This is not a misprint. For years, Driesell included Malone's picture in the media guide among those former Terps playing in the NBA. Malone never suited up at Maryland after signing with the Terps in the spring of 1974 out of high school in Petersburg, Virginia. Malone was on campus for a short time before an offer came from the ABA's Utah Stars to play for $1 million. Driesell told the man-child center that if he played one year in college, the offer would double. It was one of the few lines Driesell used over the years that didn't work.

34 Cole's Going-Away Party

As retirement parties go, the one Maryland held on the first Sunday night in March of 2002 had all the trimmings.

Instead of blowing out candles, the No. 2–ranked Terps blew out the opposition, the Virginia Cavaliers, who had also been there for the very beginning of Cole Field House as Maryland's home court in 1955 and would be there for the last ACC home game at Comcast Center in 2014.

But the last game at Cole was special.

"The one thing I remember is that Virginia played really well," Gary Williams recalled more than a decade later. "We were on a roll by then, having gone undefeated at Cole that year, we didn't want to lose the last game. We played great, and that building deserved that. We were a great offensive team at times that year, and everything fell into place that day."

Many of those who had played such a big part in turning what started out as a large but not intimidating home court were also back for the festivities, closing it out with a memorable pass-the-ball ceremony among some of the program's biggest names.

"I'm sad because it's still a great place," said one of them, former ACC Player of the Year Albert King. "I wish Cole could go on forever."

Recalled Williams, "What made it special was that a lot of the great Maryland players were there that night. Bud Millikan was there, my coach. Tom Young was there. It made that event special."

Mary Humelsine, a 1939 graduate whose father managed the construction of the arena named for Board of Regents Chairman William P. Cole, was there for both the opening game and the closing game.

"And I'll be here when they open the new arena, too," she said that night.

As often happens at these types of affairs, there was one notable person missing that night.

Despite the pep band playing one last rendition of "Amen," a song that Maryland fans got to associate with postgame celebrations during Lefty Driesell's 17 seasons in College Park, Driesell was not in attendance.

"He should be here," said former star Tom McMillen, whose arrival two years after Driesell signaled the rise of the program to national prominence.

Whether it was Driesell still being hurt for the way he was dismissed 16 years before or for the fact that he had never properly been recognized for his role in the program becoming a national power, it was a huge blemish on an otherwise spectacular night.

Millikan, whose own arrival at Maryland coincided with Cole's opening in 1955, came up from his home in Atlanta for what might have been his last visit to the campus. Al Bunge, one of Millikan's early stars, came from his home in Oklahoma.

More familiar faces such as Keith Booth and Adrian Branch all took part in a postgame ceremony that followed a 20-point rout of the Cavaliers.

"That's exactly what we wanted to do, close out Cole with a win," said Juan Dixon, then a few weeks away from leading the Terps to a national championship and breaking Len Bias' all-time school scoring record. "The ceremony at the end was a great experience for me. There are a lot of great names up in the rafters. A lot of great guys came through this program."

The program ended with junior point guard Steve Blake being comically lifted by teammate Tahj Holden for a dunk.

"I was told after the game I was going to be involved," Blake said of his ad-lib basket. "As soon as Tahj gave me the ball, a few guys told him to pick me up."

The night also included one last fist pump from Williams, who would turn 57 the following day. Amid the cheers, there were plenty of tears as the Terps closed out their nearly five-decade history with a record of 486–161.

"It's difficult because obviously this place means a lot to me," Williams said.

Courtside seats that night were selling upwards of $2,000 each.

Longtime booster Bob Schaftel of Baltimore, a 1962 graduate, vowed to save his ticket stub as he did for his first game at Camden Yards and Cal Ripken's record-breaking 2,131st consecutive game.

"When my wife and I die, the kids will probably throw them out," Schaftel said.

35 College Stars, NBA Journeymen, and Busts

Not since Steve Francis has Maryland had what many considered a superstar among its basketball alumni.

Not since Buck Williams have the Terps had a player sustain All-Star status for nearly their entire career.

More than two dozen NBA players have passed through Cole Field House and Comcast Center—and before that Ritchie Coliseum with Gene Shue.

Few have ever achieved the greatness they did in College Park.

While that is often the case for many college stars making the transition to the NBA, and for many other college programs as well, it is particularly true of the Terps.

Here's a list of those at the top of the list:

Joe Smith: The National Player of the Year as a sophomore and the No. 1 overall pick of the Golden State Warriors in 1995, Smith finished second to Damon Stoudamire for Rookie of the Year and averaged 18.7 points his second year. But a trade midway through his third year started a vagabond 16-year career that saw only brief glimpses of his early stardom.

Chris Wilcox: If Smith was nearly a finished product as a college player when he left, Wilcox was still a work-in-progress when he decided to go after helping the Terps to their only NCAA title as a sophomore. Drafted eighth overall by the Los Angeles Clippers, Wilcox had a productive three-year run with the Seattle SuperSonics before the team moved to Oklahoma City, but he never did much after that. He eventually retired because of a heart ailment when he was 31.

Albert King: A schoolboy legend in Brooklyn before he ever arrived at Maryland and a central figure in the book aptly titled *Heaven Is a Playground*, King was the No. 10 overall pick of the New Jersey Nets in 1981. He wound up playing nine seasons with four teams, but averaged just over 12 points in a career overshadowed by brother Bernard.

Juan Dixon: One of the greatest competitors ever to play at Maryland, Dixon went from being a 160-pound redshirt as a freshman to the school's all-time leading scorer. After taking the Terps to their lone NCAA title, Dixon played seven non-descript years in the NBA, averaging in double figures just once over a full season.

And the busts…

Jerrod Mustaf: After being the team's leading scorer as a sophomore, Mustaf's decision to turn pro was questioned before he became the 17th overall pick in the 1990 draft, taken by the New York Knicks. Mustaf barely played in New York and was traded after one season to the Phoenix Suns, where he lasted three seasons and was released amid allegations that he was involved in

Joe Smith rises up on Massachusetts forward Lou Roe in a 1994 NCAA tournament game. (Carol Francavilla)

the murder of a young woman whose parents claimed had been impregnated by Mustaf.

Jordan Williams: It's hard to put Williams on this list of Maryland stars turned NBA journeymen, since his pro career was so brief. Many—including Gary Williams—thought the 6'10" power forward was making a huge mistake when he announced he was turning pro after his sophomore year. It turned out to be the case, as he was picked in the second round by the Nets and saw his career last all of one season and 43 games.

36 Top 10 Transfers

1. **Byron Mouton:** Given his role on the 2001 team that reached the Final Four for the first time in school history and the 2002 team that won Maryland's only national championship in men's basketball, the 6'6" forward has to get consideration for the top spot on this list. Though his numbers were not big—9.6 points and four rebounds as a junior after transferring from Tulane, 11.1 points and five rebounds his senior year—he was the quintessential glue guy who did a lot of the defensive dirty work and always seemed to come up with huge baskets, including a couple in the NCAA title game against Indiana when Juan Dixon cooled off after a hot start.

2. **Dez Wells:** After starting out making the all-Atlantic 10 freshman team at Xavier, the 6'5" guard was accused of rape that spring. Local prosecutors wound up not pressing charges, and Wells came to Maryland late that summer. Wells immediately became one of the leaders of a young Terp team that won 25 games and advanced to the semifinals of the NIT. After the

team struggled when Wells was a junior, five players with eligibility left, and the players who came in—particularly freshman point guard Melo Trimble—embraced Wells' leadership. Wells became a first-team all-Big Ten selection by the coaches despite missing a month of his senior year with a broken wrist. Wells led the Terps in scoring in each of his first two seasons and finished second behind Trimble as a senior.

3. **Ben Coleman:** Talk about making an immediate impact. After transferring in from Minnesota, where he played two years, the 6'9", 235-pound Coleman led the Terps to an 82–80 double-overtime win over unbeaten UCLA at Cole Field House. Coleman helped Lefty Driesell to his first win over the Bruins in four tries by scoring 27 points on 12 of 13 shooting and pulling down 12 rebounds. Though that might have been the high point for Coleman in his two seasons with the Terps, he had a very solid career, averaging over 15 points and eight rebounds a game while being a second scoring option to Adrian Branch as a junior and then leading the team in scoring (right ahead of rising star Bias) as a senior

4. **Steve Francis:** He was one of the few one-and-done Terps to ever make it through College Park. After stops at two different junior colleges, one in Maryland and one in Texas, Francis returned home to Takoma Park, about a 10-minute drive to Cole Field House. Francis, Stevie to everyone, became one of the most popular and exciting players in history, averaging 17 points and 4.5 assists while leading the Terps to the Sweet 16. He left as the No. 2 player taken in the NBA draft to the Vancouver Grizzlies before engineering a deal to the Houston Rockets.

5. **Matt Roe:** The 6'5" shooter came to College Park for his final year in 1990–91 after being frustrated with his role at Syracuse despite averaging 11 points a game as a junior. Along with Walt

Williams, Roe helped keep the Terps competitive (17.8 points a game) as Gary Williams rebuilt a program hampered by the NCAA probation he inherited from his predecessor, Wade. If not for Roe, the Terps would have really been in trouble when Walt Williams, one of the top scorers in the ACC, broke his leg early in the ACC season. One of the highlights for Roe was leading the Terps to a 104–100 win with 29 points on 11 of 16 shooting over a North Carolina State team that featured Chris Corchiani, Rodney Monroe (from St. Maria Goretti), and Tom Gugliotta.

6. **Rasheed Sulaimon:** He went from being grudgingly accepted by Maryland fans who couldn't ignore or forget the three years he spent at Duke to becoming one of the most respected during the 2015–16 season, when he played second fiddle to Melo Trimble offensively while becoming one of the team's best defenders and leaders. While he sacrificed his scoring—averaging around 11 points a game—he got his career-high with 28 points in a loss at Minnesota.

7. **Robert Carter Jr.:** He joined Sulaimon and freshman Diamond Stone as the new starters on a team that won 27 games, reached the Sweet 16 for the first time since 2003, and managed to be called underachievers. He led the Terps with nearly two dozen double-figure scoring games, but he finished the year plagued by offensive inconsistency and foul trouble before announcing that he wouldn't return for his redshirt senior year in order to turn pro.

8. **Rudy Archer:** He played one season (1987–88) and helped the Terps reach the NCAA tournament for the only time in Bob Wade's three seasons in College Park. Archer played well in his only postseason experience before leaving the school for academic reasons. He will be long remembered as the player who eventually helped bring Wade down after the coach had

one of his assistants give Archer rides to a local junior college, a violation of NCAA rules.

9. **Richaud Pack:** After starting his career playing two seasons for Isiah Thomas at Florida International and then a year North Carolina A&T, where he graduated, Pack joined the Terps in 2014–15 with the idea of being "the Energizer bunny" off the bench. But an early-season injury to Wells, and Pack's ability to transform himself into a tough perimeter defender, helped the 6'4" guard start most of the year. He was great at keeping the ball moving in the offense and proved to be one of the off-court leaders in Maryland's 28–7 turnaround season.

10. **Garfield Smith:** One of the better—and star-crossed—players of Gary Williams' early tenure at Maryland, he came to the Terps as a tough, street-wise junior in 1990 out of New York— by way of a junior college in Kansas—and averaged more than 10 points and five rebounds in each of his two seasons with the Terps. The highlight was a night when Smith hit his first nine shots and threatened to knock his coach out of the record books before missing late in the game against Southern Cal. He had his senior year shortened by a broken leg midway through the year.

37 Most Memorable Wins over Duke

March 11, 1984: Lefty Driesell won his first ACC tournament championship, over Duke, 74–62. Junior Len Bias led the Terps with 26 points by hitting 12 of 17 shots. It was Maryland's first ACC tournament title since 1958.

March 1, 1995: With Gary Williams in a Maryland hospital room with pneumonia and Duke coach Mike Krzyzewski home recuperating from back surgery, Joe Smith scored a career-high 40 points and tipped in the game-winner at the buzzer. Said teammate Exree Hipp, "Superman was in the building tonight."

February 27, 2001: Maryland had gone 1–5 since blowing a 10-point lead and losing to the Blue Devils in overtime earlier in the season. Seemingly headed for another defeat, Juan Dixon led a second-half comeback that resulted in a 91–80 win for the Terps on Senior Night at Cameron Indoor Stadium. Dixon finished with 28 points and five steals and the Terps ended the game on a 41–20 run.

March 14, 2004: After finishing the regular season with a 7–9 record in the ACC, the Terps were on the bubble to make the NCAA tournament. A day after helping his team come back from a 19-point deficit against North Carolina State in the semifinals, sophomore guard John Gilchrist led Maryland to a 95–87 overtime win over Duke.

March 3, 2010: Maryland scored the game's first 12 points on Senior Night at Comcast Center and eventually lost all of its 14-point lead, but senior guard Greivis Vasquez scored 20 points— including a driving bank shot that put the Terps up for good—and Jordan Williams added 15 points and 11 rebounds in a 79–72 victory over the No. 4 Blue Devils that helped the No. 22 Terps tie Duke for the ACC regular-season title.

38 Had Lefty Not Come

Lefty Driesell was always a favorite target of fans at Cameron Indoor Stadium. During his 17 seasons at Maryland, Duke students would show up with faux bald pates in honor of the follicly-challenged Driesell.

But what would have happened if Driesell had taken former Duke athletic director Carl James' long-standing offer to coach the Blue Devils after bringing little Davidson to national prominence long before Stephen Curry was born?

And, more importantly, what would have happened to Coach K?

According to Driesell, James had a standing offer to coach the Blue Devils.

"He was my hall master when I was at Duke and every time we'd play Duke [when he was at Davidson], he'd say, 'C'mon Lefty, this is where you belong,'" Driesell recalled of James, who ironically later became his athletic director at Maryland.

The last time James made the offer came shortly after Driesell had agreed to take over in College Park in the spring of 1969.

"I told him, 'I can't back out on that,'" Driesell recalled.

Even before Driesell had that conversation about Duke, he said he was approached years before by legendary N.C. State coach Everett Case, who offered to make Driesell his successor if he came as an assistant to Raleigh for one season.

"He said he'd sign me to a five-year contract and he'd retire after one year," Driesell said. "I also was also [offered] the Florida job. I turned down three jobs that won the national championship."

While Bucky Waters, who was hired away from West Virginia after Driesell turned James down, did a pretty good job his first two

Lefty Driesell summons his team during a workout at Atlanta Omni in preparation for the Atlantic Coast Conference tournament on March 8, 1985. (Bob Jordan)

seasons in Durham by taking the Blue Devils to the NIT, things went south after that.

James, who would also become the commissioner of the ACC late in his career, didn't have a second shot at the Lefthander.

By the time he made another coaching change in 1974, Driesell had turned the Terps into a national power. James then hired Bill Foster, an East Coast guy who had somehow found his way out to Utah after coaching at Rutgers.

During this time, a bright young coach with a hard-to-spell name was building his reputation at Army.

In a story in the *Duke Chronicle* when Mike Krzyzewski was hired, it was reported that the correct way to pronounce the 33-year-old coach's name was Kre-shev-ski.

Duke athletic director Tom Butters kiddingly said later that he could have introduced his new, relatively unknown hire as "Coach Who?" The headline in the student newspaper read, "This is not a typo."

Krzyzewski reportedly beat out Boston College's Tom Davis, Mississippi State's Bob Weltich, Old Dominion's Paul Webb, and Foster's top assistant, Bob Wenzel. Butters denied speculation that the job had been offered to another coach.

"There is no doubt in my mind that Mike is the most brilliant young basketball coach in the country," Butters said. "Mike was my first choice and he received unanimous approval by the athletic council."

Interestingly, Maryland beat Duke seven of the first 10 times the teams played after Krzyzewski was hired, including in the 1984 ACC tournament final that was Driesell's lone championship during his time at Maryland. The Blue Devils won the last three games of Driesell's career in College Park.

"I beat Duke more than Duke beat me at Davidson and Maryland," Driesell said.

What might have happened to the legacy of Coach K had Driesell taken the job?

Butters reportedly zeroed in on Krzyzewski at the insistence of associate athletic director Steve Vacendak, who had played under the legendary Vic Bubas in the 1960s and was the point guard on Duke's 1966 Final Four.

At the time of his hiring, Krzyzewski was considered one of the up-and-coming coaches on the East Coast after reviving the Army program that had fallen on hard times after Bob Knight left for Indiana and Krzyzewski, his point guard, had graduated.

Interestingly, another young East Coast coach was a much hotter name. Jim Valvano had just taken Iona to two straight NCAA tournaments. Valvano's team at the little New York school had toppled both Kansas and soon-to-be-national-champion Louisville in Madison Square Garden during the 1979–80 season.

North Carolina State hired Valvano, who within three years won a national championship in Raleigh.

Three years into Krzyzewski's tenure, the local media along Tobacco Road thought Butters should have fired "Coach Who."

More than 30 years, five NCAA championships, and more than 1,000 victories later, Duke obviously made the right choice.

Yet it's interesting to think what might have happened if Driesell, a Duke alum, had accepted the long-standing offer of James or the one Everett Case made to him a few years before that.

The coaching careers of at least three men—Driesell, Krzyzewski, and Valvano—might have turned out much differently.

39 Trivia King

If there was a trivia game about the history of Maryland basketball, Mike Grinnon would likely be a stumper to this question: Who is the only men's player to be a part of both a national championship team and an ACC tournament champion for the Terps?

Grinnon was a little-used freshman during the 2001–02 season that culminated with Maryland's NCAA men's basketball title. Though his playing time increased marginally over the next three years, Grinnon is remembered for the free throws he hit to help beat Duke in Greensboro, North Carolina, as a junior in 2004.

"The teams that I played on those four years were some of the best teams in the program's history so I was playing with and competing against some really good talent," Grinnon said in a 2012 *Baltimore Sun* series to commemorate the 10-year anniversary of the NCAA championship. "There was a lot of talent that came in on the teams after me—Nik Caner-Medley, Chris McCray, D.J. Strawberry, Mike Jones—that had a lot more potential to elevate their game to the next level than the role player that I was."

Grinnon said that he watched Maryland's loss to Duke in the 2001 NCAA semifinals in Minneapolis on television but didn't understand the magnitude of that defeat (a game in which the Terps led by 22 points) until he got to College Park that summer.

"It was so amazing to see that the goal and the mission of the team was the same—it was to win a national championship," Grinnon said. "Anything other than winning a national championship was really failure."

In the preseason workouts, Grinnon was handed a T-shirt that read "Atlanta, Ga., 2002 National Champions."

"I still have it to this day. We'd work out in it every single day," Grinnon said. "The leadership that Juan Dixon portrayed and Byron Mouton showed was so remarkable."

Grinnon did not play in either of the Final Four games, but he has vivid memories from that weekend in Atlanta.

"Kansas almost blew us off the court in that semifinal game," Grinnon said. "When Coach Williams called that timeout, and it was probably before the first TV timeout we were down eight or 10 points to start. In that huddle, he didn't say a word. We all just sat there and composed ourselves. It was almost a silent timeout with no words being expressed. We came out and took it from there. That was kind of something special that stuck out in my mind."

Then came Monday night against Indiana.

"The thing that sticks out in my mind is just being in the locker room before the national championship game and the nerves," he said. "It was like silent and everyone was so focused. No one was really talking to one another. It was so surreal."

What Grinnon recalls more than his big free throws was the defense he played in overtime against Duke guard J.J. Redick in the 2004 ACC title game in Greensboro, North Carolina.

"The personal highlight of my career was absolutely that game, but contrary to belief, the more exciting moment for me was that I had to guard their leading scorer for every second of overtime, and he did not get one shot off," Grinnon said. "Personally that was more of an accomplishment than hitting the free throws."

Grinnon came to Maryland out of St. Dominic's High on Long Island, with hopes of becoming a starter with the Terps, but he never averaged more than the 11 minutes a game he played as a senior. Grinnon is realistic about the way his career panned out.

"Always throughout my career I had the mentality that I was going to be a prime-time player," he said. "I know some people might think otherwise, but I always went out there to be competitive and have a major impact on the team. I knew I was going to have to earn my stripes because I was playing behind some future NBA players. I knew with Byron [Mouton] graduating, there was going to be the tremendous opportunity to get playing time after my first year."

It didn't happen, as Gary Williams had perhaps his best recruiting class ever coming off the two straight Final Fours.

Grinnon, who graduated with a degree in communications in 2005 and manages a staff of financial planners in Northern Virginia, has no regrets.

"Do I think things could have played out a little bit differently? Sure, but at the same time Coach Williams was definitely fair with the way he treated me," Grinnon said. "I had a very special and unique relationship with Coach Williams and the coaching staff."

40 Elmore, Walton, and Uncle Sam

By his senior year at Maryland, Len Elmore had already established himself as one of the best big men in the country. As a sophomore, he had set a school single-season rebounding record of 11 a game.

Injured toward the end of his junior year, Elmore spent the summer before his senior year getting ready for the season-opener against UCLA, coming off its seventh straight national title, and fellow senior Bill Walton.

In the 1973 NCAA title game against Memphis State in St. Louis, the 6'11" Bruins junior center had scored a Final Four record of 44 points, making 21 of 22 shots and pulling down 13 rebounds.

"I took the video tape of that game home and I watched it just about all summer in the basketball office," Elmore recalled. "I studied Bill's moves the whole summer. There's nothing he could do that would surprise me."

When the Bruins went early to their star player, Elmore said he blocked Walton's first two shots. On his third shot, Walton faked Elmore into the air and drew a foul. But Elmore had certainly done his homework.

"I think he shot 8 for 24 in that game," Elmore said. "He did get 27 rebounds, but that's because he never left the paint. That freed me up because I kind of stretched the floor, shot from the free throw line, the elbow, got some easy looks there."

Elmore finished with 19 points and 14 rebounds, setting the tone for a season in which he was named first-team All-ACC center. But Tom McMillen, Maryland' leading scorer, and rising star sophomore John Lucas combined to hit a total of five of 23 shots.

At the time, McMillen was sweating out the Rhodes Scholar selection process—he would become Maryland's first and last athlete to earn that honor—and was distracted by his father's quickly fading health. McMillen's father, a physician, died a couple of weeks later.

With UCLA leading by eight with 3½ minutes to go, the Terps staged a comeback and closed to within a point in the final minute. In possession with a chance to win, Lefty Driesell called a timeout.

"We're in the huddle, and he calls it for McMillan, and I'm the one that was scoring, but they call the play for Lucas to drive baseline and kick it back to Tom somewhere," Elmore recalled.

As Lucas drove the baseline, UCLA forward Dave Meyers handchecked the Maryland point guard out of bounds. Pac–8 referee Booker Turner never blew his whistle. The Bruins won 65–64 for their 65th straight win at Pauley Pavilion.

"We weren't going to get that call," Elmore said. "Booker Turner's nickname was 'Booker Bruin.' We knew if we played them on a neutral site, or at our place, we might have beaten them by 10."

The Terps went on to go 23–5 and finished the season with the now-iconic 103–100 overtime loss to North Carolina State, which ultimately interrupted UCLA's run of national championships behind superstar junior David Thompson.

Given that the Terps were No. 4 when they met the Bruins at Pauley and were No. 4 when they faced the Wolfpack in Greensboro for the ACC tournament championship, there's a chance that they might have met UCLA if they had been invited to the NCAA tournament.

"I think that's when the NCAA tournament committee realized that they were making a mistake not inviting the best teams in the country," Elmore said.

Elmore did get something out of the trip to Westwood.

The day before the game, Elmore spent a few hours with Walton at the player's apartment.

"I wanted to see what kind of guy he was," said Elmore, who had followed another UCLA legend, Lew Alcindor, at Power Memorial High School in New York. "Both of us had some of the same political bent, kind of activist views."

The conversation eventually turned to the two sleek Italian bicycles in the hallway outside Walton's apartment. When Elmore asked Walton where he got them, the answer came back "Uncle Sam."

At the time, UCLA booster and benefactor Sam Gilbert was not a household name, on the East Coast at least. Walton had to explain to Elmore that they weren't a gift of the U.S. Army.

"I admired them, and the next thing you know, I get one in the mail, unsolicited, from Sam Gilbert," Elmore said. "I never rode it. It just sat in my family's garage. I kept it for a long time, but I never rode. I kind of felt a little bit like I was breaking a rule or something."

41 End Game for Gary

When the news came, late on a Thursday afternoon in early May of 2011, his friends and former players were caught by surprise.

Gary Williams was retiring.

"It's the right time," Williams said in a release that day.

Ed Tapscott, whose own coaching career began as a part-time assistant and full-time law student at American University 30 years before, seemed more stunned than anyone despite the fact the two longtime friends had talked about life after coaching.

"I, of course, said that he should coach until they pry the cold, dead fingers off his clipboard, simply because that's what I know him as," Tapscott said.

But as the time has passed since Williams made it official during an emotional press conference the following day at Comcast Center, it seemed to make sense.

"If you leave a little early, it's better than leaving late," Williams said that day, as students cheered him, as he left with one final fist pump.

Maryland athletic director Kevin Anderson, who said he thought he had talked Williams out of his decision a few days before, said that Williams seemed to be "at peace" with his decision.

While his relationship with Anderson appeared to be good—something he did not have with former athletic director Debbie Yow, who had left the year before to go to North Carolina State—there were other factors pushing him out the door.

A day before Williams made his announcement, sophomore center Jordan Williams had an announcement of his own: he was foregoing the last two years of NCAA eligibility to turn pro—against his coach's advice, as it turned out.

Gary Williams had recently been married for the second time—a change in lifestyle for a man who was estranged from his first wife when he first arrived at Maryland 22 years before.

And, perhaps, most significantly, the landscape had changed so dramatically in college basketball that many fans felt Williams' time had passed because of the emphasis on AAU.

The weekend before his announcement, Williams had spent time trying to convince a Kansas State transfer named Wally Judge that he should come to College Park.

"Gary went through that this weekend [with Judge] and probably thought, *Whose butt do I have to kiss? This kid should want to come. Here I am playing this game that I have no desire to play.* I think that's a portion of it," a friend said at the time.

Said another, "I think he's tired of kissing kids' tails and AAU coaches' tails."

There was a lot of speculation about what ultimately drove Williams out of the coaching business at age 66—a factor itself—but Williams has always been vague, often saying that there were a "number of reasons" for his decision.

Those who had seen him age, as many college basketball coaches appear to do, more rapidly than those who had left what had increasingly become a young man's business now see a more relaxed, happier, and seemingly healthier person.

"I didn't feel good. I went to the doctors and everything," Williams said a few days before being enshrined in the Naismith Memorial Basketball Hall of Fame in August of 2014. "If coaching was like being a professor, where they give you a sabbatical for a year, I could have coached more. I never wanted to cheat the game. I couldn't do the job that I wanted to do. I was 66. It wasn't like I was 50 and quitting."

Keith Neff, who had been close friends with Williams since his early years at Maryland, said that a coach who had been well-respected for playing by the rules (unlike a few of his contemporaries, some of whom have since been sanctioned or investigated by the NCAA) was finally going to get a chance to enjoy the riches of his life.

"He's accomplished everything," Neff said the day before Williams' press conference. "He's going to walk away having done it his way. He outlived Debbie."

42 Ex-Dookie, Terp for Life

The night he was first introduced to Maryland fans at Xfinity Center, Rasheed Sulaimon's greeting was, to be expected, mixed. No one was rude to the graduate transfer, and no mention was made of where Sulaimon had played his first three seasons of college basketball.

Five months later, everything had changed for a player who had started his career at Duke and nearly saw it end there as the first Blue Devil ever dismissed by legendary coach Mike Krzyzewski. Based on his stay in College Park, Sulaimon had either been railroaded by Coach K or had grown up under Mark Turgeon.

By the time he had finished his one season at Maryland, Sulaimon was respected for his work ethic, beloved by many of his younger teammates for the guidance he showed them, and, in the eyes of some fans, the most valuable player on a 27-win, Sweet 16 team.

Maryland's somewhat disappointing finish to a season of over-hyped expectations had nothing to do with Sulaimon.

As the backcourt partner to Melo Trimble, Sulaimon helped turn the sophomore point guard into a better all-around player and helped carry the Terps at times offensively when Trimble struggled with a nagging hamstring injury during the second half of the season.

As the big brother to Diamond Stone, Sulaimon helped keep the freshman center from getting too big a head after a 39-point outburst in his Big Ten debut and made sure Stone didn't stray off the court amid the temptations of college life for a big man on campus.

As the most experienced Terp in terms of postseason experience, Sulaimon helped the Terps overcome second-half deficits in their first two NCAA tournament games and carried them to an early lead in what turned out to be a season-ending loss to Kansas in Louisville, Kentucky.

Yet as much as Sulaimon gave the Terps, he felt he got even more in return.

"Last year I had no idea where I was going to be. Just the way that everybody embraced me and accepted me and gave me the opportunity to be a part of something bigger than myself again—to be a part of a team, I think that's one of the special things in life," Sulaimon said.

"That's a special relationship and the special bonds that you have the opportunity to create. I wouldn't change anything for the world. I'm just so happy these guys gave me an opportunity to be a part of their locker room, and open up to me and pick me up when I was down."

As he had done all season, Sulaimon spent more time talking about his teammates than he did himself after his final college game.

"That was one of the first thoughts that came to my mind, making sure the guys were okay," said Sulaimon, who was the team's leading scorer with 18 points against the Jayhawks in his final game. "As an older guy, I kind of view these guys as my brothers. As a big brother, when your brothers are hurt, you want to make sure they're okay.

"They can look at the big picture, look at everything we accomplished, look at the positives, and take all the great memories that we created this year. For the guys coming back next year, hopefully they extend this team. It's going to be a drastically different team, hopefully we're still going to be a part of it."

Despite being in the same situation after his freshman year at Duke as Trimble and Stone found themselves in at Maryland, Sulaimon wouldn't advise them what to do, leaving it to the players, their families, and Turgeon, who "developed a great bond and relationship with every one of those he recruited."

Still, Sulaimon said that the bond he made with his Maryland teammates was unbreakable.

"As a brother, if they need my opinion, I'm there for them with anything. Ten years down the line, I'm there for them and I'd like to think and I know they'll be there for me too," Sulaimon said. "I'll hold my comments to myself, but if they trust me with helping them, I'm there for them."

43 The Star-Crossed Legacy of Ernie Graham

There are two meaningful numbers in Ernie Graham's Maryland career.

The number for nearly everyone who saw Graham play from 1977 through 1981 is 44, the amount of points the 6'8" forward poured in as a sophomore against North Carolina State in December of 1978.

The number that is mostly forgotten, though, hangs from the ceiling of the Xfinity Center is 25, the jersey Graham wore and was honored by Maryland a few years before his son, Jon, wore it as well.

The elder Graham would much rather be known for what will be a permanent place in College Park than what—in this age when three-point shooting has become commonplace—might eventually be broken.

"I've never wanted to be known for one game," Graham said. "Records ought to be broken. I wanted to be somewhere permanent in the history of the University of Maryland."

The decision by athletic director Kevin Anderson to honor Graham—as much for the way he resurrected his life after years of admitted drug abuse as for anything he did on the court—helped the healing process.

"It helped me become comfortable in my own skin," Graham said.

Nearly a decade before the NCAA adopted the three-point shot, Graham hit 18 of 26 shots and eight of 10 free throws—in a span of 25 minutes—to lead the Terps to a 124–110 win.

"I know I would have been looking for the three-point line. It's so close, it's almost like a free throw," Graham said. "I don't know if it would have helped me or hurt me…it may have ended up being a distraction."

Known mostly as a scorer, Graham was the school's fourth-leading scorer when he left Maryland with 1,607 points but was overshadowed by teammate Albert King, who was first at the time with 2,058.

"I didn't play my freshman year but five minutes [a game], and these statistics were still there," Graham said. "I wasn't just a scorer. I was a guy that wanted to win and I did whatever it took to win."

What Graham said that most don't realize is that he was a pretty fair defender and passer too.

"With all due respect, I had the toughest [defensive] assignment every game—whether it was a power forward, shooting forward, or shooting guard, I had to play 'em," Graham said.

"People said I didn't play defense, but when I left Maryland I was second or third in steals [actually first with 123]. They said I never passed the basketball, but I was third all time in assists [346]." Graham said that his legacy was impacted by politics, most specifically a relationship with Lefty Driesell that soured when Graham left without graduating and caused ill will on both sides.

When he learned that his jersey number was going to be honored during the 2011–12 season along with Johnny Rhodes—in large part because of lobbying from former state senator Frank Kelly—Graham said he was caught by surprise and left ultimately disappointed.

"It happened in a second," Graham said. "And none of my teammates came, none of my coaches came."

His teammates, though, speak about him favorably.

Greg Manning, who came into Maryland the same year as Graham and still calls Graham "a dear friend," said he doesn't remember the specifics of that record-setting night.

"It had to be something cool because they still talk about it," Manning said.

But he does have clear memories of Graham.

"He could score, he was a guy that way back…when there weren't many players like you that were his size," Manning said. "He could back you down, he could shoot the jump shot, he had a great handle, and he was a really good college player."

The legacy of Ernie Graham and the Terps changed a couple of years later, when Jon Graham, then a sophomore at Penn State, was granted a medical hardship to return to Baltimore.

The younger Graham was added to the roster by Mark Turgeon and he became one of the emotional leaders of Turgeon's first NCAA tournament team at Maryland as a senior in 2014–15.

"It was wonderful, it was awesome," the elder Graham said of his son's career as a little-used Terp.

That Graham was there to witness his son's college career was a remarkable part of his story. Already smoking marijuana as a 13-year-old in East Baltimore, Graham graduated to cocaine and later heroin.

It contributed to Graham never fulfilling his potential as a pro, drafted in the third round by the Philadelphia 76ers but never playing a game. It also led to an estrangement with Driesell.

"It was non-existent," Graham said of his relationship with his former coach. "We're okay now."

With the help of his wife, Karen, and his two sons, Ernie Jr. and Jon, the elder Graham turned his life around. He speaks to schoolkids about the dangers of drugs.

Mostly, he is grateful to be back in the Maryland family. Even after Jon graduated following the 2014–15 season, the Grahams were semi-regular visitors to Xfinity Center.

"[Mark] Turgeon gave my son an opportunity that I'll never forget, and Kevin Anderson engineered getting my jersey up. I have nothing but the highest praise for the university at this point."

44 Gary and His ADs

Gary Williams came into the Maryland job in the spring of 1989 with a reputation as being one of college basketball's rising stars. In taking over at his alma mater, Williams was aware of the ongoing NCAA investigation into the program under former coach Bob Wade.

Lew Perkins, who had arrived in College Park two years earlier, assured Williams that the Terps were only going to get a "slap on the wrist" from the NCAA. That slap turned into a punch in the gut—a three-year probation that was the toughest since the SMU death penalty—and nearly ruined Williams' career.

It didn't help his relationship with Perkins, which ended when the athletic director, who would be cited in the NCAA findings for having a "lack of institutional control," left for the University of Connecticut before the probation was announced.

That started a feeling of "mistrust" between Williams and his two future bosses at Maryland, Andy Geiger and Debbie Yow.

While everyone talks about the bad marriage between Williams and Yow—one that somehow managed to last 16 years—the four-year relationship between Williams and Geiger was not great either.

Williams was at a team banquet in the spring of 1994 when word got out that Geiger would be announced later that week as the new athletic director at Ohio State, Williams' former school of all places. What Williams couldn't know at the time was that the new AD would be Yow, who was at Saint Louis University at the time.

At the time of her hiring, Williams said that her ability to raise funds at Saint Louis would be a plus, given Maryland's $6 million deficit, as would her background as a women's basketball assistant coach.

"It can be a positive because you can talk to her about a problem and she can understand it," he said.

Despite Williams turning the program around shortly after Yow arrived—the Terps went to the Sweet 16 in each of the next two years—their relationship seemed to sour. It didn't matter that the basketball program's continued success was the lifeblood of the athletic program as football struggled.

Yow kept changing football coaches—from Mark Duffner to Ron Vanderlinden to Ralph Friedgen—as Williams' program became a national power. When the Terps finally matched some of that success when Friedgen's first team unexpectedly won the

ACC title and went to the Orange Bowl, he was rewarded with a 10-year contract extension when Georgia Tech inquired about his availability.

"Even though the basketball team got to the Final Four the year before, she said, 'This is the greatest thing that ever happened at the University of Maryland since [I've been here],'" Williams said.

Though Williams had signed a deal of similar length in 1998—one that reportedly paid him a base salary of $675,000 that could reach the $1 million salary Friedgen was given if the basketball team won a national championship—Williams always felt that Yow favored Friedgen because she hired him.

"You persevere. What do you do?" Williams said in the winter of 2016. "The only thing I should have done, I should have gone after her job in 2002 [after the Terps won the NCAA tournament]. It took her two years to give me a new contract. Billy Donovan got a new contract from [Jeremy] Foley two weeks after he won his first national championship. Just stuff like that."

Williams added that his constant battles about budget—reportedly one of the smallest in the ACC despite the team's national profile—and a feeling that Yow also treated the women's basketball program and coach Brenda Frese as equals to the men's program despite its non-revenue status were more than a little frustrating.

"It took a lot out of me dealing with her, it took a lot out of me every day," he said.

Yow's defenders say the same thing and finally, when the chance to return to her home state came when the N.C. State job opened in July of 2010, Yow jumped. The sniping between the two continued, as Yow accused Williams of "sabotaging" the hiring process when she finally hired Mark Gottfried the same year Williams retired.

45 Gary's Night with Mr. Naismith

The over-under on how long it would take Gary Williams to wipe away his first tear or choke on his words was about two minutes tops, maybe even a minute.

So much for his tough-guy image that he carried with him for more than 30 years on the Division I level, 22 of them at Maryland. Williams often showed his soft side.

Williams did it when he returned to College Park from Ohio State in 1989, vowing to bring the program back to prominence. He did it again five years later when the Terps returned to the NCAA tournament.

And, of course, he did it the day he announced he was retiring.

But this time, on the stage of the Symphony Hall in downtown Springfield, Massachusetts, on the night he was inducted into the Naismith Hall of Fame in August of 2014, it seemed to be different.

"It's a great thrill, a very humbling experience," Williams told a packed house that included nearly 100 family members, former players, assistants, and friends.

Williams credited his Collingswood (New Jersey) High coach, John Smith, for "keeping me out of trouble" and former high school teammate Stan Pawlak "for teaching me how to work hard."

He also credited former NBA great and fellow Hall of Famer Billy Cunningham, who presented Williams, with unknowingly putting him on a path toward a career in coaching.

Recalling a game he played as a Maryland sophomore against North Carolina when Cunningham was a senior and one of the Atlantic Coast Conference's big stars, Williams said he tried to take a charge after Cunningham blew past teammate Neil Brayton and went in for a dunk.

Gary Williams stands on stage during the Naismith Memorial Basketball Hall of Fame class of 2014 announcement in Dallas. (Charlie Neibergall)

"Next thing I saw was his Converse shoe going over my shoulder," Williams said with a laugh. "Billy was dunking and I think he was smiling at the same time. Right about then—thank you, Billy—I started thinking about being a coach."

That story, and the way he told it, was typical of Williams' dry and often self-deprecating sense of humor. For all the chip-on-the-shoulder bravado he showed on the sideline, Williams had never been afraid to get off a good one-liner—even at his own expense.

Walt Williams, one of the former players who attended the festivities that night, said of his former coach, "No matter what type of player he had, he'd get the most out of them and even more.

"If you start piling up the number of players he could affect in that way, you can have some pretty good teams. That's why he got away with so many years of not having top recruits and still compete at a high level."

Mike Lonergan, who spent one season as an assistant coach under Williams as he transitioned himself from being a Division III coach at Catholic University in Washington to Vermont (and now at George Washington), said that Williams' spotless record is rare these days.

"The more corrupt our sport gets at the college level, I think the better his legacy is because people know he was above board, he wasn't a cheater," Lonergan said. "To win for a long period of time, it's hard to survive in this business.

"I think even some of my friends who weren't Gary lovers appreciate him more now."

Another old-school guy, Dr. Naismith himself, would certainly approve.

46 He's the Juan

Upon his induction into the Maryland Athletics Hall of Fame in 2012, Juan Dixon said in an interview with the *Baltimore Sun*, "No one ever thought that a skinny guy from Calvert Hall would be in the Maryland Hall of Fame. We had a lot of naysayers, but Coach [Gary Williams] believed in me."

Though Dixon left Baltimore as Calvert Hall's all-time scorer, few thought he would be able to accomplish the same thing in College Park. But when he left after leading the Terps to the 2002 national title, Dixon had bumped the legendary Len Bias down a spot in the record books.

Dixon's road might have been filled with doubters, but never self-doubt.

From the time he arrived at Maryland as a skinny, 6'3", 150-pound freshman in the fall of 1997, you could tell there was something different about the way Dixon was wired. Many often pointed to his tough upbringing—his parents both were heroin addicts who died of AIDS—but those who knew him say that he was born that way.

After redshirting his first season, Dixon made more of a contribution with his attitude as a freshman than as a scorer.

"Juan Dixon has a great future here," Williams told the *Sun* early that season. "He plays hard no matter what happens out there. Be it a turnover or a missed shot, he keeps on going full speed. It's important for other players on the team to see that."

The biggest jump came between his freshman and sophomore years.

Playing behind All-American Steve Francis as a freshman, Dixon was thought to be nothing more than a three-point shooter, and a streaky one at that. Even early in his sophomore year, Dixon was struggling.

But after missing 21 straight three-pointers early in the season, Dixon used one of the moves he had worked on all summer to hit the first of many big shots of his Maryland career.

It came against Illinois, a mid-range jumper with 6.3 seconds left to give the Terps a win. It came 11 days after Dixon had missed a potential game-winner against Kentucky.

The shot was the result of the work Dixon had put in over the summer.

"He'd developed a reputation as a three-point shooter and needed a new dimension," Williams said. "But I've told a lot of guys to do stuff over the summer, and it never got done. That's not a problem with Juan. You know he's going to work. He just loves to play so much. So many guys get out there [on the court], and it looks like someone is forcing them to play. If you watch Juan for two minutes, you know that's not the case."

"If you want to be the best, you get the ball [at the end] and you take that shot," Dixon said. "You can't be afraid to fail in that situation. Hey, Michael Jordan probably lost 900 games. But he was never afraid to fail, and he won a whole lot more than he lost. I've learned from that. The big guys are the ones who take those shots, and keep taking those shots. I want that to be me."

The rest, as is often said, is history.

By the middle of his sophomore year, Dixon had clearly taken the baton from Francis as Maryland's go-to player and was a rising star in the ACC. Despite an early-season shooting slump and mid-season ankle injury his junior year, Dixon led the Terps to the first of back-to-back Final Fours.

Then came a senior year that saw Dixon break Bias' scoring record of 2,149 points during the second round of the NCAA tournament and then, along with fellow senior Lonny Baxter, take the Terps to the national title.

"Coming into this school, a lot of people knocked Coach Williams for recruiting me. I had a lot of critics," Dixon said after becoming the school's all-time scorer. "I had a gift of putting the ball through the hoop, and I just kept working on it and kept trying to have fun doing it for four years. It's a tremendous feeling and a great accomplishment."

47 Bias Would Have Been Jordan's Rival

As crazy as it sounds, as difficult as it to compare, many believe that Len Bias would have become Michael Jordan's rival had he been able to fulfill the promise he showed in four seasons at Maryland.

Bias was Jordan's successor as the best player in the ACC, and one of the best players in the country. A little taste of that rivalry came when Bias was a sophomore and Jordan was a junior, in what became a much-talked-about showdown at Cole Field House.

Like Jordan, who was picked third in the 1984 draft, Bias might have come into the NBA with a bit of a chip on his shoulder after being chosen behind North Carolina center Brad Daugherty.

There was one difference: while Jordan had to turn the Chicago Bulls into challengers to the Detroit Pistons "Bad Boys" dynasty and eventually into legitimate contenders, Bias was set to join a team that won a NBA title nine days before he was drafted.

In putting together their reports on Bias—reports that were later scrutinized after his death—Celtics general manager Jan Volk said that comparisons were made to Jordan.

"Our scouting reports said that compared to Michael, Bias was a better outside shooter, might not handle [the ball] as well, but he was bigger and tougher," Volk told the *Baltimore Sun* in 2006.

If anything, the Bulls dynasty that produced six titles over an eight-year period might never have happened no matter how dominant a player Jordan became. If anything, the Celtics and Bulls would probably have traded Eastern Conference titles on a yearly basis.

The pressure on Jordan to lift the Bulls back to respectability would never have happened to Bias, who would have likely been brought along in the team's celebrated sixth man role.

Before his own death in 2007, Dennis Johnson said that Bias might have helped prolong the careers of several Celtics, most notably Larry Bird.

"They probably would have been able to phase us old guys out a little bit at a time," said Johnson, who at 31 was a little older than Bird and McHale and younger than Parish. "It would not have been as much of a strain."

Longtime *Boston Globe* columnist Bob Ryan said that just as John Havlicek was the bridge player between the Celtics dynasty in the 1950s and 1960s, and Dave Cowens became the bridge between the 1960s and 1970s, Bias would have filled that role as well.

"I saw him as a [James] Worthy level, maybe not first-team all-league, but a guy who would have been in All-Star Games and would be just outside the upper echelon, a guy who would have been a major star, maybe not an inner-sanctum star," said Ryan. "But who knows, he might have been that great."

Len Elmore, whose own pro career had ended two years before Bias was drafted and had begun working as a college basketball analyst, said Bias had a dimension the Celtics sorely lacked, particularly in comparison to the "Showtime" Los Angeles Lakers.

"He could also beat you off the bounce, which is one thing that on a consistent basis those Celtic teams didn't have," Elmore said. "He could isolate and drive to the basket and beat you with that athleticism. Larry was Larry, but he didn't have that dimension that Len had."

As Jordan had to work on his outside shot to complete his game, Bias would have had to work on his defense. Playing with defensive stars such as Dennis Johnson, McHale, and Parish would have likely rubbed off on Bias.

"He would have learned the game at a higher level," said Johnson.

Volk also said Bird, who was so excited about the Celtics drafting Bias that he planned to go work with him at rookie camp, would have been the perfect mentor.

"One of the real beauties of Larry Bird on our team was that he had such a large personality that his presence put perspective to everybody and allowed big egos to interact very effectively. That's just because of who he was and how he carried himself," Volk said.

That relationship never was forged. Eventually, the Celtics filled the void left by Bias' death by drafting Reggie Lewis in 1987. Six years later, after succeeding Bird as captain, Lewis was dead after suffering a heart attack.

Dave Gavitt, who took over as Celtics president in 1990, said that team tried unsuccessfully to get some salary cap relief from the NBA after both players died by asking for a chance to sign another player.

The team's request was denied in both cases.

"Jerry Colangelo said, 'Don't take this personally; this is not about green, it's about Red,'" Gavitt said. "Within a year after the Reggie Lewis tragedy, they did change the rule."

Since the Celtics reached the NBA Finals in 1987, when they lost to the Lakers in six games and the Eastern Conference finals in 1988, when they lost to the Detroit Pistons in six, Boston had been to the playoffs 11 times before winning another championship in 2008.

"I had said at the time in the days after [Bias'] death that this was going to impact the franchise for a very long time, 10 years or longer, but that the effects of it would probably not be felt for a couple of years," said Volk, who left the team in 1994. "I think it affected us for a very long time."

48 Jack and Joe, Kings of the Press Box

The press box at what is now called Maryland Stadium—formerly Byrd Stadium—is named after the athletic department's two patron saints of public relations, Jack Zane and Joe Blair.

Polar opposites in terms of physical stature and personality, Zane and Blair worked in College Park for 75 years combined. Put it this way: they knew where all of the skeletons were buried.

Blair came to Maryland in 1950 after graduating from the University of Missouri, and Zane became his student assistant in the sports information office until his graduation in 1953.

While both wound up leaving for a while—Blair to become the publicity director for the Washington Redskins on two separate occasions, Zane to work in a similar capacity at George Washington from 1963 through 1969—they eventually found their way back to Maryland.

Zane returned around the time Lefty Driesell became the head coach. As large and loud as Zane could be, Lefty was larger-than-life and louder than just about anybody.

"Lefty was a little off the wall with the media whether he won or lost," Zane recalled in the spring of 2016. "Sometimes he didn't want to talk and sometimes you couldn't get him to stop."

Zane recalls the game at South Carolina that ended with the infamous fight when he was trying to walk down to the basement of the gym where the team was getting dressed.

"I knew Lefty was not going to talk to the press—no way," Zane said. "There was not a snowball's chance in hell of him talking to media after that happened."

Zane figured out a way.

After a security guard refused to let him go down to the visitor's locker room on orders from the South Carolina athletic director, Zane found the AD, who told him that the media was ready to talk to Driesell in the press room.

"I said, 'Do you want Lefty standing there waiting for your coach [Frank McGuire] to come out and all the media right there?'" Zane said. "He said, 'You've got a point. I'll come and get him when he's finished.'"

Eventually, they agreed to allow Zane to escort the media down to the locker room.

"I knew what was going to happen next," Zane said. "I go down and walk in the locker room and Lefty is talking to one of the players. He said, 'No media in here.' I said, 'You just made my job easy.' He asked, 'What do you mean?' I said, 'The South Carolina AD said you cannot talk to any reporters.' Lefty said, 'Nobody's going to tell me who I can talk to. You get 'em down there.' We went down there, and Lefty was great.'"

Zane, who worked at Maryland full-time until his retirement in 2003 and continued to work there part-time for several more years, could be an intimidating presence, not afraid to call young reporters into his office and dress them down if they wrote a story he—or one of his coaches—didn't like.

Blair was much the opposite. Much smaller than Zane, Blair's reputation among the Washington media covering the Redskins for long stretches over three decades saw him as much more of a confidante, willing to share a story and a drink (or two) and a tip.

Known for wearing bow ties when he dressed up or Bermuda shorts when he dressed down, Blair always had a cigarette dangling from his mouth, lit or unlit. Before each game against North Carolina at Cole Field House, Blair used to go outside and share a quick smoke with legendary Tar Heels coach Dean Smith.

When Blair died after suffering a stroke at age 72 in November of 1995, hundreds packed the campus chapel to celebrate his life. While he was never married—"these teams were his life," longtime lacrosse coach Dick Edell said of Blair—at least 18 friends named their sons after Blair.

At Maryland, Zane and Blair proved to be an effective partnership.

More like Joe Friday and Bill Gannon of *Dragnet* fame than Bud Abbott and Lou Costello, Zane and Blair had a special connection. When Blair was forced to retire after the 1982 NFL season and moved to Florida, Zane heard that his former mentor was looking for work.

"He said, 'Why are you calling?'" Zane said. "I told him I was looking for a full-time assistant, but you could have your choice—football or basketball. He said, 'I've got to close my apartment up, I've got to close my bank account out.' I said, 'I didn't mean tomorrow, anytime you want to leave down there, you come up and I'll hold it for you.'"

The next day Blair called back.

"I said, 'Where are you?'" Zane said. "I'm at my apartment. He was in town. He said, 'Anything you want me to do tonight or tomorrow?'"

Jack and Joe were back in business.

49 Jack Heise, Bob Novak, and the Fastbreakers

Early in Lefty Driesell's tenure at Maryland, the new coach was not happy with the support his team was getting on the road. He would be given upwards of 75 to 100 tickets for Terp fans, but often couldn't find many takers.

Enter Jack Heise, a Washington attorney and Maryland grad who had been a basketball team manager in the late 1940s.

"Jack Heise and a guy named Les Smith got a meeting with Lefty and said, 'We need to get you a booster club,'" recalled John Rymer, a 1958 Maryland grad and longtime fan. "Lefty wanted to have that pack of Maryland fans down in North Carolina and South Carolina."

According to Rymer, Heise and Smith began recruiting fellow grads interested in following Driesell's program on the road to contribute $1,000 each. They became known as "the Fastbreakers" and from that group of around 50 forged a small group that made nearly every road game.

The original group eventually grew to include famed syndicated columnist and political television pundit Robert Novak, whose connection to College Park was the same as it was all the local sports teams. Based in Washington, D.C., Novak lived close by.

"Heise and Novak were particularly faithful on the road," said Rymer, who eventually in joined the group.

Members of the Fastbreakers were easy to spot even before the road games began.

Greg Desroches, who was the club's second president, said that he wanted "to give some definition, visibility, notoriety" to the group and came up with the idea of wearing their own uniform:

a navy blue blazer with thin red trim around the lapels, as well as hard-to-ignore pants.

"The blazers were very understated, but then we had these red, dark blue, and white plaid pants," Desroches said, laughing at the memory. "It was fine for the time. It was the kind of outfit that looked okay on me because I was 28 or on a George Raveling or Joe Harrington, but not on somebody that weighed 300 pounds."

Even Novak, the ultraconservative, wore his Fastbreaker pants.

"When we would come into a place, the students would howl," Desroches recalled.

Two of Rymer's favorite stories happened the year after Len Elmore and Tom McMillen graduated.

The first took place when the Terps travelled to Raleigh to play North Carolina State and star David Thompson. Maryland had never beaten the Wolfpack since Thompson arrived and were not expected to win that year with N.C. State ranked No. 2.

"Mr. Elmore had watched Lenny get beat umpteen times by David Thompson and came down to the game in Raleigh and he led us in cheering," Rymer said.

The Terps, ranked No. 8 at the time, finally beat the Wolfpack 98–97.

A few weeks later, after victories over the three other North Carolina schools, the Terps played North Carolina at Carmichael Auditorium. "We had a whole bus of fans and everybody had a little broom," Rymer recalled. "They let us in for some reason with the brooms."

The Maryland fans got to raise their brooms in victory after a 96–74 win in Chapel Hill—one of the worst home losses the legendary Dean Smith ever took at North Carolina.

Even after Driesell was forced to resign in the wake of star player Len Bias' death in 1986, Heise and Novak and the Fastbreakers remained loyal supporters during the three-year tenure of Bob Wade.

Some of the Fastbreakers eventually broke into a group called "FOG"—Friends of Gary—when the former Terp captain and point guard took over the floundering program in 1989. More than anyone, Heise was considered the team's ultimate fan—"Mr. Maryland" he would be called.

"Jack was there in good times and bad times," said Barry Desroches, whose brother married Heise's daughter.

The year Maryland won its national championship in 2002, Novak didn't miss a single game, often making his television appearances on *Crossfire* via remote. Heise missed only one, a road game at Oklahoma four days before Christmas.

"His wife Jackie told him that if went, he didn't have to come home," Barry Desroches recalled.

Heise and Novak died in 2009, less than two months apart.

Those pants are somewhere deep in storage in Greg Desroches' house, but now and again he is reminded of them. One time came during the 2015–16 season when John Lucas made a rare visit to College Park for a game.

"He said, 'Greg, Greg, it's so good to see you,'" Greg Desroches said. "John said, 'I'm amazed I recognized you without your Fastbreaker pants.'"

50 It's Always a Holliday with Johnny

If there has been a fixture in College Park over the past 35 years, it wasn't the school's seven football coaches or four men's basketball coaches, as much as it was the man broadcasting their games— Johnny Holliday.

The indomitable Holliday, who is closing in on 80 but has the voice and vigor of a man half his age, started as the team's radio play-by-play man in 1979 after Tim Brandt left to become a TV sports anchor at WJLA in Washington.

Holliday, whose real name is John Holliday Bobbit, had spent the first half of his professional life as a fulltime disc jockey whose work was later included in the Rock and Roll Hall of Fame and part-time musical theatre leading man who got into sports announcing through his connection to Art Modell.

After starting out a disc jockey at an all-black radio station in Miami in the late 1950s, and eventually working his way to middle-of-the-road stations in upstate New York, Holliday found himself in Cleveland in the early 1960s.

Working in a town where legendary disc jockey Alan Freed launched a musical genre that came to be known as rock and roll, Holliday picked up extra money as a spotter for the visiting teams during NFL telecasts.

There was a doubleheader and Modell asked Holliday to be the PA announcer for the first game between the Washington Redskins and Philadelphia Eagles before the Browns—led by the legendary Jim Brown—took the field at Cleveland Stadium.

"The PA announcer had died in the off-season, and Art Modell asked me to do the other game, and the main spotter was going to do the Browns game," Holliday recalled. "Modell calls down after the first game and asks me to do the second game as well."

After moving to New York City, Holliday's career was put on hold when the station where he worked went to an all-news format. He then landed in San Francisco, where he also served as the PA announcer at home games for the Oakland Raiders and San Francisco Warriors.

"That's where my friendship with Rick Barry started," Holliday said of the Warriors' star.

Holliday had a barnstorming basketball team that featured the Hall of Fame player.

"Rick Barry used to say that Johnny was the only player that he ever played with that took more shots than he did," Gary Williams joked.

When the musical format changed—"I didn't want to play the bang-bang music," said Holliday—the station director arranged for Holliday to move to Washington, D.C. Aside from playing the middle-of-the-road rock Holliday preferred, the station, WWDC, also had the rights to the Redskins, Senators, and Bullets.

"Tony Roberts and I did the pregame show for the Senators," said Holliday, who now does the pre- and postgame shows for the Nationals.

Holliday eventually started doing play-by-play on Navy football and George Washington basketball. After moving over to WMAL, Holliday found himself the new play-by-play man for the Terps in 1979. By then, Lefty Driesell was going into his 10th season and was something of a local icon.

Recalling his first meeting with Driesell, Holliday said, "I was kind of intimidated by him like everyone else."

In those days, Driesell would tape his pregame show the day before the game.

"I asked if we could do it the day of the game and I didn't know how he was going to react," Holliday said. "I asked him why he didn't do it the day of the game, and Lefty said, 'Nobody ever asked me.'"

Holliday only had a couple of "flare ups" with the Lefthander. One came in a game when the Terps blew a 14-point lead.

"He said, 'You didn't have to say that, you could have said we played haaaard, we played tougggggh," Holliday said, trying to imitation Driesell's Tidewater drawl.

Johnny Holliday, who has been calling Terps games since 1979, works the NCAA South Regional tournament in Nashville on March 21, 2003.
(Al Behrman)

Then there was a game when Holliday had the audacity to mention that legendary DeMatha High coach Morgan Wootten had taught Maryland point guard Dutch Morley how to shoot free throws.

"He said, 'By the way, Morgan Wootten didn't teach him. I taught him,'" Holliday recalled. "He [Driesell] wasn't stupid, he was dumb like a fox."

Holliday loves to tell the story of taking one of his daughters, Kelly, to a road game in Georgia. It was right after one of the team's stars, Herman Veal, was accused of sexual assault and Duke fans had thrown condoms on the court when Veal was introduced in the starting lineup.

After warning his daughter that Driesell might not be in the best mood, Kelly came out beaming.

"Dad, he's the sweetest man. He's like a father figure to his players," Kelly told her father.

Holliday was there the day Driesell was forced to resign, a few months after star player Len Bias died from what was determined to be a cocaine overdose. After Driesell, his wife, and daughter left Cole Field House, Holliday drove to the coach's house near the campus.

"He was crushed, he talked about Lenny being like a son, and he said, 'I'll take the blame [for his death],'" Holliday recalled. "I felt so bad for him."

Former radio partner Greg Manning, who played for Driesell and worked next to Holliday for 16 years, said of Holliday, "He's so good, he's so talented, he can do anything. He can make anybody feel at ease. He's like Dick Clark. He never changes."

Gary Williams, whose entire 22-year career at Maryland was done with Holliday as his play-by-play man as well as the host of his radio and television shows, said that the longtime voice of Terp sports would even be more appreciated if he worked in more of a college town.

"It's true about a lot of things connected to college sports in this area," Williams said. "So many things are going on, sometimes you don't appreciate a guy like Johnny Holliday. You look at Cawood Ledford, he was in Kentucky, Woody Durham at North Carolina, there's not much competition in those places for the media."

51 Lefty Deserves the Hall

Can the criteria for the National Collegiate Basketball Hall of Fame in Kansas City, Missouri, and the Naismith Memorial Basketball Hall of Fame in Springfield, Massachusetts, be so different?

Even so, Lefty Driesell deserves to be in whatever hall or monument or museum there is dedicated to college hoops.

Driesell was a member of the National Collegiate Basketball Hall of Fame in 2007—one of three coaches inducted in its second class. On his third try as a finalist in 2016, Driesell was rejected again by the folks representing Dr. Naismith.

Why?

It couldn't be his record.

When he retired early in the 2003–04 season from Georgia State, Driesell's 786 victories ranked fourth overall behind three coaches who might vie for space on college coaching's Mount Rushmore—Adolph Rupp, Dean Smith, and Bob Knight.

Everyone might think Driesell's college career started at Maryland—it didn't.

Those who have followed the Lefthander know that it began at Davidson, where he twice took teams to the Elite Eight and—if not for North Carolina's Charlie Scott hitting a jumper to beat the Wildcats in 1969—might have also taken them to the Final Four.

Driesell never won a national championship, as 2016 inductee Tom Izzo did with Michigan State in 2000. Driesell's teams never went to the Final Four, as fellow Naismith rejectee Bo Ryan's Wisconsin team in 2014 and 2015.

But none of them had their best team denied entrance into the NCAA tournament—as Driesell's 1973–74 Maryland team was—because of a rule that stated only conference champions got invited. The Terps might not have won—this was the UCLA era after all—but Driesell would have had more chances.

A sparkling record is not the only path into the Naismith Hall of Fame—you can get in as a contributor as well.

Driesell's contribution to modern college basketball used to be as October 14 became October 15 and teams were allowed to practice. Now it, like many other rules and regulations the NCAA mandates, is exactly 45 days before a team's first game.

It's a little thing called "Midnight Madness."

Why do teams such as Michigan State stage "Late Night with Tom Izzo" and why does nearly every team across the country hold some sort of event to officially start preseason practice? Because of Lefty and what he first tried in College Park in 1971.

Maybe someone else would have eventually had the seemingly harebrained idea, except that Driesell beat everyone to it. While that might be the most tangible legacy of Driesell's career, it's actually not the most significant.

How about turning down the National Invitation Tournament after the 1973–74 Terps lost in overtime to David Thompson, Tom Burleson, and North Carolina State in the classic 103–100 Atlantic Coast Conference tournament final in Greensboro, North Carolina?

By rejecting the NIT, which at the time was nearly as popular as the NCAA tournament because it was played at Madison Square Garden, Driesell forced the NCAA to look at expanding the field to 32 teams, which was done the year after the fourth-ranked, 23–5 Terps stayed home.

And then there's the matter of Driesell's personality. If this was a personality contest—and not a popularity contest because Lefty, like another 2016 rejectee, Rollie Massimino, was definitely for many an acquired taste—Driesell would be a shoo-in.

Like Dickie V.

In an age when college basketball lacks oversized characters on the sidelines, ESPN analyst Dick Vitale often fills that void from his broadcast table at courtside. Vitale's inclusion had nothing to do with what he did in his brief coaching career at the University of Detroit and with the Detroit Pistons, but with what he did in bringing college basketball back to popularity with ESPN.

Guess what? Driesell's courtside shenanigans—from his famous stomp to his victory sign to his wild declaration about turning Maryland into "the UCLA of the East"—also helped popularize the game back in the 1970s. He was to Maryland and the ACC what Al McGuire was to Marquette or Lou Carnesecca was to St. John's.

Both McGuire, who won a national championship with Marquette in 1977 (three years after being the first coach to be ejected from a championship game) and Carnesecca, who took St. John's to the 1985 Final Four, are members of the Hall of Fame.

While they have had their differences in recent years—mostly over Lefty's less-than-appropriate remarks about the court at Comcast Center being named after Gary Williams—the man who coached Maryland to its only national championship was asked about Driesell.

"I think it was so emotional during that time [when Driesell was forced out] that sometimes Lefty doesn't get the credit he deserves," Williams said in 2001. "When he came there, I had just played there. There was no marketing. We weren't a major program. Lefty is the reason Maryland became a major program."

And why he deserves to be in the Hall of Fame—the one in Springfield, Massachusetts.

52 Life after Maryland for Lefty

As the NIT selection committee was trying to figure out first-round matchups for its 1990 tournament, a reporter called Manhattan athletic director Jack Powers, the chairman, with an obvious suggestion.

"Why don't you put James Madison at Maryland and bring Lefty back to College Park?" the reporter asked.

"I don't know if we can do that. Maryland is still paying a part of Lefty's salary," Powers said.

"If you do, you might not have enough seats in Cole Field House," the reporter said, "You might need Byrd Stadium."

Powers passed on the idea, bringing Massachusetts and a young John Calipari to Cole. Plenty of good seats were available, which led to the Terps getting sent to Penn State for what turned out to be a second-round loss.

Whether or not Maryland officials wanted Driesell back on campus, fans would have to wait more than a decade for the first matchup between the Lefthander and his old school.

By then, in 2001, he had moved on to Georgia State, where he had done the same thing at the little Atlanta school that he had done at his first three coaching stops: bring the program to the NCAA tournament.

The selection committee that year didn't pass on the chance of a potential story line. The No. 11–seeded Panthers needed to pull off an opening-round upset to face the third-seeded Terps. They did, beating No. 6 seed Wisconsin after falling behind by 16 in the first half.

"I was rooting for Lefty because it's been so long since he's been in the tournament," Williams said the day before the game.

"He's one of those people that is important to the history of college basketball. Look at him. He's 69. All he has ever wanted to do was coach basketball. That's his life. That's who he is.

"As far as playing against Lefty, I'm sure there are a lot of stories and a lot of things have been written. We're playing Georgia State, and it's an NCAA game. When it comes time to play, it's Maryland vs. Georgia State. It's not Lefty vs. Maryland."

Driesell took a similar tact.

"Y'all are trying to make something out of nothing," he said. "Y'all make it out to be some vendetta. It's just a basketball game, and it's going to last 40 minutes, and somebody's going to win and somebody's going to lose. I don't care who we're playing. I got a paycheck from Maryland for, what, 17 years.

"They paid me for nine years after I left. They bought me a house at the beach and a boat and cars and all of that stuff. So I have nothing against Maryland. I have a lot of friends there. Tomorrow when we tip it up, we're going to war. After the game, we'll kiss and hug each other."

At least one of his players got a sense that this was not just a typical game for Driesell, even with what was at stake.

"It would definitely be a gift to [Driesell] to come away with that win," Shenard Long, who had started his career at Georgetown, said. "I don't know how much he's concentrating on it. He tends to hide his emotions a lot. He's trying to make us think it's just another game. But I know it's going to be very special for him."

The Terps won 79–60, moved on to the Sweet 16, and eventually to their first Final Four before losing to Duke in the semifinals. A year later, when Maryland made it back to the Final Four in Atlanta, Driesell was there rooting for the school that forced him to resign 16 years before.

"I think it was so emotional during that time that sometimes Lefty doesn't get the credit he deserves," Williams said. "When he came there, I had just played there. There was no marketing. We weren't a major program. Lefty is the reason Maryland became a major program.

"He was the guy that put the seats on the floor. He started Midnight Madness, did so many things to market the program. He was great for the university. He was blamed by some people for what happened with Len Bias, which was totally wrong. Whoever the basketball coach was there at the time was going to share in the blame."

Driesell, who would retire the following season, admitted that he would be pulling for the Terps.

"Gary has done a good job. I enjoy watching them play," said Driesell. "I'm not going to throw a big celebration if they win, but I would like to see it. I still have a lot of friends there."

53 Getting the Scoop

Being the beat writer on Maryland men's basketball on and off for more than 30 years, I have earned my share of scoops.

One of the more interesting stories that was first disclosed under my *Baltimore Sun* byline involved the sanctions leveled against the Terps after Gary Williams was hired to clean up the mess left by Bob Wade.

A few weeks after the NCAA came on campus to hold a joint press conference with university president William E. Kirwan and athletic director Lew Perkins, one of my sources in the athletic department called me to vent about the penalties Williams' program was going to suffer.

As my source—a close associate of Perkins—told me about the three-year probation that included a two-year ban from postseason tournament play and a one-year ban from appearing on live television (meaning that the Terps couldn't play in the ACC tournament)—the only mix-up came when he said that the probation would start immediately.

I called the three people that I knew would be in the loop on this: Perkins, Williams, and Kirwan. None of them would confirm—or deny—the accuracy of my information, Kirwan politely warned me, "You know, Don, there are only about four of us who know, so be careful who you use as a source."

While my source called back the next morning to apologize for speaking incorrectly about when the sanctions would start, the story had already hit the presses. Since this was long before the Internet made news a 24/7 proposition, that's the way it stayed until Maryland had scheduled a news conference of its own to go over the sanctions.

I was greeted at the news conference by sports information director Herb Hartnett, who pointed at me and said, "You're wrong, you're wrong, you're wrong. If this was a baseball game, you'd be batting .100." As it turned out, given that all my facts were correct except for the starting date, I told him, "I think I would be batting about .900."

A few days later, I was walking through a crowd at the ACC tournament in North Carolina when Kirwan came toward me. Recalling our conversation a few nights before, I was relieved to see him smile. He gently grabbed my arm and whispered into my ear, "Good source."

Hearing that, my batting average just went up about 50 points.

Things settled down for a few months, but the following season I got word that Maryland had committed a secondary violation under Williams. I had trouble getting the information, so I chose to wait until I got it right. The *Washington Post* reported—incorrectly as it turned out—that Williams had sold recruits Terp clothing at "deeply discounted prices."

It turned out that a little-used player had not filled out his NCAA scholarship forms properly and was not eligible.

The next day, Maryland held a press conference where Williams chastised the *Post* for publicizing incorrect information.

One of my bigger scoops was the result of the ongoing feud between Williams and athletic director Debbie Yow.

Coming off a semifinal loss to North Carolina State in the 1997 ACC tournament, the Terps were headed to Memphis to play the College of Charleston. Yow and her husband, Bill Bowden, were on my plane, which connected through Cincinnati.

During the layover, Yow asked me, cryptically, "What is he going to do about them?"

Yow either thought I knew what she was talking about or was trying to give me the beginning of a story. I answered her back with the same vagueness, "I don't know, what do you think he's going to do to them?" She said, "Bench 'em for a half. It's too big to bench for the whole game."

When I got to Memphis, I sought out Greg Manning, the former point guard who was Johnny Holliday's color analyst in those days. I asked him who and what Yow was talking about. "Oh, you didn't hear, Terrell Stokes and Laron Profit blew curfew Friday night, and Gary found out about it after the game Saturday."

I spent the next two hours getting reaction from Williams, the two players, and several of their teammates. Obinna Ekezie was so upset that I had to calm him down so as not to attract attention from other reporters. I calmly went back to the press room and banged out the story about Williams benching the two for the first half of a game that the Terps would wind up losing.

Jody Foldesy, a young reporter, came by and asked very innocently, "You got the scoop?"

I smiled, and said, "Yup."

That night, the beat writers went for ribs at the Rendezvous and music at BB King's.

I didn't say a word.

The next day, Foldesy sought me out.

"You really did have the scoop," he said with a smile.

By the way, I never did thank Debbie.

54 Lonny's Phantom Foul

If there was one play in Maryland's 2001 NCAA tournament semifinal defeat to Duke that many fans—not to mention Gary Williams—lament, it was the fifth personal foul called against Terps center Lonny Baxter.

"Everybody always asks me about that call, that foul," Baxter said in the spring of 2016. "You can't change it. It is what it is."

It came with a little under three minutes left and Maryland, which had led by as many as 22 points in the first half, had fallen behind the Blue Devils by five points. Baxter posted up against Duke center Carlos Boozer, who also had four personals at the time.

"He actually started to raise his hand after the whistle, thinking they were going to call it on him," Baxter recalled a decade later, in a series of stories with the *Baltimore Sun* to commemorate the 2002 national championship. "Those kinds of things happened against Duke."

During his brief career in the NBA, Baxter said that he joked about the call with the former Duke star.

During the CBS telecast of the game, color analyst Billy Packer—whom many Maryland fans thought didn't like the Terps dating back to his playing days at Wake Forest—was incredulous that the foul had been called on Baxter. Replays showed both players jostling for position near the basket.

"I just couldn't see it," Packer said on the telecast.

Neither could Williams.

After seeing the foul called on Baxter, Williams did one of his trademark pirouettes and yelled toward the press table, "How bleeping bad do you guys want Duke in the final?"

Williams screamed in the direction of Big East commissioner Mike Tranghese, who was not only a close friend of the Maryland coach dating back to Williams' years at Boston College but was also the chairman of the NCAA tournament selection committee.

Baxter's comments about Duke getting calls also played out in the championship game two nights later, when a potential third personal on star guard Jason Williams late in the first half was not called after Williams rode the back of Arizona star Jason Gardner.

Baxter said that he never heard Gary Williams' comment, but added, "I'm happy they called that foul on me because it fired us up for the following year when we won it."

Recalled Baxter more than a decade later, "There were just a lot of iffy calls in that second half."

Gary Williams didn't wait long to have his players start thinking about revenge. Shortly after the Terps arrived back in College Park, they went straight to Cole Field House wearing T-shirts that read, "2002 NCAA Final Four, Atlanta, Ga, National Champions."

Baxter said that the Terps used the defeat at the Metrodome to inspire them going into the following season.

"We felt like we had been robbed, we felt like we should have been in the championship game the year before," Baxter said. "We were determined that if we were to get back there again, we wouldn't let it slip through out fingers like it did."

55 Maryland's Biggest Wins

1. **1958 ACC tournament final.** The Terps came from seven down at half behind the hot shooting of Charles McNeil to beat defending national champion North Carolina 86–74 to become the first team outside the state of North Carolina to win the tournament.
2. **1984 ACC tournament final.** After losing three times in the final under Lefty Driesell, the Terps beat Duke 74–62 behind a very motivated Len Bias, who scored 27 points in a year he thought he should have been voted All-ACC first team.
3. **1986 overtime win over No. 1 North Carolina in Chapel Hill.** After a shocking 0–6 start in the ACC, the Terps had won four of five but were still in need of a win at the brand-new Dean Dome. Behind 35 points from Bias, the Terps gave Driesell his first win over a top-ranked team.
4. **1990 win at North Carolina.** In his first season at Maryland, Gary Williams finished a regular-season sweep of the Tar Heels and legendary coach Dean Smith. Sophomore Evers Burns finds a mop in the Dean Dome and brought it back to the locker room.
5. **1993 opening game win over Georgetown at USAir Arena.** The Terps came from nine points down in the second half to shock the No. 13 Hoyas on their home court behind 26 points from unknown freshman Joe Smith and a game-winning runner in overtime by Duane Simpkins.
6. **1994 second-round NCAA tournament win over Massachusetts.** Having made the NCAA tournament for the first time under Williams, the Terps avenged a defeat to the Minutemen earlier in the season to advance to the Sweet 16.

7. **2001 win at Duke.** After blowing a 10-point lead in the last minute and losing at Cole Field House in overtime earlier in the season, junior Juan Dixon led the No. 16 Terps past the No. 2 Blue Devils and added insult to injury by kissing the Duke insignia at midcourt.

8. **2001 NCAA Elite Eight win over Stanford.** Behind regional MVP Lonny Baxter, the 11th-ranked Terps beat the No. 2 ranked Cardinal to reach the Final Four for the first time in school history.

9. **2002 NCAA final over Indiana.** In a game marked by long scoring droughts by both teams, the Terps survived the Hoosiers 64–52 with senior Juan Dixon capping off his legendary career by being named the Final Four's Most Outstanding Player.

Gary Williams and Juan Dixon enjoy their biggest win, a 64–52 over Indiana on April 1, 2002, to claim the national championship.

10. **2004 ACC tournament final win over Duke.** Capping off a weekend of comeback wins against teams within the state of North Carolina, the unranked Terps beat the No. 5 Blue Devils as sophomore John Gilchrist gave Williams his first ACC tournament championship.

56 My Favorite ACC Venues

One of the reasons why the ACC is not the ACC anymore doesn't just have to do with the fact that there are more former Big East teams in the league than ACC originals. It also has to do with the arenas in which some of those teams play.

The biggest charm in the old ACC had to do with the variety of venues.

It didn't seem the same when the Sports and Entertainment Arena replaced Reynolds Coliseum at North Carolina State, when the John Paul Jones Arena supplanted University Hall at Virginia, or when Comcast Center made Cole Field House irrelevant.

Older fans, and media members, preferred the old places.

While some buildings grew on me—the Dean Dome being at the top of the list—my favorites tend to have roots back in the 1950s and 1960s rather than in the new millennium.

Aside from Cole, here are my top four:

Carmichael Auditorium (North Carolina): Maybe it was the fact that the only game I ever saw in this venerable gym featured Michael Jordan and Ralph Sampson, when the Tar Heels and Cavaliers were fighting not only for supremacy in the league but in the whole country.

Maybe it was because the game itself came down to the end, with Jordan singlehandedly leading a comeback by scoring the game's last nine points and then swooping in over the 7'4" Sampson for an offensive rebound to seal the deal.

You could feel the ghosts in this place, but you couldn't hear yourself think. The game I saw, a 64–63 win for the No. 4 Tar Heels over the No. 3 Cavaliers, the Virginia players didn't even come out for the starting lineup introductions because it was so damn loud.

Reynolds Coliseum (North Carolina State): How many college basketball arenas were initially built to handle an annual congregation of farmers? That was the case with Reynolds, which came about after local farmers saw their outdoor meeting rained out one year in the early 1940s.

It took a while to get the funding together, but the end of a steel shortage during World War II and the hiring of legendary coach Everett Case in 1946 eventually got the arena finished. Part of the mystique was in its low-slung roof, which made the place look more like a plane hangar than a gym.

Though I got to see some pretty good games there from the early 1980s—watching the 1982 NCAA champion Tar Heels pass through during the East Regional—to the opening of the new building in 1999, I really would have liked to see a high school phenom named Pete Maravich work out there while his father, Press, was coaching the Wolfpack.

Cameron Indoor Stadium (Duke): While a place many consider one of the meccas of college basketball has to be on this list, its position in the middle of my top five is on purpose. The first few times I ventured in, I loved every second I was there. By the time Maryland played its last game there in 2014, I couldn't wait to leave.

In the mid-1980s, the Cameron Crazies seemed cute and creative. I didn't even mind getting hit in the jaw with a tennis ball being slung back and forth from one part of the student section clear across the court to the other. Having the Blue Devils fall on me after being body-surfed through the crowd was a bit annoying, I must admit.

By the end of my nearly 30-year run of going to games there—and I saw a ton of great ones, including the Jeff Capel half-court shot to send the Terps to double OT (though I was in the press room writing a North Carolina victory story)—I had tired of their act. As I said to one fan after he was deliriously happy about beating Maryland by a point in the last visit in the ACC, "Not our rivals, my ass."

Smith Center (North Carolina): My feelings about the Dean Dome are nearly the opposite of those I have about Cameron. They have nothing to do with the fans, but about the atmosphere. I once compared the two, writing that you felt you were going to a rock concert in Durham and a museum in Chapel Hill.

Eventually, the "cheese and wine" crowd that former Florida State star Sam Cassell spoke of in the early 1990s was replaced by the raucous fans you see today. It was partly the result of a snowstorm, when only the students showed up for a game against Maryland and school officials realized what an asset it was to have them sit near the court.

When I returned there during the 2015–16 season for the ACC-Big Ten Challenge, it felt like home. The powder blue décor that once seemed so overdone was comforting, the students were loud and booed only one Terp loudly—former Duke player Rasheed Sulaimon—and I hated leaving.

57 Nightmare at Cole

Ask Gary Williams which was his toughest defeat in 22 seasons at Maryland, and he'll probably start with the 2010 NCAA tournament second-round loss to Michigan State.

That's the one that ended with a Spartan player ducking on the inbound pass and Korie Lucious nailing a three-pointer to ruin a spectacular Greivis Vasquez-led comeback by the Terps.

The second toughest?

While most will bring up the NCAA semifinal defeat to Duke at the 2001 NCAA Final Four, when the Terps saw a 22-point first-half lead steadily whittled away in the second half of a 95–84 defeat, there's more than a few fans who will mention another loss to the Blue Devils earlier that season.

It came at Cole Field House in late January.

As Williams' buddy, future Ravens owner Steve Bischiotti, was getting ready for the Super Bowl in Tampa, the eighth-ranked Terps welcomed the second-ranked Blue Devils to College Park before a sellout crowd.

Leading by as many as 15 points in the first half and by 10 with 54 seconds left, the Terps watched as sophomore point guard Steve Blake fouled out with a little over a minute remaining, and the Blue Devils stormed back behind star senior Shane Battier and, after forcing overtime, won 98–96.

For years, Maryland players hated talking about that game even more than the Final Four game.

"I knew it wasn't over, but I thought we had it in hand," Blake said that night. "This is definitely the worst loss I've ever had. I just feel terrible. My body is drained. You get excited to have something, then you get it taken away."

The Terps lost for only the second time in 15 games because they lost their composure down the stretch and got few favors from the officials, who whistled Maryland for 31 fouls, compared to Duke's 21.

Junior center Lonny Baxter was on the bench early after getting called for a questionable touch foul. Terence Morris (13 points) fouled out early in overtime, following Blake to the bench. No Duke players fouled out.

"I wish I could talk about that, but I can't," Blake said.

Duke took 42 foul shots, converting 32. Maryland made 20 of 28, and missed key attempts in crunch time.

"You've got to play for 40 minutes against Duke. We played for 38 or 39," junior forward Byron Mouton said.

Down by 10 and in desperate straits, Duke began fouling the Terps, who responded with hesitation. Backup point guard Drew Nicholas missed three of four free throws in the final minute of regulation to give the Blue Devils the opening they needed.

"This is probably the most stunning game I've been a part of," said Mike Mardesich, who finished with four points. "We saw ourselves with a nice lead with a couple of minutes to go and we started playing a little passive. We gave it away."

Said Terps coach Gary Williams: "The test as to whether we're a good team will be how ready we are to play Virginia on Wednesday, because that's going to be a very difficult game. This is very disappointing, but as I said before the game, I've been here before. Don't let this take you away from your next nine ACC games."

Maryland certainly learned its lesson that night.

And another against Duke in Minneapolis.

58 My Favorite Big Ten Venues

Though I had been to a several Big Ten arenas before Maryland joined the league in 2014, they were mostly names and places I had heard about for a long time. Even those that I had visited for games were a distant memory.

I had been to Crisler Arena in Ann Arbor in 1990 as part of a short-lived career as a color analyst for Westwood One, but what I remembered most was waking up to the news that Mike Tyson had lost to Buster Douglas in Japan.

I had been to the Kohl Center in Madison in 2003 for the NCAA tournament, but my only memory of that trip was watching Indiana beat Duke on television at a sports bar near the arena.

I had been to Assembly Hall in Bloomington in 2010 when Maryland played Indiana, but that was Tom Crean's first year coaching the Hoosiers, and the place didn't seem to have the same energy as I could recall feeling from games I had watched on TV.

Having been through the league in Maryland's first two seasons, here are my top four outside of the Xfinity (neé Comcast) Center:

Assembly Hall (Indiana): It was interesting to see the difference in the five years from my last visit to when Maryland played there in 2015. The place was packed, the energy was back, and those candy-stripe pants, even worn by some fans, made it fun.

At least it did for the Hoosiers. While both that game and the one during the 2015–16 seasons were blowout victories for Indiana, even the Maryland players said after the first one-sided loss that it was the best venue they had played at during their first season.

The odd shape—jutting out at one end and then going straight up all around—was weird to see on television, but it seemed to add to the home-court advantage for the Hoosiers. It's by far the loudest building in the Big Ten with only Xfinity coming close.

Mackey Arena (Purdue): This might be the most underrated arena in the country. The first time Maryland played in West Lafayette, Indiana, the students were on winter break. When the Terps returned in 2016, they were back and wearing black.

There's the historical significance, of course, with its location on John Wooden Way in honor of the most famous Boilermaker of all. (Sorry, Rick Mount fans.) The mini-museum dedicated to the Wizard of Westwood was an unexpected treat.

Breslin Center (Michigan State): This was the first place Maryland played as a member of the Big Ten, and the fact that the game went into overtime (with the Terps winning) certainly made it memorable.

Just as happened at Purdue in Maryland's first trip, the students were still on break. Though impressed with the size of the crowd for a late afternoon game two days before New Year's, I didn't get a full taste until the "Izzone" was back in full force.

That happened in 2016, and the fans certainly played their part in helping the Spartans pull away at the end of a close game. But I have to admit my favorite thing about the Breslin Center is that the DJ plays "Hava Nagilah," a traditional Jewish wedding song.

I have no idea why, and neither does he.

Pinnacle Bank Arena (Nebraska): Given the fact that Nebraska is a football school, and it seems more suited to house an NBA team than a college team, this place is rocking.

The first time the Terps went to Lincoln, the Cornhuskers had lost seven straight, and the arena was sold out. Last year's sellout came the night after a huge snowstorm blanketed the state. Both games went down the wire—the Terps won both—and the fans had a lot to do with helping the home team.

I can't imagine what will happen if Tim Miles gets the Cornhuskers completely turned around, but this place illustrates the difference between the Big Ten and ACC in that even the football schools with spotty basketball histories have.

59 Replacing a Legend Isn't Easy

Mark Turgeon knew what he was getting himself into when he took over for Gary Williams in May of 2011.

"Gary Williams was Maryland basketball," Turgeon said during his introductory news conference. "And I hope 15 years from now, 20 years, however long this lasts, that you're going to say Mark Turgeon was Maryland basketball."

Five years into his tenure, Turgeon has done an admirable job in getting the program back on track.

His record—114–59, including 55–16 from 2014 through 2016—is slightly better than the last five years of Williams' tenure, when the Terps went 108–61. That Maryland reached the Sweet 16 in 2016 for the first time since 2003 took a huge turtle off his back.

But as others have found out in college basketball, replacing a legend isn't easy.

Forget those who tried to replace John Wooden at UCLA or Dean Smith at North Carolina or Bobby Knight at Indiana.

How about coaches who were hired to replace those considered a tier below, Hall of Famers like Williams would eventually become, but not legends? Many of them succeeded on the basketball court, but not in the court of public opinion.

Look at the career of Tubby Smith, who won a national championship in his first year after succeeding Rick Pitino at Kentucky, reached the Elite Eight his second year and two other times while making the NCAA tournament in each of his 10 seasons in Lexington.

Smith finally came to the realization that he wasn't going to be as revered or respected as Pitino—or Adolph Rupp—and left for Minnesota before moving on to Texas Tech and now Memphis.

Look at the career of Rollie Massimino, the first of seven coaches who have been at UNLV since Jerry Tarkanian left in 1992—eight if you include Chris Beard, who took the job 19 days in the spring of 2016 before going back to Texas Tech, where he had been an assistant for Smith.

Seven years removed from his NCAA title at Villanova, Massimino lasted two seasons before finishing out his Division I coaching career with a mostly unsuccessful eight-year run at Cleveland State. Even the coach who replaced Massimino at Villanova—Steve Lappas—never came close to finding the success Daddy Mass had with the Wildcats.

Which brings us back to Turgeon.

As much as Maryland fans seemed to get on Williams toward the end of his 22-year reign in College Park for lackluster recruiting and inconsistent results, the current fan base at Maryland started getting a little testy when the Terps went from winning 25 games and reaching the NIT semifinals in Turgeon's second year to going 17–15 for the second time in his first three seasons.

When five players with remaining eligibility left following the 2013–14 season, many questioned Turgeon's future and job security, though his initial eight-year contract that paid him more than $2 million annually still had five seasons remaining.

"I have so much confidence in myself, the people around me, and this great basketball program," he said at the time. "I don't feel any pressure. I'm more relaxed today than at any point since

I took the job. And I mean that. The hardest part is explaining it to recruits."

As for the impatience of the fans, Turgeon said, "If they weren't mad, then I wouldn't want to be here. I like that the fans care enough to say bad things or say great things. I know just how I feel day to day. I'm in a much better place. I'm happier. I feel great about all the things that have happened this spring.

"I'm going to miss the guys [who left], but I feel great about everything. The hard part was going through it and waiting for summer school to get started and to where we are now. I think I'm really going to enjoy being between the lines with this group next season."

As things turned out, the arrival of freshman point guard Melo Trimble was the single biggest catalyst for turning around the program. The Terps, picked to finish 10th in their first season in the Big Ten, came in second and beat league champion Wisconsin in their only meeting.

After returning to the NCAA tournament for the first time in five years, expectations for the 2015–16 season were the highest they had been since the year Maryland won the NCAA title. The addition of transfers Robert Carter and Rasheed Sulaimon were supposed to more than offset the graduation of Dez Wells.

Things didn't turn out exactly as planned. A season-ending injury to sophomore guard Dion Wiley right before the opener, a lingering injury to Trimble that led to a second-half shooting slump, and a lack of rebounding and defense from Carter and freshman center Diamond Stone contributed to a good—27–9 and a Sweet 16 berth—but not memorable season.

The pressure will be back on Turgeon in 2016–17, proving that it's hard to replace a legend.

60 Rhodes Scholar

Though Tom McMillen didn't help the Terps become "the UCLA of the East," as Lefty Driesell had promised, the team won the NIT when he was a sophomore and went to the Elite Eight when he was a junior.

Individually, McMillen's two-season scoring average of 20.3 during his junior and senior years is the highest in school history, and despite only three years on varsity, he is in the top 10 in both scoring (1,807) and rebounding (859).

McMillen's most significant achievement might have been in becoming the school's first and only Rhodes Scholar.

The Rhodes Scholar came about after McMillen interviewed with Georgetown University president Father Henle—the morning after the No. 4 Terps crushed the rebuilding Hoyas by 32 his senior year.

"We killed Georgetown, and I walk into the interview, and the chair of the committee is always a non-Rhodes scholarship, and it was Father Henle, and I said, 'Shoot, I've lost this thing,'" McMillen recalled.

"But it turned out to be a positive because we had three or four minutes of the interview when we were turned out about basketball. It took some of the pressure off."

Being a Rhodes Scholar turned out to be a positive—though tiring—experience as well.

Going to school in Oxford, England, McMillen signed with an Italian team in Bologna. Twice a week, he would fly to Rome, get picked up by a team official or teammate and driven to the game. He would be on the first flight out in the morning back to London.

"It was a pretty difficult schedule," McMillen said. "But we had about 8,000 fans at every game, we sold out every game. I was probably at the time one of the highest-paid athletes in Europe and here I was doing it part-time."

61 Tennis, Anyone?

Only those who attended Maryland during the early and mid-1970s, or followed World Team Tennis in the late 1970s, remember John Lucas the tennis player.

While certainly not as good with a racket as he was with a basketball, Lucas was good enough to be a two-time All-American and WTT mixed-doubles champion.

Lucas, who played six years on the men's pro tour while starting his NBA career, got his start at a young age in Durham, North Carolina.

"When I was in the third grade, my father and mother were both school principals," Lucas said. "The high school where my father was the principal was right up the hill from where we lived, and when I came home, he would have me come up to the gym."

Carl Easterling was both the boys' basketball coach and the tennis coach.

"He took time and taught me a set shot, he also taught me how to play tennis, and he gave me a future," Lucas said.

While in high school, pro tennis star Arthur Ashe heard about the African American teenager in North Carolina and tried to convince Lucas to attend his alma mater, UCLA. Fellow North Carolinian Henry Bibby, who was a star basketball player for the Bruins, talked to Lucas about following him to Westwood.

North Carolina coach Dean Smith was also interested in Lucas, but it came after the local star outplayed future Tar Heel Walter Davis in a postseason All-Star Game in Charlotte after their senior year. But Lefty Driesell got the inside track on both schools.

"Neither school was going to allow me to play both, so I had to pick which [sport] I wanted," Lucas recalled. "Coach Driesell didn't really have an issue."

Lucas said that Darrell Royal, Maryland's tennis coach at the time, "had never seen me play tennis." The coach didn't even know about his talents on the tennis courts until Lucas showed up at Maryland.

After starring for the Terps in basketball as a freshman, word spread quickly about Lucas playing tennis.

"We used to have crowded tennis courts," Lucas said.

As the school's No. 1-ranked tennis player in both singles and doubles, Lucas won the ACC singles titles as a sophomore and senior and teamed with a Venezuelan named Freddie Winkleman to take the league's doubles titles as a freshman and junior.

"The ACC was pretty loaded—Virginia, Clemson, North Carolina," Lucas said. "I think we finished third and fourth."

Lucas travelled the Association of Tennis Professionals (ATP) tour for the first six years of his 14-year NBA career. He also teamed with Dr. Renee Richards (formerly Dr. Richard Raskin) to win the World Team Tennis mixed doubles title as teammates on the New Orleans Nets.

"We went 29–1," Lucas said.

62 Maryland's Top Walk-Ons

Varun Ram set some sort of unofficial Maryland and NCAA record toward the end of the 2015–16 season, when he was honored for the second time on Senior Night.

After graduating as a double-major in neurobiology and physiology the previous season, Ram returned as a graduate student in global supply chain management for another season.

Ram, who transferred to Maryland after his freshman year at Division III Trinity University, left as one of the most popular—and productive—walk-ons in school history.

The 5'10", 160-pound point guard played in 63 games—also a record for a player who spent a portion of his career paying his own way—and had one signature moment.

It came in the 2015 NCAA tournament opener, Maryland's first NCAA tournament appearance in five years, in the final seconds against Valparaiso.

After not playing the first 39 minutes, Ram was inserted on a key defensive possession and wound up stripping a Valpo player as he was about to take a go-ahead three-point shot.

The Terps wound up winning by three.

Ram's role increased as a senior when he found his way as the third or fourth guard behind starters Melo Trimble and Rasheed Sulaimon for a good chunk of the season.

On Senior Night, in a rout of Illinois, Ram hit his final field-goal attempt as a Terp, a straightaway three-pointer that brought a standing ovation from the sellout crowd.

Here are the rest of Maryland's starting five of celebrated walk-ons.

Mike Thibeault: He filled in as a backup point guard on some of Gary Williams' early teams in College Park that had been depleted by transfers after the program was placed on NCAA probation. He was known as a volume shooter—launching 22 shots in 56 minutes his first season—and a pesky defender.

Norman Fields: A 6'0" guard who played from 1995 through 1999, Fields appeared in 52 games and scored a total of 66 points. After leading the Terps in total shooting with a combined percentage of 60.5 as a junior, Fields shot a team-low 37.2 percent as a senior.

Earl Badu: Though he played in just 18 games over three years and scored only four points, the 6'0" guard is remembered most for being a part of two Final Four teams and scoring the final basket ever in a men's game at Cole Field House against Virginia in March of 2002.

John Auslander: After spending a season at UNC-Greensboro, Auslander joined Mark Turgeon's first team as a sophomore and played in 14 games that season. Injuries limited his career, but he made enough of an impression that he was hired as a valued graduate manager and played an integral role on two NCAA tournament teams.

63 A Different View of Lefty

Of all those who played for Lefty Driesell over the course of his coaching career, Greg Manning might have the most interesting perspective.

After he was finished playing, Manning eventually got into athletic administration and became the athletic director at Georgia State, where he was Driesell's boss for the end of the coach's career.

"He treated that job like he was at Maryland. There was no difference," said Manning. "It was 24 hours a day. I would get a call from Coach, at least twice a week, and it might be on Sunday afternoon, and he absolutely had to see me. He absolutely wore me out. He attacked it like he was in the ACC."

Manning said that Driesell constantly was trying to come up with gimmicks to raise the program's low profile.

"He had a notepad with at least two pages full of ideas," recalled Manning. "Ninety percent of them were like something that was from Mars. The other 10 percent were terrific. I would say, 'We can do this,' and he would say, 'How about the other 50 I've got on here?'"

Finally, in 2001, Driesell took a 28–4 team filled with transfers from bigger schools to the NCAA tournament. Georgia State was shipped out to Boise, where Driesell's team was seeded 14th and would meet Wisconsin in the opening round.

"I turned to our president after the first five minutes of the game and I said, 'We're better,'" Manning recalled. "'We've got better players. We're going to win.' And I'll be darned, we win that game and who do we play next? We play Maryland."

Manning still believes that if Georgia State's star big man, junior forward Thomas Terrell, "doesn't get in foul trouble we beat Maryland. He had a team. We were really good. It was a pleasure to watch."

Manning loves to tell the story about how Driesell used to recruit to Georgia State, a commuter school in downtown Atlanta.

"Lon Krueger was the coach of the Hawks, and he would come over and be watching our practice," said Manning. "One day, early on, Lon was sitting there and he said, 'You're not going to believe this. Coach Driesell brought one of his recruits over.'"

Driesell would show them the Hawks' practice facility and the CNN Center.

"He would tell them that's where they're going to play and never ever show 'em our arena," Manning said. "Lon would ask me, 'Can you believe that?' And I would say, 'Of course I can believe it.' Who else would even think of that?"

64 Greatest Game Ever?

When Villanova's Kris Jenkins hit the game-winning three-pointer to beat North Carolina in the 2016 NCAA championship, there was an immediate explosion on Twitter over whether the showdown in Houston was the greatest college basketball game ever played.

Len Elmore has heard it all before.

He heard it in 1992, when as an analyst on the CBS telecast of the East Regional final between defending national champion Duke and Kentucky at the Spectrum in Philadelphia, Christian Laettner capped off a near-perfect performance with a last-second turnaround jumper right inside the three-point line.

(Near-perfect because while Laettner will forever be remembered for his perfect stat line of 10 of 10 on field goals and 10 of 10 on free throws, he will also be forever remembered for his less-than-perfect on-court manners when it came to stepping, however lightly, on Aminu Timberlake's chest.)

Elmore also heard it through a string of other down-to-the-wire and buzzer-beating victories in the NCAA tournament.

Among them, the 1982 North Carolina–Georgetown championship game that launched Tar Heel freshman Michael Jordan's legend and the 1983 title tilt between North Carolina State and heavily favored Houston, which was won when Lorenzo Charles redirected Dereck Whittenburg's air-balled three-pointer in for a buzzer-beating dunk.

Elmore is a perfect judge when it comes to this contest, since he was on the court at the Greensboro Coliseum for nearly the entirety of Maryland's 103–100 overtime loss to North Carolina State in the 1974 ACC tournament championship game.

"Beauty is in the eye of the beholder," Elmore said. "The thing that made the '92 game so special was the sudden-impact ending."

That it kept Duke's chances of a repeat alive played into the significance of the outcome, as well as the fact that Laettner, whom many consider one of the 10 greatest college players of all time, even outdid himself after hitting a huge game-winner two years earlier against Connecticut in the Sweet 16.

"Jenkins' shot didn't have the same thing riding on it as Laettner's because if Laettner misses, they're done," Elmore said. "To me, it's less pressure. It was a well-played game for the most part, up and down, and give Carolina credit for coming back from double-digits down."

Elmore said that Marcus Paige's "crazy, double-pump shot from three" to tie the game was reminiscent of Sean Woods' "double-clutch shot" that kissed high off the backboard to put Kentucky ahead of Duke with seconds remaining in the 1992 game.

While Jenkins' launch certainly had its own explosion— including the confetti streaming down from the ceiling of the RNG Center before the referees could even review if the shot would count—the fact that it broke a tie right before the final horn takes away some of the drama.

At least it does in Elmore's eyes.

"When you look at Jay Wright and people were commenting on how cool he was," said Elmore, who was at the game, "well, think about the situation. They had the ball in a tie game, and it's either: we make the shot and we win or we miss and we're going to overtime. I think the wheels were turning [in Wright's head] about what they were going to do in overtime, not thinking they were going to make that shot."

Mo Howard has a different viewpoint—and a unique perspective—when comparing the 2016 NCAA title game to others in contention as the greatest game ever, including the 1974 Maryland–North Carolina State game.

Like Elmore, Howard was in Houston to watch it live because his son, Maurice Jr., is an assistant on Wright's staff.

Howard said that it was similar to the Villanova win over Georgetown in the 1985 NCAA final at Rupp Arena, which is considered among the greatest upsets in Final Four history.

"There's no way the Villanova kids should have been in the game," he said. "It should have been like Villanova playing Oklahoma [a 44-point rout].

"For them to even hang around in the game and have leads in the game was just beyond my comprehension. I thought North Carolina was going to kill 'em. I said to my son repeatedly, 'When you face a team that has multiple highly skilled big guys, I think you guys are going to have a problem.' It didn't happen that way."

Howard believes that what made the ending of the Villanova–North Carolina game so special was that the winning play didn't involve a Hail Mary pass like the one Laettner took from Grant Hill, but one "that they practiced every day. This wasn't any great X-and-O call by Jay Wright."

The Hill-Laettner play—which ironically happened in Philadelphia—"might have been more dramatic," Howard said, "but in terms of importance of the moment and all the plots and subplots surrounding that game, the best game I've ever seen on any level was that game. It was one for the ages, man."

65 Maryland's First Great Big Man

For more than a decade, Al Bunge had the reputation as the best player ever to come out of Maryland, certainly its best big man.

For nearly two decades, the 6'7¾" center from New Jersey held the school's single-game scoring record of 43 points.

Bunge's stature as the best big man to play for the Terps ended when Lefty Driesell brought Tom McMillen and Len Elmore to College Park in the fall of 1970.

Bunge said that he almost didn't go to Maryland from his small high school in New Jersey. But Bunge decided to go after one of his high school rivals, Charlie McNeil, took a scholarship to play for Bud Millikan. They were roommates in College Park for four years.

"I had never seen a college basketball game, I had never seen a college football game," recalled Bunge. "We didn't have a television in those years, and nobody I knew did either."

His record was erased more than 18 years later when Ernie Graham torched North Carolina State for 44 points.

Even Bunge admits that his record was not that big a deal.

Asked what he remembers about that game as a senior, Bunge said, "Not an awful lot except that it wasn't too hard. It was Yale. We scored a whole bunch of points, and I didn't play the whole game."

Bunge's jersey number (54) was never honored, as Graham's eventually was in what had even more to do with politics than points.

Bunge might have been as deserving, given that he started on Maryland's first ACC tournament champion team in 1958 in Raleigh, North Carolina after finishing fourth during the regular season and was an All-ACC player as a senior. The Terps beat both

North Carolina, the defending national champions, and Kentucky that year.

Had it not been for an ongoing battle with ulcerative colitis and anemia, which was discovered when Bunge was a freshman, he might have had an even better career, college and pro.

"It almost killed me at the end of my freshman year. I was rushed to the hospital in Baltimore," Bunge said. "It affected me every year I played. That's ancient history."

Walter Bellamy pulls down the rebound on a shot attempted by Maryland's first great big man, Al Bunge (54), during the first game of the Bluegrass Invitational tournament on December 28, 1959.

Bunge, who was also recruited to play football for Jim Tatum at Maryland, said that he lost nearly 50 pounds, dropping down to 165 during his freshman year. Bunge said he had repeated transfusions during his career in College Park, usually toward the end of each season.

"When I came back as a sophomore, I couldn't run up and down the floor," Bunge said. "I had a transfusion, and that made me better for most of the year. When we got to the end of the year, my anemia started coming back."

As a sophomore, Bunge collected a career-high 22 rebounds in a game against Georgetown, but his weight dropped under 200 pounds by the time the Terps played in the NCAA tournament, losing to Temple in the East Regional semifinal in Charlotte, North Carolina.

"We got beat by three or four points [71–67]. Guy Rodgers and Hal Lear were All-Americans, and their big center was a guy named Van Patton who was about 250 and he just beat the living crap out of me," Bunge said. "I could hardly play. I didn't play half the game. I always said if I was healthy, we would have won."

The next two years, the Terps fell just short, losing against Virginia in 1959 and N.C. State in 1960 in the ACC tournament.

"I think we would have won the ACC when I was a junior and senior if I had been healthy," said Bunge.

Bunge's selection to the All-ACC team as a senior, along with his 43-point outburst against Yale, helped earn him an invitation to a prestigious postseason All-Star Game at Madison Square Garden.

Some of Bunge's East teammates included future NBA stars Jerry West of West Virginia and Lenny Wilkins of Providence and Tom Stith of St. Bonaventure. Among those on the West team was Cincinnati's Oscar Robertson, who Bunge said he guarded for most of the game.

"I think we held Oscar to something like 11 or 12 points, but they weren't all against me," Bunge said.

Bunge heard from a number of NBA teams, including the New York Knicks, Syracuse Nationals, Fort Wayne Pistons, and Philadelphia Warriors. Claiming territorial rights to Bunge, the Warriors drafted him No. 7 overall to join a team that featured a second-year seven-footer named Wilt Chamberlain.

He never played a game.

Bunge said that he got into a contract dispute with Warriors president and general manager Eddie Gottlieb over the team paying for the health insurance he needed because of his anemia.

Instead, Bunge took an offer from Phillips 66 Oilers, the Oklahoma-based oil company barnstorming team of pro and semipro players. He wound up working for the company for more than 30 years, even moving to company headquarters in Bartlesville, Oklahoma.

The years and distance from his days in College Park lessened the connection he had to College Park. He does not remember when he heard Graham had broken his scoring record, but in those pre-Internet years the news didn't reach Oklahoma immediately.

His most interesting connection to the current program is that one of his daughters, Tracy Bunge, was an All-American softball player at Kansas at the same time that Mark Turgeon was the team's starting point guard.

Turgeon said that he remembered Tracy Bunge, but had no idea her father once held the Maryland school scoring record.

"That's pretty neat," he said.

66 The Shot

More than a decade later, Drew Nicholas will be stopped in airports, gas stations, banks, and health clubs by Maryland fans, or simply college basketball fans who want to talk about "The Shot."

Of all the shots Nicholas had taken before that Friday night in March of 2003 in the opening round of the NCAA tournament, and all those he took in a nine-year pro career in Europe, nothing came close.

Nicholas still has vivid memories of the circumstances that led up to his game-winning, run-off three-pointer to beat UNC-Wilmington in Nashville.

"I remember everything about it," Nicholas said.

There was the UNC-Wilmington player who had two free throws to put the Seawolves ahead of the defending national champions with five seconds remaining.

"I thought we were in pretty good shape because he was a 40 or 45 percent foul shooter," Nicholas said. "He makes the first one and I said, 'Oh man, don't let him make the next one.' And he makes the next one, and obviously we're down one."

Nicholas remembers Maryland coach Gary Williams drawing up a play designed to have senior point guard Steve Blake take the inbound pass from Tadj Holden and take it as far as he could before shooting.

"During the timeout, there was a little worry, and I was thinking, *I can't let my college career end like this in the first round of the NCAAs the year after we won the national championship*," Nicholas said.

Nicholas remembers being the secondary option off the inbound pass and telling Holden that he would go back and get the ball if Blake was covered.

"He just kind of nodded at me, and the play happened, and that's all she wrote," Nicholas said.

Nicholas, who had hit a game-winning three-pointer "from pretty much the same spot" to beat N.C. State on the road earlier that season, dribbled it as far as he could and let it fly from about 20 feet on the right side.

"I needed to get something up there," Nicholas said. "I am pretty sure that in my entire college career I had never taken a three-pointer off one leg like that."

And he remembered thinking something that he would finally admit years later. Because he was being pushed toward the right-side court and shooting left, he thought the ball was going to sail wide.

"I tell people all the time, when I let it go, I thought it was an air ball," he said.

Gary Williams has vivid memories of The Shot.

"That was right in front of our bench. He was two feet away from me when he made the shot," Williams recalled. "The thing I really remember is that he really got squared up, his shoulders were exactly where they should be for that angle for the shot. He shot a pure jump shot. People think he threw it up there. It looked like a 15-footer the way he shot it. All great shooters can do that."

Though he said that the sequence was almost like having "an out-of-body experience," Nicholas also has memories of the shot's aftermath that saw him run off the court and seemingly out of the arena.

In truth, Nicholas turned left and found his way to an area behind the courtside seats.

"I was out of there," he said. "I just shot it and I was going so fast, I was kind of going in that direction. I just took off running. I remember thinking, *There's no way in hell I'm letting the refs tell me that wasn't good.*"

The celebration continued right there.

"It was either Blake or Andre Collins, and one of those guys grabbed me and we fell to the floor, and I couldn't breathe for a couple of seconds," Nicholas said. "Everybody was either on top of me or grabbing me, and I do remember Coach Williams going nuts."

When the Terps returned to the arena the next day to get ready for their second-round game against Xavier, some of Nicholas' teammates urged him to try that shot again. Nicholas declined.

"I was one for one and I would never shoot that shot again," he said. "I still haven't shot it."

Interestingly, when Maryland played Michigan State in the Sweet 16, it came down to nearly the same situation, and Nicholas found himself close to standing near Spartans coach Tom Izzo.

"I remember Izzo telling me, 'No way you're getting this basketball,'" Nicholas recalled. "He had somebody behind me and somebody in front of me. Blake could get the ball easily, and I remember watching Blake's shot, and it looked as good as any. He had a much cleaner look."

As the years went on, and the tape of Nicholas' shot kept getting replayed every March, Nicholas thought about the last-second shots he had watched as a kid growing up on Long Island.

Along with UCLA guard Tyus Edney's full-court dash with 3.8 seconds left to beat Missouri in 1995—en route to the Bruins winning the national title—there was of course Christian Laettner's shot to beat Kentucky in the 1992 Elite Eight game.

"I think this is where my hatred for Duke started, when Laettner hit the shot," Nicholas said.

No shot Nicholas hit during a productive professional career come close to duplicating the magic of that March night.

"That was the pinnacle," he said. "It doesn't get any better than that. If it does, it's a helluva career for whoever hits two of those shots."

67 Diamond Stone Briefly Shining Bright

In Maryland basketball lore, it will be remembered as the night Diamond Stone had his coming-out party—and his going-away bash—on the same evening.

It was the night of December 30, 2015, and Stone did his best to dismantle Penn State, rewrite the program's record books, and show the lone NBA scout in attendance that he might be ready sooner rather than later.

If the first half was a continuation of what Stone had done the previous five games in a reserve role—scoring seven points—the second half was an indication of what might be in store.

Stone scored 32 points in the half, including 14 of his team's last 23, as the then–fourth-ranked Terps overcame 34 minutes of offensive ineptitude with six minutes of perfection.

The come-from-way-behind 70–64 victory over improving but still lowly Penn State will long be forgotten in the scheme of the 6'11" center's career.

That Stone erased Joe Smith's 23-year old scoring mark for freshmen—something Melo Trimble had fallen two points shy of tying the season before—was only part of the record book rearranging.

The second half point total by Stone, which was part of a 39-point, 10-of-15 field goal shooting, 19-of-25 free throw shooting performance, also knocked Ernie Graham out of the record books.

In his own record-breaking performance, Graham had gone for 30 in the second half of his 44-point explosion against North Carolina State in 1978.

Two other former Terp stalwarts who often made a living at the foul line, Tom McMillen and Keith Booth, had their respective records for free throws made and attempted wiped away.

Stone, who described himself as a "pretty humble kid" despite a Twitter page that identified the former Milwaukee schoolboy star as "All Eyes On Me," said that he didn't care about the record.

"I really don't pay too much mind to it," he said with a smile after the game. "It was just a regular game to me, a Big Ten game, and we're trying to win the Big Ten. We've got to get ready for Northwestern Saturday."

But it was a big deal to others, none of whom were surprised at what Stone had done.

"I think Diamond likes the bright lights, he likes the stage, he likes to be challenged, and we were extremely challenged today," Maryland coach Mark Turgeon said. "He was terrific."

Only an inconsequential missed free throw with 19 seconds to go prevented Stone from joining six other former Terps—Graham, Smith, Al Bunge (43), Greivis Vasquez (41 in a triple-overtime win at Virginia Tech), Len Bias (41), and Gene Shue, who scored 40 or more twice—in a fairly exclusive club.

Walt Williams, whose record of seven straight ACC games with 30 points or more included his own career-best of 39 points, joked on the postgame radio show that his best offensive game in College Park was the result of more than 15 shots.

"I probably took 15 shots by halftime," the Wizard said.

Robert Carter Jr., whose own collegiate high at that juncture was a 21-point game as a sophomore at Georgia Tech, said that Stone was probably not that impressed by it himself.

"He thinks he's supposed to be great every game," Carter said, "just talking to him in practice and telling him to work hard, his time is going to come, and tonight was his time."

As things turned out, the Penn State game didn't foreshadow that many outbursts the rest of the season. He had a more normal, yet still impressive, 22-point, 11-rebound performance in a road loss at Michigan.

The rest of Stone's freshman year was more typical, especially for a big man. After a string of 12 straight double-figure scoring nights, Stone had two in single digits before finishing the season with 22 of 27 back in double figures.

Stone finished the season, and his Maryland career as it turned out, with a subpar five-point, four-rebound, foul-plagued performance against Kansas in the NCAA tournament's Sweet 16, the first trip there for the Terps since 2003.

How will Stone's one season in College Park be remembered? For the hype that accompanied his signing, the bursts of offensive brilliance that usually came in bunches, and the thought of what might have been had he stayed past his freshman year.

68 Steve Blake, NBA Lifer

Shortly after Maryland won the NCAA title in 2002, Steve Blake went to Gary Williams and asked what he thought of the junior point guard putting his name into the NBA draft as sophomore forward Chris Wilcox was doing.

Bad idea, the coach told him.

Blake listened, returning to College Park for his senior year. It turned out to be good advice, as Blake was drafted in the second round by the Washington Wizards—the same team that had taken Juan Dixon in the first round the previous June.

More than a decade later, Blake was the only Terp from that team left in the NBA.

Long after Dixon's seven-year career ended in his second stint with the Wizards in 2008, long after Lonny Baxter left to become a basketball vagabond in Europe, even after Wilcox went from lottery pick to journeyman and saw his 10-year career shortened by a heart condition, Blake kept going.

"There were two things about Blake—he was quicker than people thought he was, and the other thing is that he's bigger, he's 6'3", he's not a 6'1" point guard," Gary Williams said. "I knew just being his coach that he was very perceptive as far as basketball. If you told him something, he would really look at it and if he agreed with it, he could execute it very quickly."

Williams said that during Blake's time playing under Phil Jackson with the Los Angeles Lakers, Jackson told him, "Steve Blake picked up the Triangle Offense quicker than any player he ever coached. That's a pretty good endorsement right there."

For several years, Blake has even run into former Maryland fans who thought he was retired, too.

"Should I be retired?" he asked during an interview with the *Baltimore Sun* in the summer of 2015, shortly after being traded twice in a matter of days and landing with the Detroit Pistons, his ninth NBA team.

"I do take it year by year, but when I do look back, I definitely see how blessed I am to have taken the paths I've taken, having grown as a player and [to] understand the NBA to where I can stick around and fit in. I feel very lucky and blessed to have had that."

Blake left Maryland as its all-time assist leader with 972—200 more than Greivis Vasquez—and fourth in steals. But what helped Blake stay in the NBA as long as he did was the fact that he improved his three-point range, as a career 38.3 percent three-point shooter, and his defense.

One of the reasons the Los Angeles Lakers signed Blake in 2010 to his most lucrative NBA contract—a four-year, $16 million deal—was that superstar Kobe Bryant remembered what a pest Blake had been while playing for Portland and the Clippers.

Steve Blake throws an arm around Juan Dixon after they defeated Kansas 97-88 in the 2002 NCAA semifinal. (David Martin)

It didn't hurt that Blake's last game of the 2009–10 season after being traded during the year from the Trail Blazers to the Clippers was against the Lakers and Blake had the first—and what turned out to be only—triple-double of his career.

"They'd just won two championships, and I was thinking that I was going to be able to get a ring. I had other options as well. Nothing's given. I love my experience there, but we didn't win a championship," Blake said.

Constantly reminded that his more famous college backcourt mate didn't last nearly as long in the NBA as he did, Blake said that the response from fans was "understandable," but quickly added that: "Juan was amazing, and he had a successful NBA career.

"Maybe if he had different opportunities he would have played longer, but he had a nice long career. Of course, I would have thought he would have played a lot longer than me. Chris had a long career, too, but I'm lucky enough to keep playing a long time, too."

When he was traded by the Trail Blazers on Draft Night in 2015 to the Brooklyn Nets, many figured he would finally call it quits since his family—including his parents and a couple of his sisters—moved to Portland. Then, a couple of days later, he was traded to Detroit.

"It's the first trade that's a shock to the system a little bit," he said. "When you're planning on staying somewhere or you want to stay somewhere and you really have no say in the matter and you find out you have to go somewhere else, it's tough for you professionally but mostly for the family. The second one I kind of knew it was coming so it wasn't a total surprise."

While many expected Blake to be cut in training camp, early-season injuries to point guards Brandon Jennings and Spencer Dinwiddie opened the door for the 36-year-old veteran to stick around. It also probably helped that no-nonsense coach Stan Van Gundy appreciated Blake's work ethic and professionalism.

Blake wound up playing in 58 games as well as the first-round playoff loss to the Cleveland Cavaliers, averaging around 17 minutes a game. He had his best month—averaging nearly seven points, five assists, and two rebounds a game, including 13 points and six assists against the Cavs in the regular season finale—as the Pistons won three of their last four to earn the eighth and last playoff spot.

Said Blake, "I'm definitely a more mature player. I guess throughout my NBA career, I learned the game a lot. I knew that if I wanted to play a long time I needed to shoot the three. That was a given, but I've always been a pass-first point guard, that's kind of the way I've always played, understanding the NBA concept. I've always understood my role within the teams to do my job well so they would want to keep me around."

His old college coach is not surprised to hear that Blake wants to keep going into the 2016–17 season.

"If there's one word to describe Steve, it's consistent," Williams said. "Even when he was playing with us, his consistency was incredible. I think a lot of people missed that. Even Billy Packer, who trashed Blake during the semifinals and finals [in 2002]. I don't think he appreciated what Blake did for our team."

69 In a Wink, Francis was Gone

Until Diamond Stone made a one-season cameo at Maryland in 2015–16, the last "one-and-done" to play for the Terps was Steve Francis.

It was a different deal back then. Francis, who had spent two years at different junior colleges trying to get his NCAA eligibility, arrived in College Park in the fall of 1998 and was gone by the spring after helping the team reach the Sweet 16 and then getting drafted No. 2 overall by the Vancouver Grizzlies and then traded to the Houston Rockets.

Just as his journey at Maryland was over quickly—as quick as the nickname "Wink" Francis had carried with him since his days growing up near the campus in Takoma Park—his NBA career seemed to have a similar trajectory. A fast rise followed by an equally speedy exit.

By the time he made the first of three straight All-Star game appearances in 2002, Francis had gone from being some sort of college supernova to a player who was suddenly being put in the same sentence—and same starting West Conference backcourt— with a rising star named Kobe Bryant.

"He's the best point guard in the NBA," John Lucas, a former No. 1 overall pick himself, said that season while coaching the Cleveland Cavaliers.

By the time he reached that All-Star game in Philadelphia, something seemed to be missing for the player everyone had started to call "Stevie Franchise."

The Rockets were losing and would ultimately trade Francis a couple of years later to the Orlando Magic.

The medical issues and injuries that would wind up derailing his career and forcing him into premature retirement after a few mediocre seasons were beginning to take their toll.

The enthusiasm Francis seemed to carry with him from the time he played his first game at Cole Field House and then into the NBA appeared to be waning.

When a reporter who had known Francis since his Maryland days questioned whether was still having fun, he snapped.

"When was the last time you saw me play?" he said. "What was the difference between then and the first time you ever saw me play? The joy is not gone. It's never gone anywhere."

But then, slowly at first and then quickly, it was gone.

And so was Stevie Franchise.

A series of cost-cutting trades and knee problems that took away his explosiveness as it did for other young NBA stars from Penny Hardaway to Tracy McGrady—for whom he was swapped and shipped to Orlando—eventually turned Francis into a shell of what he had been.

After playing parts of two perfunctory seasons with the New York Knicks, at one point teamed with another fading star, Stephon Marbury—and then a short-lived return to the Rockets and getting cut by the Grizzlies (perhaps the basketball gods' way of getting back with him for refusing to go to Vancouver out of Maryland), Francis was gone, trying briefly and embarrassingly to resurrect his career in China.

In a 2010 *Slam* magazine article titled "What the hell happened to Steve Francis," the former three-time All-Star and one-time Rookie of the Year didn't seem to accept that his career was over.

"My agent won't allow me to go out and play streetball because I have nothing left to prove out there, so I work out at my court at home with my two-year-old son," he told *Slam*. "I'm still able to get out on the [NBA] court and bust somebody's ass…. If a team calls me up and is interested, give me two weeks and I'm ready to rock. The money has to be right though."

Asked about his second stint with the Rockets, Francis said, "They signed me back and they had me playing behind somebody that wasn't even drafted—Skip to My Lou [of street ball fame, also known as Rafer Alston]. You can't let a three-time NBA All-Star rot on the bench. It really rubbed me the wrong way."

Of his even shorter stay with the Grizzlies during training camp, Francis said, "Why would I need to showcase myself at this point and prove myself to a team that wasn't winning and play behind two players [Mike Conley and Kyle Lowry at the time] that haven't proven themselves? My agent worked out a deal to get me out of there."

In recent years, Francis has appeared to find some peace, trying to do work on his foundation, growing his family in Houston, and staying in touch with a place he fondly called home for a year. True to his boyhood nickname, he is "Wink," hard to pin down for more than a moment or two.

70 Bias Finally Makes Maryland Hall of Fame

The first sign of softening came during the 2013–14 season, with his picture on a game ticket when the Maryland men's basketball team played Tulsa. It was athletic director Kevin Anderson's way of testing the temperature to see how fans felt about the late Len Bias.

With a positive reaction, the movement to get Bias into the Maryland athletics Hall of Fame had taken hold.

In July of 2014, the school announced that Bias would be one of seven to be inducted.

"We just felt like the time was right," said Kevin Glover, a former Maryland football star and the head of the M Club, which oversaw the process. "We all know it's a very sensitive issue. A lot of changes were made to the university back in the day because of this situation [Bias' death]."

The decision to induct Bias, who left as the school's all-time leading scorer before being passed by both Juan Dixon and Greivis Vasquez, came more than 28 years after the 6'8" forward died from what was called a cocaine overdose in his dormitory suite following the 1986 NBA draft.

Bias had been selected by the soon-to-be world champion Boston Celtics with the No. 2 pick.

Longtime coach Lefty Driesell, who called Bias' death "tragic," said that the recognition of his former star was long overdue.

"He wasn't a drug addict," Driesell said. "He had come back from celebrating becoming a multimillionaire and he didn't know what he was doing, and it killed him. If he had died in an auto accident or drowned swimming, he would have been a hero. He was one of the greatest kids I ever coached."

First eligible in 1986, Bias was denied entrance for more than two decades because of a bylaw in the Hall of Fame voting that candidates who brought "embarrassment or disrepute" to the university could be denied, though it was not guaranteed.

Former sports information director Jack Zane, who had served in both voting and nonvoting capacities on the Hall of Fame committee, said he opposed Bias' candidacy simply because of the bylaw regarding off-court issues but added, "I think he deserves it based on what he did on the court."

On the night of the ceremony that October, university president Wallace Loh thanked the Bias family for allowing their late son to be honored. Relations between Maryland and Bias' parents, whose younger son Jay had been shot to death a few years later at a suburban mall, were strained for many years.

Loh said it was a "great honor" to include Bias in the Hall of Fame. Former teammate Keith Gatlin, who left Maryland as the school's single-game assist record holder largely because of Bias, said that "I think it's special for his family and I think, for the university, to heal."

Walt Williams, who grew up idolizing Bias and was still in high school when Bias died, summed up the feelings of many who had called for his induction.

"The way his life ended was tragic, but he did other things," Williams said. "He was a great player. He gave a community a sense of pride. He made other players behind him want to come here. You look at the players that came after—myself, Jerrod Mustaf,

Juan Dixon, Keith Booth—all of those guys would credit some portion of why they came here [to] Len Bias. So his legacy goes on and on. Even to this day, you still hear players talk about him that never saw him play before."

Sadly, there are some Maryland students who have no idea who Bias was or where he lived—and tragically died—in Washington Hall. When one student was asked if he knew that he was living in the same quad as Bias, the response was typical.

"I didn't," the student said. "I also don't know who Len Bias is."

The quad itself has no mention that Bias lived in room 1103 or when and how he died. Today, the quad is home to barbeques, sunbathing, and volleyball games on a turf court.

71 Addition by Subtraction

Within weeks after Maryland finished a disappointing 2013–14 season with a 17–15 record, five players with remaining eligibility announced plans to leave the program.

Fans questioned third-year coach Mark Turgeon's future in College Park. Turgeon took the high road and didn't bad-mouth the malcontents, saying he would have to "look in the mirror" about how he was running his program.

Turgeon liked what he saw, not only in the mirror, but what was in store.

The departures of Seth Allen, Shaquille Cleare, Nick Faust, Charles Mitchell, and Roddy Peters—all of whom had been starters at one time or another the previous season—paved the way for Maryland's revival.

It was the ultimate case of addition by subtraction.

It was also addition by addition.

"I think the pieces fit," Turgeon said that summer as the new team started to work out. "I feel like we have some really, really good pieces. When you're putting a team together, it's all about pieces…. We've added guys who have a really good feel for the game."

The biggest addition was point guard Melo Trimble, who became the first point guard that Turgeon fully trusted since taking over for Gary Williams. While others who came in that summer didn't make as immediate an impact, the chemistry was apparent for everyone to see.

Rather than compete with star guard Dez Wells for points and praise, Trimble quietly molded his game with the rest of his teammates. Rather than radically alter the way he ran his program, Turgeon confidently continued to do what worked for him at Wichita State and Texas A&M.

"I have so much confidence in myself, the people around me, and this great basketball program," he said. "I don't feel any pressure. I'm more relaxed today than at any point since I took the job. And I mean that. The hardest part is explaining it to recruits."

As things turned out, he didn't have to do much explaining. Picked to finish 10th in their first season in the Big Ten, the 28–7 Terps were a surprising second behind Wisconsin and beat the Badgers head-to-head on the court as well as for top recruit and Milwaukee native Diamond Stone.

Even after Wells graduated, the Terps continued their progress. While some were left disappointed by the team's 27–9 record and first Sweet 16 appearance in 2015–16 after Maryland was one of the early season favorites to win a national championship, Turgeon proudly points to a 55–16 record since Trimble took over as the point guard.

Jake Layman, the only member of the 2012 recruiting class to finish out his career, proved prescient in his words during the summer of 2014. Even before a nearly new team would play its first game together, Layman had a pretty good feeling.

"If we build a culture around here that's going to get guys to work hard and focus on one common goal, I think we'll be fine this year, and I think we're heading in that direction," Layman said.

72 Just Shy of a Record

Of all the accomplishments by Maryland basketball players over the years, the most remarkable might have been by Walt Williams.

Though Williams' streak of seven straight games scoring 30 points or more during the 1991–92 season was one off the ACC record by Len Chappell of Wake Forest, it was done when the Terps had little to play for but pride, and Williams was the only real threat opposing teams had to worry about.

While he was yet to coach the likes of Joe Smith or Juan Dixon or Greivis Vasquez, future Hall of Fame coach Gary Williams said at the time that "I've never coached a player on a roll like this" and called the streak by the 6'8" guard "the best I've seen."

Walt Williams, who wound up averaging an ACC-best and school-record 26.8 points a game as a senior, said toward the end of the streak, "There are some nights when you feel like everything is going in. I've had that feeling for a while. It's a comfortable feeling."

The shooting streak, which included Williams scoring what became a career-high 39 points, came after he was moved from point guard to shooting guard, the position he would play for 11 years in the NBA after being drafted seventh overall by the Sacramento Kings later that year.

"I don't think he was a definite lottery pick as a point guard," one NBA scout said at the time. "But he's getting closer to being a sure thing because of what he's done lately. He's proven he can score."

What was remarkable was Williams' efficiency during the streak. He made 81 of 135 shots from the field, 32 of 58 from three-point range. It meant he was averaging 33 points a game on an average of just more than 19 shots.

In the 39-point game, which came against Wake Forest, Williams made 15 of 21 shots from the field, five of seven three-pointers, while being guarded alternately by two 6'8" forwards. If not for some foul trouble, Williams might have broken Ernie Graham's school record of 44 that still stands.

"That was as fine a performance as I've seen in my years in coaching," former Wake Forest coach Dave Odom said after the Demon Deacons pulled away to an 86–76 victory.

Gary Williams said a lot had to do with Walt Williams' versatility.

"You could play him at four different positions," Gary Williams said. "You couldn't come down and know where he was going to be every time down the court. With his ball-handling ability, if he got a matchup with say the 4-man [power forward], he couldn't guard Walt because Walt handled the ball too well. You had a point guard on him, we'd post him up and back him down. It was incredible."

If his old coach has any regrets, it was that Walt Williams' streak came when the Terps were on probation and off television.

"A lot of people didn't have a chance to see it unless they went to the games, and not many people went to the games," Williams said.

There was also the relationship Walt Williams had with his teammates.

"From managers on up to the other guys that started with him, Walt was probably as well-liked a player as any guy I've ever coached," Gary Williams said. "There's very few people that ever said anything bad about Walt. It never went to his head. Walt was always Walt."

Some of it started when Walt Williams stayed after the program was placed on probation following his sophomore year.

"For a guy not to transfer with what was going on, that's incredible," Gary Williams said. "That would never happen today."

Admittedly, a lot of Williams' success came from his teammates setting screens to free him.

"To do what he's done, you have to get screens and you have to learn how to use those screens," Gary Williams said. "It seems he gets better at that every time out. The other guys have done a great job getting Walt the ball. A lot has to do with Walt's popularity. If you don't like a guy, you don't always see when he's open."

Said Walt Williams: "The fellows are getting me open, and Kevin [McLinton] is doing a great job getting me the ball. The defense is on me, so [the screens] almost have to be perfect."

Williams also credited another member of the Maryland team for helping him. During a playful game of one-on-one after practice one day, team manager Matt "Buck" Morin suggested to the team's star that his shooting motion was causing the ball to float toward the basket with a sidespin rather than a backspin.

"I just told him that sometimes his hands drifted off instead of following through," recalled Morin, a stocky 5'7" former CYO player whose girth led to Williams giving him the nickname of the now-iconic John Candy character, Uncle Buck.

After scoring 33 points against North Carolina in Maryland's next game, Williams credited Buck.

"I think Walt gave me too much credit, but that's the kind of guy he is," said Morin, who would go on to become a successful high school coach in the area. "He's become a great player and a great friend."

Said Walt Williams: "He was out there working just as hard as I was."

There was also another reason cited for Williams suddenly becoming one of the hottest shooters in the country.

After the streak was finally stopped when Williams scored 21 points in a two-point loss to Georgia Tech, Gary Williams said that his star player had lost one of the contact lenses he started to wear right before the streak began.

"Quite a coincidence, isn't it?" said Williams.

The Yellow Jackets—mostly future NBA player Jon Barry—harassed Williams into a four-of-13 first half and limited him to just five shots in the second half by face-guarding the Maryland star. "We didn't want him to get a good look at the basket," Barry said.

"It was just a bad game," Williams said.

73 Maryland's Biggest Villains

A lot of animosity can be built up over 50 years of college basketball, and Maryland fans have their favorites—or non-favorites as the case may be.

In a sport where players come and go every four years (or even shorter now), coaches are typically the ones who feel more of the wrath on the road.

For that reason, Frank McGuire might have been the first villain to find his way to College Park, first to Ritchie Coliseum with North Carolina and eventually to Cole Field House with South Carolina.

Dean Smith, who had been one of McGuire's assistants in Chapel Hill and eventually took over when McGuire went to South

Carolina, replaced his former boss at the top of the list for years, only to be surpassed after he retired by Duke's Mike Krzyzewski.

But how about the players?

There are obvious ones, typically tied to the two or three teams that Maryland fans hated the most—North Carolina and Duke, and for a while in the 1960s, South Carolina. The three that stand out all wore Duke uniforms, and two even played on the same team.

Christian Laettner is at the top of anyone's list. If there was a homecoming game each year with a team made up of the most hated rival players, the former Blue Devils star would be invited by everyone—maybe even by some of his old teammates.

"Laettner kind of liked it," Grant Hill said. "He used to taunt the crowd. He embraced it. He loved it, being the villain, the bad guy."

There is a good reason why Laettner, one of the greatest college players ever, had an ESPN 30 for 30 documentary titled *I Hate Christian Laettner* in his honor. But Laettner actually was a class—not crass—act when it came to the Terps.

After an undermanned Maryland team hung tough with the top-rated Blue Devils after Walt Williams fouled out and lost at Cameron Indoor Stadium 91–89 during Laettner's senior year, the Duke center praised the Terps—and was typically blunt.

"There were a lot of things we didn't do, and you have to give Maryland credit," said Laettner, who finished with 30 points. "I guess I was a little surprised the way they came back. We probably relaxed a little when Walt Williams fouled out. But we showed our poise and we made some shots."

Then there was one of Laettner's teammates. Though Laettner was certainly Public Enemy No. 1 during his career at Duke, point guard Bobby Hurley was considered equally annoying by Maryland fans, especially whenever he made facial gestures after getting called for a foul.

Mostly, Terp fans didn't like the way Hurley led the Blue Devils to victory whenever the teams played.

Maryland played Duke nine times during Hurley's career and never won. It certainly had a lot to do with the fact that Krzyzewski's team was never ranked lower than 14th and the Terps were still coming out of the throes of the probation that resulted from Bob Wade's three-year tenure.

Hurley even broke the NCAA record for career assists the last time he played Maryland, on Senior Night at Duke in 1993.

"It makes me feel good to do something that nobody has done before," said Hurley "Hopefully, I'll get a few more this year so I'll make it hard for somebody to catch me. It really shows how fortunate I am to play with so many great players over the last four years."

How can you hate a guy like that?

As for the third member of this group, JJ Redick, Maryland fans finally got a bit of revenge for what Laettner and Hurley did to the Terps. Maryland beat the Blue Devils three times in nine meetings during Redick's time in Durham.

Of all the verbal abuse he took during his career at Duke, Redick said that Maryland fans were "the worst."

Toward the end of one of Duke's wins at Comcast Center, during Redick's junior year, Maryland fans stood behind one of the baskets and led a "F… you, JJ," chant as the Blue Devil guard was about to shoot free throws.

Years later, Redick looked at a video of that game and watched as he talked trash with Baltimore Ravens owner Steve Bisciotti, who was a courtside regular during Gary Williams' later years at Maryland.

In an article for ESPN's Grantland, Redick said, "He was talking noise to me the whole game, and I was just yapping back. I watch video now of me in college, and I just think, *What are you doing, man?*"

During his visit there as a senior, Maryland fans chanted obscenities about Redick's younger sister and shouted out her cell phone number. Years later, long after he left Duke, Redick admitted that he might have had something to do with the vitriol.

"I probably deserved it," Redick said. "I was sort of a [jerk]."

74 A Star in the Making

Pete Holbert was going into his junior year at Maryland when he was joined by two incoming freshmen on an Urban Coalition summer league team in Washington.

One of them was a gangly 6'8" forward from Prince George's County named Lenny Bias. In a league made up mostly of college and pro players—including the Washington Bullets rookie team—Bias was the leading scorer.

"You had all the best college players, all the local pro players, and all the local playground legends that didn't make it," said Holbert, who had been a McDonald's All-American coming out of high school in Fairfax, Virginia. "These were grown men."

Bias averaged 36 points a game, most of his points coming on dunks.

"He dunked on everybody," Holbert said. "He was better than the Bullets' rookies, Greg Ballard and Charles Davis. He was just killing these guys. That was the best shape I ever was in my life, and I scored 21 points a game and I thought I had a great summer. I was just being overshadowed by this guy."

Coming in for the 1982–83 season, Bias played briefly behind Adrian Branch at small forward. During an early season one-point win at Canisius, Lefty Driesell didn't even put Bias in "until the end of the game, I think he had two points,'" recalled Holbert.

By the time the Terps were scheduled to play third-ranked UCLA at Cole Field House 19 days later, Bias was in the starting lineup.

"He was nervous, he was rushing, he was missing his shots," Holbert said. "It went into overtime—I fouled Kenny Fields to put it into overtime—and Lenny scored all 10 of our points in overtime. It was like, 'This guy's really going to be good.'"

Bias would start 12 more games as a freshman. On a 20–10 team led by Branch and Ben Coleman that lost in the second round of the NCAA tournament to Houston and Phi Slama Jama, Bias averaged an unspectacular 7.2 points.

"I don't think he was that confident," Holbert said.

Even after leading the Terps to the ACC tournament title and being named most valuable player as a sophomore, Bias seemed to lack self-confidence. Holbert, who roomed with Bias for two seasons, said that Bias received an invitation to try out for the 1984 Olympic team and turned it down.

"I asked him, 'Lenny, why aren't you going?' He said, 'They've already got that team picked,'" recalled Holbert. "I said, 'Lenny, there's not 12 guys in the country better than you.'...I said, behind Michael Jordan and Sam Perkins, the third-best guy on that team is Wayman Tisdale, and you're better than Wayman Tisdale.'"

Holbert said that it motivated Bias, who would tell people he got "snubbed" by Olympic coach Bobby Knight. By the time Holbert returned after graduating, Bias had changed both physically and in terms of his self-confidence.

"He just got bigger and stronger, and there was no stopping him," Holbert said. "That's when the light switch came on. Was he that much better between his sophomore and junior year? Probably not, he got a little stronger, and his jump shot got better. He was the same player."

Holbert said that Bias "got even stronger" before his senior year, and his game progressed.

"He wasn't out partying. He was in the weight room getting ready to be an NBA player," Holbert said. "No one has a body like that and is out doing coke every night. You could put a case of beer in his refrigerator, and it would last a year."

Though Holbert admits that their friendship didn't endure as Bias' star rose, he was still shocked—and saddened—when he heard that his former teammate and roommate had died suddenly two days after the 1986 NBA Draft.

At the time, Holbert was working in Virginia Beach, Virginia, and was on the road when he got a call from his mother with the sad news.

"I just got one of those military bag cell phones, and my mom called me at like 7:30, 8 o'clock in the morning, and she said, 'Where are you?'" recalled Holbert. "I told her, 'I'm getting ready to make calls, I'm in my car.' She said, 'Pull over to the side of the road.'

"She told me Lenny died, and it might be cocaine-related. I said, 'Mom, that doesn't make any sense because Lenny's freshman year he wouldn't even drink a beer, and his sophomore year he might occasionally have one or two beers in the off-season."

75 Most Underrated Players

While some of Maryland's long-ago stars have been mostly forgotten, there are even more who played for the Terps that were largely overlooked for their accomplishments, even while they were in college.

At the top of that list is, perhaps, Johnny Rhodes.

Coming in the same year with Exree Hipp and Duane Simpkins, a year before Keith Booth and Joe Smith, Rhodes was a key player on the two straight Sweet 16 teams that led the program's revival in the mid-1990s.

While Smith and Booth went to the NBA as first-round draft picks—Smith for a 16-year career and Booth to get a ring as a member of the 1997–98 Chicago Bulls—Rhodes never earned a penny as a true professional.

His only time in the spotlight after leaving Maryland came when he and Hipp briefly played for the Harlem Globetrotters, which seemed so out of character for the low-key, no-frills Rhodes.

"He was probably the best player I coached who never played in the NBA," said Max Goode, who coached Rhodes in postgraduate prep school and later coached at the Division I level.

Rhodes left Maryland as the school's and ACC's all-time leader in steals (344) as well as in the top 10 in scoring (1,743 points) and assists (437) and as the school's all-time rebounding guard (704).

Admittedly, Rhodes doesn't know if would have been mature enough to handle playing in the NBA.

"I could have been one of those guys who made a lot of money and didn't have a penny to show for it," Rhodes said the night his jersey was hung from the rafters in Comcast Center in 2012.

Rhodes said that he wondered why it took so long for his jersey number to be raised years after Smith and Booth had theirs honored.

"I try to look at the positive side right now. Truth be told, I appreciate it now more than I would have a few years ago. I am very thankful."

Rhodes, who started his own construction company, said that not getting to play in the NBA "helped strengthen me in other areas in my life."

Here are some other overlooked Terps:

Derrick Lewis: He played center at 6'7", 195 pounds and left Maryland in 1988 as the school's all-time shot blocker with 339, 83 more than Terrence Morris, as well as its third-best rebounder with 948 behind Len Elmore and Lonny Baxter. He was famous for using his elbows in order to wedge his way inside, once getting rebuked in the middle of a game by legendary North Carolina coach Dean Smith, and did a lot of the dirty work for more-talented offensive players before becoming the team's top scorer as a senior.

Eric Hayes: Though he came in with more fanfare than Greivis Vasquez and seemed happy to play second fiddle to the volatile Venezuelan because of his own quiet personality, the 6'4" guard had a fairly productive career in College Park, finishing as the school's all-time leading free throw shooter (87 percent) and sixth all time in assists (513) while scoring more than 1,200 points.

Jim O'Brien: After being only one of four players who answered Lefty Driesell's famous "We Want You" ad in the *Washington Post* in 1969, the red-haired shooter affectionately known as "Bozo" hit the game-winner to upset South Carolina as a sophomore, when he led the Terps in scoring, and was a solid second option behind Tom McMillen his last two seasons.

Tom Roy and Owen Brown: It's hard distinguishing between these two frontcourt players who were known mostly for their defense and rebounding on some of Driesell's best teams in the mid-1970s. Roy averaged 11 points and 11 rebounds as a senior in 1975, and Brown averaged close to 15 points as the second option that year behind John Lucas. Brown tragically died during a pickup game at age 22 a few months after graduating.

76 The Short Honeymoon with "The Jewish Jordan"

As Maryland fans were celebrating a string of victories during the 1998–99 season, a high school phenom was lighting it up in the strangest of places: a Jewish private school in Baltimore.

Tamir Goodman, a skinny 6'3" guard with red hair and ridiculous range, had started getting some attention when reporters showed up to do stories on a future star who wouldn't be able to play on Saturdays once he reached college.

Goodman got on Maryland's radar when a former ref turned basketball businessman named Paul Baker sent a tape to Billy Hahn, then Gary Williams' top assistant in College Park.

After watching the tape, and aware that at least one other ACC school (Clemson) was interested in Goodman, Williams offered him a scholarship without ever watching him in person.

Shortly after Goodman accepted the offer, his team at the Talmudical Institute happened to be playing a game at Cole Field House against Bishop McNamara, a local Catholic school not among the local powers.

Goodman went four for 34 from the field.

Williams went berserk.

Pulling Hahn into his office that afternoon, Williams said, "What were you thinking?"

Despite all the attention Goodman was attracting—including a cover story in *Sports Illustrated*—Williams knew he wasn't an ACC player, though at the time many thought Goodman was better than redshirt freshman guard Juan Dixon.

As the months went on, and Goodman's stock had plummeted during an injury-plagued summer, Maryland tried to convince him that he should turn down the scholarship offer and look elsewhere.

Williams and Hahn told him that not being able to play or practice from sundown Friday to sundown Saturday would be a problem.

"It was very discouraging," Goodman after meeting with the Maryland coaches in early September of 1999. "It would have been better off if they would have said [in January] 'we would love to have you as a player, but I'm not sure the Sabbath can be worked out.' I would have said 'thank you' and moved on. You don't promise a kid a birthday present and then not give it to him."

As things turned out, Williams' assessment of Goodman's game was correct. He wound up going to Towson, where he played less than two years before getting into a physical altercation with former Tigers coach Michael Hunt and leaving the school to play professionally in Israel.

At one point slated to play for the country's most prominent team, Maccabi Tel Aviv, Goodman never regained the shooting touch that brought him such attention in Baltimore. One local writer said of Goodman that "he threw up enough bricks to put up a building."

Three years after Goodman's honeymoon with the Terps ended, Dixon led Maryland to the national championship.

Goodman said he didn't watch.

77 Terp Heroes

Separated by more than 40 years, Lefty Driesell and Alex Len shared something other than their association with Maryland basketball.

Both the former longtime coach and two-year center saved lives in heroic rescues under far different circumstances.

Driesell was fishing with two friends off the Delaware coast in the summer of 1973 when he noticed some townhouses that were on fire. After bringing the boat in, Driesell knocked on doors and even broke one down, watching the lone occupant, a woman, run out screaming that an intruder had come in.

Len was lounging with friends in the Dominican Republic after finishing his season with the Phoenix Suns in the spring of 2016 when one of them was caught in a riptide and went under the water. Len rushed in from the beach and helped bring his friend to safety.

Neither thought of himself as a hero.

While a judge who witnessed Driesell's actions in Bethany Beach claimed the then-42-year-old coach was a hero in saving the lives of at least 10 children, Driesell said he wasn't, saying, "We were just trying to get the kids out. I was lucky we were fishing right in front of the houses."

The NCAA disagreed with the Maryland coach, awarding him its Medal of Valor.

The NBA might do something similar in the near future for Len.

The 7'1" center from Ukraine was relaxing on a beach at the Hard Rock Hotel and Casino near Punta Cana and spent most of his vacation indoors because of windy, rainy weather.

On the afternoon before they were to leave in April of 2016, Len and his three friends were near the water and had been warned to stay out of it by the locals who knew how dangerous the tides could be.

After coming in from a short swim in which one of his boyhood friends had briefly gone under, Len told another friend, Jay Johnson, to "be careful" when he went in.

Despite the advice, Johnson figured that a good hearty swim would tire him out for the flight back to the U.S. After jumping to avoid one wave, the next wave pulled him in and pushed him some

40 yards from the shore. Though he considered himself a good swimmer, Johnson thought he was "going to die."

After first thinking Johnson's call for help was a joke, the Suns center realized the seriousness of the situation and, seeing his friend's obvious distress, went back in the water. Johnson's body was shutting down in the freezing water.

"By the time I got to him, he was halfway passed out," Len said. "He couldn't swim. He wasn't moving. If I would've come a couple minutes later, he probably would've drowned."

With the help of a lifeguard who was brought in after Len raced into the water, a floatation device reached Johnson. Len admitted that he started to panic as the water became too much for him as well.

Had Len been 6'1" and not 7'1", Johnson might have died. It was only after Len was able to stand with his own head above the water that the group was successful in pulling Johnson back to the shore.

Johnson, who runs a charitable foundation called Gametyme, said that his flirtation with death will make him focus on helping disadvantaged children. Johnson made the story about Len's heroism public.

Like Lefty Driesell did all those years before, the 25-year-old basketball player said he was not a hero.

"I didn't feel like it at the moment," Len said. "I was just trying to help Jay."

78 Lonny Goes Back to Back

While most fans remember Juan Dixon winning the Most Outstanding Player when Maryland won the national championship in 2002, the player who helped deliver the Terps to back-to-back Final Fours was Dixon's big sidekick, Lonny Baxter.

As emotional and intense as Dixon could be, Baxter was equally stone-faced and seemingly laid-back. But that was just a facade for a player who was among the steadiest and statistically efficient as any who has ever worn a Terp uniform.

"When I was at Maryland, I just played with a ton of pride," Baxter recalled in the spring of 2016, a little over a year removed from a pro career spent mostly in Europe. "That's just what motivated me every night. Just wanting to do it for my state of Maryland."

After Baxter, then a freshman, was part of a center-by-committee to replace Obinna Ekezie after the senior was injured late in 1998–99 season, Baxter showed that he was a big-game player when he put up 16 points in a second-round NCAA tournament game against Creighton.

"I didn't know what to think when Obinna went down," Baxter said. "I couldn't believe it happened. Coach told me I didn't have to try to do everything. He told me I didn't have to be a hero. He said 'because Obinna is not going to be able to play the rest of the season, don't go out and try to do this and that. Just play your game.'"

Baxter wasn't highly recruited coming out Springbrook High School because he weighed more than 270 pounds. He spent a year at Hargrave Military Academy in Virginia, which Baxter said gave him the needed discipline.

"Being in military school just me a lot of structure," he said. "If you could stay there for a whole year, you could do just about anything. Getting up in the morning, marching to the mess hall, it was just different than what I was used to. It was the first time I ever went away from home. It helped me mature a lot. A lot of guys would do things to get kicked out. I did what I had to do to get to the next level."

Baxter started to show as a sophomore what that game was. It was mostly confined to a 10-foot square, where as teammate Terrell Stokes said, "When he catches the ball, he can take two or three people with him to the basket."

The flashes Baxter showed came toward the end of a mostly frustrating foul-plagued year that saw him average 6.8 points. That became the building block on which one of the best careers by a Maryland big man was carved.

Not only did Baxter put up remarkably consistent numbers his last three years—averaging better than 15 points and eight rebounds—he seemed to be at his best in the biggest of games. As a junior he was named the MOP in the West Regional by scoring 50 total points against Georgetown and Stanford.

A year after helping the Terps reach their first Final Four in school history—only to have the infamous "phantom" foul called against him in the second-half referee-induced collapse against Duke in the semifinals—Baxter did it again as a senior, scoring 29 points in an epic East Regional final win over Connecticut to earn a second straight MOP.

"It means a lot," Baxter said of his two straight MOPs, the only player in NCAA history to do so. "I never worried about my individual achievements, but doing that was big because it showed that I could play with anybody in the NCAA during my time. I was just making history. That's what you come to school for. That's what you want to do."

Baxter wound up two rebounds shy of becoming the first player in Maryland history to score 1,500 points (1,858, good for seventh all time) and 1,000 rebounds (second only to Len Elmore). His last game, coming in Maryland's 64–52 championship win over Indiana in Atlanta, was typical of Baxter: 15 points, 14 rebounds, and three blocked shots.

"He's so physical," Indiana coach Mike Davis said of Baxter that night. "He was just kind of bulling our guys out of the way. He would step in real hard. He got the ball point-blank. Once you get it point-blank, there's nothing you can do."

Baxter admitted that he was thinking about what happened the year before against Duke, perhaps affecting him in the team's 2002 semifinal win over Kansas when he got into foul trouble and played just 14 minutes.

"People asked me whether the Duke game was out of my mind," Baxter said after the Indiana game. "I was like, 'No, it won't be until I win a national championship.' Now it is, because we won tonight."

Though Gary Williams could sense Baxter's frustration, "the thing about Lonny is that he never changes what he tries to do."

Baxter would never come close to duplicating in college what he did in the pros, where he was drafted in the second round by the Chicago Bulls but didn't last long before finishing out most of his pro career in Europe, including one stop in Siberia.

"I don't regret college or anything," Baxter said. "It was the best four years of my life, and we just finished it off the way it should be done."

79 The Night Gary and Coach K Went Missing

The setting seemed a bit bizarre that night at Duke. The crazies were there, in full voice, though two of the rivalry's largest figures—yes, it was a rivalry—were absent.

It was March 1, 1995, and the Terps had gone to play at Cameron Indoor Stadium without fifth-year coach Gary Williams, who was in a Maryland hospital with a serious bout of pneumonia.

"I was sedated, they were trying to figure out what was wrong with me," recalled Williams. "I was being tested for Legionnaire's Disease, viral and bacterial pneumonia. For about six days, they couldn't come up with anything. I didn't know what was going on. That was as sick as I've ever been."

Williams spent his 50th birthday in the hospital.

Mike Krzyzewski hadn't been seen for months, recovering at home from early-season back surgery. In their place were two long-time lieutenants, Billy Hahn for the Terps and Pete Gaudet for the Blue Devils.

"As an assistant, you always want to put yourself in a situation where you have a chance to become a head coach if that's what you choose," Hahn said that night.

When you have a star like Joe Smith, who was then a sophomore and on his way to becoming National Player of the Year, it makes life a lot easier. Smith scored a career-high 40, including a tip-in to win 94–92 at the buzzer.

The victory helped the Terps, ranked sixth, clinch a share of their first regular season title in 15 years. Hahn celebrated with a still-talked-about dance with sports information director Chuck Walsh on the court.

In scoring the most points by a Maryland player since Len Bias scored 41 on the same court—including 13 of his team's last 16—Smith locked up ACC Player of the Year.

"I just felt it was my night," said Smith, who had been held to a career-low six points by the Blue Devils the previous month in College Park. "I could see that their big guys were getting a little tired, so I told the fellas to get me the ball. We knew we had to keep our focus without Coach Williams here, but Coach Hahn and the other assistants did a great job."

Said Cherokee Parks, who finished with 20 points, eight rebounds, and seven blocks: "They did a great job of crashing the boards, and it was hard keeping anyone on Joe. He seemed to be in too many places at the same time."

Smith's tip-in came on a missed drive by Duane Simpkins, who as a freshman had scored on a similar play to beat Georgetown in a game that was sort of the coming-out party by the team's then relatively unknown center.

The Maryland players were so happy that they serenaded Smith in the cramped, sweaty, and happy locker room with an "I want to be like Joe" chant. Junior forward Exree Hipp said that he recalled seeing that Smith had just 17 points at halftime, then looked up at the scoreboard to see the total was 36.

"I said, 'He's scoring all our points,'" said Hipp. "Superman was in the building tonight. What a better way to end the game but on a Joe Smith basket at the buzzer."

Back in Maryland, Williams barely lifted his head off the hospital pillow to see that his team won. While he would return—a bit shakily—for the NCAA tournament and the Terps went to the Sweet 16 for the second straight year—Maryland never got its mojo back.

"I had to sign a waiver to get there. The first-round games were in Utah," Wiliams said. "Our trainer, J.J. Bush, had oxygen behind our bench in case I needed it because of the pneumonia."

It took Hahn another six years—and a trip to the Final Four—to get another chance at being a head coach. Gaudet wasn't so lucky. Krzyzewski knocked the 4–15 record his longtime assistant at Duke and Army compiled in his absence off his own record-breaking mark and fired him months later.

Williams shrugged off his illness.

"That's a great diet," he said. "I lost 20 pounds."

80 Kurtis Shultz's Georgetown Cameo

Kurtis Shultz wasn't expecting to play much, if at all, when Maryland opened its 1993–94 season against Georgetown at USAir Arena.

A 6'6", 235-pound power forward who was built more like a tight end, Shultz had been offered a scholarship only because other more prominent players were not admitted academically.

Toward the end of his freshman year, Shultz found himself in a close game at crunch time and made six straight free throws to help beat Clemson.

"I remember reading in one of the magazines this summer that those free throws were not only the highlight of my freshman year, but that they'd probably be the highlight of my career at Maryland," Shultz recalled before his sophomore year.

As Gary Williams started adding players who would lead the program's revival, Shultz was considered nothing more than a big body to toughen up the young rising stars like freshmen Joe Smith and Keith Booth in practice.

Settled into his seat on the bench for the season-opener against the Hoyas, Shultz heard his name called once, late in the first half, and as he ran to the scorer's table, he fell on his face.

"I tripped on Coach's foot," Shultz recalled after the game. "Coach Williams started yelling at me to get in the game. It was pretty funny. Little Matt Raydo started joking, 'You know that was on ESPN.'"

Shultz made a much cleaner entrance late in the game. Inserted to give a foul and put the historically poor-shooting Hoyas in a one-and-one, Shultz wound up stealing the inbound pass and setting up Smith for the basket that put the game in overtime.

Maryland won a victory Williams has long called one of the most important in his 22-year tenure in College Park.

As for Shultz, the free throws he hit as a freshman and the steal he made as a junior turned out to be the highlights of his playing career. He hurt his back as a senior and played just 12 games.

Shultz wound up making a much bigger impact on the program when he returned as the team's strength and conditioning coach and played a big part in Maryland's two straight trips to the Final Four in 2001 and 2002.

"We needed to get stronger and quicker," Gary Williams said. "Our players like the way Kurtis keeps things interesting and makes it where guys want to do the work. They believe this is the best thing for them. They believe in Kurtis."

Shultz played a big role in Lonny Baxter going from an overweight freshman to a two-time NCAA Regionals MVP, as well in helping fellow Baltimorean Juan Dixon put on the weight and the muscle to become a big-time scorer.

"Kurtis gets us ready. There's never a light day with him. He stays on us. He's what we need," Baxter said during Maryland's championship season in 2002.

"Kurtis has definitely been good for this team," said Dixon. "I'm a lot stronger. I'm taking a lot more bumps. I think I'm finishing well and I'm able to go off the dribble more because of my strength. Kurtis does his job."

81 Jake Layman, Survivor

Lone survivors often have regrets for being left behind, guilt for being the only one left standing.

For Jake Layman, the only member of a much-ballyhooed group of recruits in 2012 and the first Maryland player to finish under Mark Turgeon after starting out as a freshman, being the last man standing in this case turned out to be a pretty good thing.

Though criticized at times for his inconsistency, Layman's resiliency could never be called into question.

By the time he ended his career in the spring of 2016, Layman had tied Juan Dixon for the most games played (141), was fourth in three-pointers made (198) and attempted (547), and was both 18th in scoring (1,436) and rebounding (674).

Layman often said that he never thought about leaving in the tumultuous spring following his sophomore year, when all three of the players with whom he arrived—center Shaquille Cleare, forward Charles Mitchell, and guard Seth Allen—left along with Nick Faust and Roddy Peters.

His loyalty to Maryland coach Mark Turgeon was rewarded when the Terps went to the NCAA tournament his last two seasons, and Layman played some of his best basketball toward the end of his senior year, reviving interest from NBA scouts that had seemingly waned a bit.

"He's had a great year, he's had a tremendous year," Turgeon said toward the end of that season. "When kids say they're going to enjoy their senior year like Jake has, they usually have great years. He sees the light at the end of the tunnel and he's excited about finishing the year the right way."

The self-confidence Layman seemed to lack for much of his career, often leading to him deferring to alpha-male personalities such as Dez Wells, appeared to grow in the NCAA tournament, when Layman scored a career-high 27 points in a first-round win over South Dakota State.

When then South Dakota State coach Scott Nagy admitted after the game that the game plan to stop Maryland point guard Melo Trimble from penetrating appeared to backfire when Layman buried a slew of corner three-pointers, even Layman seemed surprised that he wasn't a focal point.

"That's crazy, when you consider that I'm one of the best players on this team," Layman said, uttering words that even his father, Tim, recalled never hearing his son say.

While his scoring dipped slightly as a senior on a team that had plenty of offensively minded players—perhaps one or two too many—his defense improved significantly and he finished with career highs in field goal percentage (50), three-point percentage (39.6), and free throw percentage (83.2).

"As a player, you can't worry about the numbers," Layman said. "As long as you're playing at a high level, while being confident, then I think the sky's the limit for anybody, and that's where I'm at right now. I'm playing very confidently."

When his career finally ended after a Sweet 16 loss to Kansas—Maryland's first trip to the Sweet 16 since 2003—Layman seemed disappointed yet fulfilled. While he understood how some would label the season a failure, he would not.

"Just to be remembered as a group that never stopped fighting," said Layman, "these 14 guys have worked hard. It's not about the season, it's about what happened before the season, workouts and lifting and spring and all those things. I'm so proud of these guys."

While a few of the players who had left two years earlier had improved their stats, none had even played in the NCAA tournament.

"I definitely made the right decision," said Layman.

As bad as Turgeon felt for his players, he probably felt the worst for Layman, who came in as a quiet freshman whose blonde hair got more attention than his basketball skills, and left as a team leader headed for the NBA. (He was drafted in the second round by the Orlando Magic, 47th overall, and then traded to the Portland Trail Blazers.)

"Jake's hard for me, it's hard for me to look at him and not start crying," Turgeon said. "A couple of years ago, everyone jumped ship, and he didn't.... Since then we've been 55–16 and been to the Sweet 16."

Standing outside the team's locker room, Turgeon recalled what he told Layman after the game, the season, and the 6'9" forward's career ended.

"I told Jake we've got it going in the right direction," Turgeon said. "We'll keep this thing rolling, and it's going to get better. We're getting better, and he should feel he's a big part of it."

82 Dez Wells Rewrites His Ending

When he arrived at Maryland in September of 2012, many Terps fans didn't know what to make of Dez Wells.

His one season at Xavier might have silenced some doubts about whether he was a Division I talent, but it raised more questions about his character.

There was his suspension for his role in a well-publicized brawl with crosstown rival Cincinnati and, of more concern, the fact that he had been kicked out of the school after a female student filed charges against him for sexual assault.

Though the charges were quickly dropped by prosecutors who felt Wells had been made a victim by his accuser and a scapegoat by a school that would later have to settle out of court with Wells for wrongfully expelling him and defaming his character, some Maryland fans were skeptical.

Even Wells didn't know what was going to happen.

Kentucky had been his first choice, but after John Calipari tried going to bat for a player who was a former high school teammate of former Wildcat star John Wall, the university president didn't like the publicity he thought might follow Wells to Lexington.

"I had no intentions of actually coming to Maryland," recalled Wells. "I just wanted to take a load off and be somewhere where it was not just about cramming in a weekend visit in 18 hours. I wanted somewhere I could let my guard down and just talk to people and see what a school actually had to offer."

He smiled.

"It worked out," Wells said. "It worked out pretty good, I'll say."

Three seasons later, Wells left as one of the most respected players in recent history.

Though Wells is never mentioned in the same way Walt Williams helped keep the program viable by staying in College Park after Gary Williams inherited a ridiculously tough NCAA probation, the 6'5" guard played an important role in the growth of the Terps under Mark Turgeon.

"I think he will be the exclamation point at the beginning of the Turgeon era," ESPN analyst Len Elmore said late in Wells' senior year. "With the departure of certain guys and other guys coming in, he's the anchor. He held the program down until they could get these other guys."

The team's leading scorer his first two years and a Big Ten first-team selection as a senior—despite missing a month of the season with a broken wrist—Wells will long be remembered at Maryland for his bravado, his toughness, and the way he willed the Terps into their first NCAA tournament in five seasons.

"One thing I've learned from this whole process is that you just have to have patience," Wells said toward the end of his senior year. "You can't rush anything that you want to last for a long time. It tested me, it tested my patience and my faith, but I feel like I've grown up so much."

The program grew up with him, jump-started by a somewhat surprising 27–9 season in Wells' senior year. While much of the credit deservedly went to freshman point guard Melo Trimble, Wells was the one Trimble and others looked for when the games got tight.

One game in particular stood out. Matched up against Big Ten favorite Wisconsin late in the season, Wells outplayed every Badger—including National Player of the Year Frank Kaminsky—to lead the Terps to a 59–53 win over the No. 4 team in the country.

Former Maryland coach Gary Williams said that Wells reminded him of some of those who had played for him.

"He just had that look that reminded me of [Juan] Dixon and [Steve] Blake and those guys," Williams said after Wells finished with 26 points, six rebounds, four assists, and no turnovers. "They would get that look. It didn't matter what happened out there; they were going to find a way to win the game."

83 Gary and the Refs

For a coach with a reputation as being maniacal and having a trash mouth on the sidelines, Gary Williams seemed to know just how far he could push a referee without getting T'd up. Some might find it surprising that Williams, in 22 years at Maryland, only got tossed twice.

"I only got one technical foul the last three years I coached," Williams said. "You make adjustments, you get to know officials, they get to know you. You gradually do it. Just like good players adjust to officials, if they call the game tight. Certain referees you couldn't say anything."

Interestingly, the two ejections came nearly a year apart—and for completely different reasons.

The first, in a road defeat at Florida State in January of 1997, Williams was thrown out by Dick "Froggy" Paparo, whose penchant for finding the spotlight himself by making controversial calls was well-documented.

After receiving a technical foul in the first half, Williams was ejected in the final minute of a 74–70 loss to the Seminoles. It turned out that Paparo, who coaches often accused of having rabbit ears, thought the Maryland coach was cursing him out.

Turns out he was yelling at one of his own players for not calling a timeout forcefully enough after the Terps had cut a 13-point deficit to three points. Fortunately for Maryland, Florida State freshman Ron Hale missed both free throws.

It marked the first time Williams was thrown out of a game as a college coach.

"I did not make the statement I was credited with there," said Williams. "I said something to Laron Profit, and the official thought I was talking to him. There was just some confusion there."

Paparo informed the ACC the next morning that he mistakenly thought Williams was yelling at him.

The following year, in a game at Duke, the Terps were called for four technicals in a span of 95 seconds as the Blue Devils, ranked first in the country, were putting together a 28–4 run. Wiliams was ejected with a little less than six minutes gone in what eventually became an 86–59 defeat.

Veteran ACC referee Larry Rose said that he gave Williams a couple of warnings for "cursing three times and he continued."

Williams had picked up his first technical after Sarunas Jasikevicius had been called for a T after complaining about a moving screen. Williams picked up another, was tossed, and Profit got the fourth.

"I found out later on that Fred Barakat had sent out a memo about moving screens," Williams said. "Nobody moved more on screens back then than Duke. They called good screens, but they were big and they would slide a little bit. They set Sarunas on a second foul for calling a little screen. I just had had it. Plus we never got any respect there. After that game, we seemed to get more down there as time went on."

Given Williams' famous temper, and the fact that Maryland always felt it was going into enemy territory whenever it played in the state of North Carolina, it's pretty remarkable that he was thrown out of only two games in more than two decades. (Contrast that to Mark Turgeon, who was thrown out of a game his first season.)

Williams always had interesting reactions to how others—media, fans, refs—reacted to him.

One of the best stories came after a Wake Forest booster complained to the school's athletic director, Ron Wellman, about Williams for using inappropriate language during an ACC tournament game. Wellman in turn sent a complaint to Maryland AD Debbie Yow, whose feud with her basketball coach was well-documented.

To keep the ACC off her back, Yow told her coach that he had to go for anger management counseling. He agreed and informed her that he was going to talk with noted sports psychologist Bob Rotella, who actually worked for the University of Virginia when he wasn't out on the PGA tour advising some of the world's great players.

What did Rotella tell him?

"He gave me some great putting tips," Williams cracked.

84 Was Dixon the Greatest Terp Ever?

Being at the top of a school's scoring list doesn't ensure being the greatest player in history.

One has to consider the era played in, whether he was eligible for three or four years or might have only stayed one or two.

Maryland fans have been debating for years over the merits of Juan Dixon, Len Bias, Albert King, and John Lucas.

Somebody might one day surpass Dixon's 2,269 points at the top of the scoring list, as Dixon overtook Bias (2,149), who had breezed by King (2,058), who had done the same to Lucas (2,015).

Dixon certainly has one distinction over any of the former Terps in the conversation: he led Maryland to its only national championship in 2002 after helping Maryland reach its first Final Four the previous year. By the time he was finished, Dixon was a part of four Maryland teams that won a school-record 110 games.

"If he doesn't score, Maryland doesn't win," said King shortly after Dixon broke the record.

Bias is the only Maryland player to be named ACC Player of the Year twice but never did get the Terps past the Sweet 16 in the NCAA tournament. As a sophomore, Bias led Maryland to its only ACC tournament title under Lefty Driesell and only the second of three in history. No one else on this list can make that claim.

King might have been the most gifted player in Maryland history and, perhaps, the most selfless in this group. Dixon, Bias, and Lucas all played with the kind of edge that drove them to greatness, while King might have deferred to others he played with more than he should have.

For Lucas' first two seasons he was part of perhaps the greatest collection of talent during Driesell's 17-year tenure. Though he would often take over practices and score at will—something Driesell would reprimand him about—Lucas was a great teammate for leading scorer Tom McMillen.

During his three years—the last of which he moved to shooting guard with the addition of freshman point guard Brad Davis—Lucas

Juan Dixon, as he was often seen with Maryland, celebrating another success.
(Ed Reinke)

averaged nearly five assists a game. None of the others are close—with both Dixon (2.6) and King (2.5) on the list of the top 20.

"Len Elmore is the best center Maryland has ever had, Tom McMillen is the best power forward Maryland has ever had, and Lucas was the greatest player I played with," said Mo Howard, who played in the same backcourt with Lucas. "Since John, Juan Dixon is the greatest player I've seen at Maryland."

What might set Dixon apart from the rest of these Maryland greats is his defense. While not a shutdown defender, Dixon had a knack for stepping into passing lanes for steals and easy layups or dunks for him or others. Dixon's 333 steals is second behind Johnny Rhodes on Maryland's all-time list.

"All you hear fans talk about is his offensive ability, but people in the know talk about his defense," King said.

What is difficult to gauge is a player's toughness. But on a team filled with overachievers who seemed to be a reflection of their blue-collar coach, Dixon was the one who most closely resembled his coach, Gary Williams.

"Juan is one of the toughest, if not the toughest, players I've ever seen," said Greg Manning, who played with King, Ernie Graham, and Buck Williams. "I haven't seen anyone compete like Juan Dixon does."

Even before Dixon led the Terps to their title in 2002, King had placed him at the top.

"No matter what happens this weekend," King said before the 2002 Final Four in Atlanta, "you put him atop anyone else because of what he's accomplished. He took Maryland to a place no one else could."

85 A Hot Ticket

In the old days, Maryland basketball was the hottest ticket in the Washington-Baltimore area—particularly after the Redskins went into nearly a decade-long playoff funk.

After a few lean years that saw Comcast Center sell out only for really big games—Duke and North Carolina to be specific—the interest returned when the Terps joined the Big Ten in 2014–15.

Considering the school's somewhat restrictive ticket policy, Mark Turgeon's team needs to keep its streak going of two straight NCAA tournament appearances.

With 4,000 tickets available for students through a lottery, more than a few undergrads have turned into high-priced scalpers for the tickets they pay a little more than $400 a year for in an activities fee.

As of 2013–14, Maryland was only one of three Big Ten schools to charge its students, and its fee was around three times what the other two schools charged. The flip side is that some schools, such as Michigan, offer a limited number of tickets for students to each game.

While most of the Big Ten games as well the first regular-season meeting against Georgetown in more than 20 years sold out in 2015–16 in College Park, the prospect of a rebuilding team for the Terps in 2016–17 could mean a return to more sporadic crowds and less of a demand on student tickets.

Given the school's system of issuing "loyalty points" for those attending games, will it put a premium on attending games against Northwestern and Penn State just to enhance the chances of seeing Michigan State and Indiana?

The only problem is that, according to students, very few follow the rules. Those who win tickets quickly turn them around, often using Facebook and other means of social media to get their message out. Given the public nature of that type of brokering, finding the culprits should not be difficult.

Reselling student tickets is against university policy.

According to a story in the *Testudo Times*, "it's a tough violation to catch, especially now that students can legally transfer tickets to one another. If two kids in the bathroom at R.J. Bentley's come to a cash sale and then transfer the ticket to the buyer's name, there's virtually nothing to be done about it."

86 Reaching the Promised Land

Right after the music ended, right after Juan Dixon heaved the game ball to the heavens—or at least toward the roof of the Georgia Dome—and right after Chris Wilcox famously mussed the salt-and-pepper hair of Maryland coach Gary Williams, Terps everywhere cried.

And then they exhaled.

It had been a long road back from the abyss.

A 16-year journey that had started in tragedy and shame on a June morning in 1986 in College Park had ended in triumph and celebration on an April night in 2002 in Atlanta. No college basketball programs had sunk as low and come back as far as Maryland in that period of time.

None really were even close.

After watching arguably the most athletically gifted player in the program's history turn up dead after a cocaine overdose in his dorm suite two days after being the second pick in the NBA draft, after seeing its longtime coach forced to resign and his ill-equipped successor fail, after getting banned from the postseason competition and even from appearing on TV, Maryland became national champions.

It took the feistiness of Dixon, who overcame his own personal tragedies to replace Len Bias as both the school's all-time scorer and the face of what Maryland basketball was thought to be. It took the fortitude of Williams, whose return to his alma mater in 1989 nearly ruined his ascending career.

And it took the faith of Terps everywhere to stick by their team—something many had stopped doing even before Bias died and Lefty Driesell was replaced by Bob Wade and eventually by Williams. By the time Maryland reached Minneapolis the previous year for the 2001 Final Four—the first in school history—the bandwagon was bulging.

But on the night the Terps had taken down Indiana 64–52 and then cut down the nets, with Williams twirling the last piece in his hand and waving it toward the crowd, he sat on the dais in the media center and, without uttering a word, basically said, "I told you so." You could see it in his eyes, and feel it in his heart.

And then the words came pouring out.

"Having played at Maryland, coming back at a time I hate to even think about, because there was so much mistrust, so much doubt about the place of the basketball program at the university," Williams recalled the next morning, "we had to work all those things out before we could even think about having a good basketball team.

"The guys who played, Walt Williams, people like that, during that time we had a lot of people keeping the crowd at Cole Field House, even though we couldn't participate in the NCAA tournament or be on television. I'll always remember those guys…I'm not sure we could have recovered if it weren't for the people involved back then."

Dixon, who saw both his heroin-addicted parents die from AIDS, personified the toughness and resilience that Williams showed as a coach, quieting those who doubted that the skinny kid from Calvert Hall would be nothing more than a bench-warmer at Cole Field House by becoming the Most Outstanding Player at the 2002 Final Four.

But he credited Williams for taking him and the others on a ride they would never experience again.

"The program came a long ways," said Dixon. "They were in a lot of trouble. Coach came in and did a great job. We're one of the best programs in the country right now."

More than a decade later, Williams is most proud of the gauntlet the Terps traveled that year—beating Kentucky, Connecticut, Kansas, and Indiana.

"Very few teams had to play those storied programs right in a row like that to win the championship and we did," Williams said in the spring of 2016. "We had a team that was really talented. I thought about this right after the game, when we were still on the court. Nobody on that team, even Juan, thought they were above anyone else. It was a complete trust. They did what they had to do to play the best basketball. You can't say that about a lot of guys."

Said Lonny Baxter, then the team's senior center and quiet leader, "We were just a bunch of guys who were very competitive. We just wanted to win and we just wanted to make our mark in the NCAA world. That's what we talked about every night, winning it all. When we stepped out onto the court, we played with a tremendous amount of pride every single night. The whole state of Maryland was watching us."

Assistant coach Dave Dickerson was the only team member—including Williams—to have been there to witness the bottom firsthand. He was a freshman the year Bias was a senior, went to the hospital with other teammates after hearing the horrible news of his death, and then was part of the rough transformation from Driesell to Wade.

Only after returning to his alma mater to work for Williams did he take his class ring out of the box and put it back on.

But he too credited Williams.

"I think Gary should be given a Purple Heart," Dickerson said. "The job he has done is mind-boggling."

Baxter said he was aware of the program's struggles, having grown up following the Terps in the aftermath of Len Bias' death.

"Gary Williams was one of the reasons why I wanted to come to Maryland, to play for that type of coach," Baxter said. "Gary really resurrected the program at the time after Len Bias had died."

And then there was Kristin Scott, Williams' only child and the mother of his three grandchildren. As a teenager, she and her father had been somewhat estranged after her parents divorced and he moved from Columbus, Ohio, where he had coached Ohio State, to College Park. But as she got older and he got a little softer, they reconciled to have a warm, deep, and lasting relationship.

"This all started at Woodrow Wilson High School in 1970," said Scott, referring to the undefeated team her father had coached to a New Jersey state championship shortly before she was born. "This isn't just about this year's team. It's about all the Maryland alumni who've waited so long and all the players who have played for him."

Tears welled up in her eyes and she smiled

"If I were him," she said, "I would quit right now."

87 Women in the Locker Room

At a time when female sportswriters were still fighting to get into the locker rooms of many professional teams, Maryland had two women beat writers, Betty Cuniberti of the *Washington Post* and Sandy McKee of the *Baltimore Evening Sun*.

When McKee got the assignment, in the summer of 1979, her first task was to introduce herself to Lefty Driesell.

"When I took that beat, the person who had the beat couldn't get an interview with Lefty," McKee recalled. "There was a conflict. He wouldn't give him an interview. I called up and got an appointment, but it was hard because he was so busy."

A somewhat reticent West Virginian, McKee admitted that she was more than a little intimidated by the prospect of covering the larger-than-life coach. On her way to College Park for a meeting, McKee came up with a potential ice-breaker.

"The morning I went down there, I drove past a florist shop and bought a bouquet of red and white flowers for him. When I got there, his secretary looked at me like I was nuts. He was having his lunch."

Just as Driesell was about to take a bite, McKee interrupted.

"I said, 'Before we start, I brought you something' and I gave him these flowers, and he was so stunned he took them and he took 15 minutes to find a vase and then he offered me half his sandwich," McKee said.

While admitting now that "it might have been a little over the top" giving flowers to Driesell, what was supposed to be a 20-minute interview turned into 90 minutes, and a strong working relationship was born.

Driesell used to make sure that McKee always got what she needed, particularly after games.

"The setup in the locker room was that he spoke at the same time the locker room was open, which was before they got out of their uniforms," McKee said. "I couldn't be in two places at one time, and I would also catch him [Driesell] as he was coming out and he always gave me two questions after everything was done. I'm convinced it was because I was nice to him after I did that interview."

McKee admits that giving a coach flowers was a little unusual and knows that some of her male colleagues who found out about it thought that it gave her an unfair advantage. To which McKee said, "Guys can sit down with him after a game and have a drink with him on a road trip, and I couldn't do that."

There were places on the road that weren't set up to accommodate female reporters.

"When you covered Georgia Tech, the visiting team's locker room was on the other side of the showers and they'd be showering, and you'd be walking through," McKee said. "It was an unbelievable time. You had to close your eyes and keep moving."

McKee covered the Terps for three seasons, giving way to another female reporter, Molly Dunham, who later became the executive sports editor of the *Baltimore Sun* after the two papers merged.

Cuniberti gave way to John Feinstein, who turned it over to Sally Jenkins. During the 1985–86 season, the Terps had three women reporters—Dunham, Jenkins, and Melody Simmons of the *Baltimore News American*.

McKee later covered the Washington Redskins (where she said she became the first female beat writer even before Christine Brennan did it for the *Post*) before going on to cover tennis, Navy football, horse racing, and auto racing before retiring in 2014.

Covering Maryland was a lot easier than covering the Redskins, some of whom refused to talk with a woman in the locker room.

"Dave Butz would escort me outside, do the interview, and then we would both go back in, and I would finish doing my interviews," McKee said with a laugh. "The Terps, I thought it was okay. The players were very nice, polite kids. They didn't feel like I was inconveniencing them."

McKee said that she is often not interviewed for stories looking into the rise of female sportswriters because she has few of the horror stories that other women encountered for several more years.

"I always thought I was treated well," she said. "I never considered being a woman a negative. So I didn't go looking for trouble. My friends tell me that if I had been more aware, I might have noticed discriminatory things."

88 Meloland

In the modern history of Maryland basketball, few players had the immediate impact that Melo Trimble did as a freshman during the early stages of the 2014–15 season.

The first McDonald's All-American to commit to play in College Park since Mike Jones in 2003, Trimble was anointed the team's starting point guard before he even stepped on campus.

It wasn't just the fact that Mark Turgeon had confidence in a player who had dominated in high school at Bishop O'Connell. With the departure of Seth Allen and Roddy Peters during a tumultuous spring exodus after the 2013–14 season, Turgeon had no other options.

"He knew he was going to play in the past, but he knows he's really the only true point guard on the roster," Turgeon said at the time. "I don't think it will change his approach to how hard he works or how disciplined he'll be…. He's mature enough; he's ready for it."

Trimble's first three games seemed to say otherwise. He did not shoot the ball particularly well (7 of 23, including 5 of 15 on three-pointers) and seemed a little tentative with his ball-handling (seven turnovers, six assists).

But the fourth game—against Arizona State in the opening round of the CBE Hall of Fame Classic in Kansas City—was a foreshadowing of his freshman year.

Trimble finished with 31 points, taking just 11 shots from the field, 14 from the free throw line. It was the start of one of the best debut seasons by a Terp.

Not only did Trimble quickly establish himself as the team's floor leader, and help Maryland overcome losing star Dez Wells for a month with a broken wrist, he became one of the top players in the Big Ten.

In a mid-January home game against Michigan State, Trimble scored 21 of his 24 points before halftime, including an ankle-breaking move on Tum Tum Nairn to set up a crossover three-pointer to close the first half.

"It felt like high school," Trimble said after a 16-point rout of the Spartans that established the Terps as league contenders for the season. "When I was in high school, games like that used to happen. Today was really special."

Said Michigan State coach Tom Izzo, "I'd have to say that he's the straw that stirs the drink," he said. "There's no question about it."

Trimble kept stirring that drink for what turned out to be a memorable freshman season in which he became the first freshman point guard to be named first-team all-Big Ten since Eric Gordon at Indiana.

Yet with the hype came the heady expectations that seemed to take their toll on Trimble as a sophomore. On a team picked among the favorites to reach the Final Four and win Maryland's second national championship, Trimble never seemed to sustain the mojo.

There were a few Melo moments: a sparkling performance after shaking some early nerves in a close loss at North Carolina in early December and a long three-point shot to beat the buzzer at Wisconsin, Trimble's first-ever game-winner, were the highlights.

A combination of a nagging mid-season hamstring injury and the pressure to live up to the early season hype—including being the preseason Big Ten Player of the Year—seemed to wear on Trimble, whose pro stock plummeted along with his 10-point drop in three-point shooting.

The decision to put his name into the NBA Draft didn't go as planned. Trimble continued to struggle at the NBA Combine in Chicago, where ESPN analysts were in agreement that the 6'3" sophomore needed to return for his junior year.

While Trimble continued to work out for a few NBA teams privately, the public sentiment was much the same: he needed to stay in college and keep trying to regain the magic from his freshman year. Finally, two hours before the deadline, Trimble announced he was coming back.

Already one of the most accomplished players in his first two years as a Terp—the only Maryland player aside from Joe Smith to score at least 500 points in each of his first two seasons—Trimble will come back looking to prove himself as he did as a freshman.

"I think Melo will play with a big chip on his shoulder," Turgeon said the morning after Trimble announced he was returning. "I thought Melo played with a target on his back last year. Melo has been a great player his whole life."

As for Trimble's stock falling, Turgeon said, "It's just the way it played out. I think there are guys who are going to be drafted ahead of Melo and I think Melo is a better player. It's just the way they saw it this year. The great thing for Melo is that he gets to come back, play point guard at the school that he loves, and continue to prove he's a great player."

Meloland was back in business.

89 How Tom Young Nearly Became Coach

When Bud Millikan was fired following the 1966–67 season, there was not much of a coaching search. Frank Fellows, who had been his assistant for a number of years, was simply promoted.

In an ACC that featured some of the best coaches in the country—led by the venerable Frank McGuire at South Carolina, well-respected veteran Vic Bubas at Duke, and a rising star in Dean Smith at North Carolina—Fellows and the Terps were overmatched.

Despite a one-point win over McGuire and the Gamecocks early in the season, Maryland finished 8–16, including 4–10 in the ACC, in Fellows' first year. The second year was worse. Despite Will Hetzel averaging a then-school-record 23.3 points, the Terps went 8–18, 2–12 in the ACC.

Tom Young, who had played on Maryland's 1958 ACC championship team after returning from the Army, had spent the two years as Fellows' assistant after being a head coach at Catholic University in Washington, D.C.

Young knew he would be looking for a job.

After Maryland and Duke lost their respective opening-round games in the ACC tournament, Young recalled walking around Greensboro with Chuck Daly, one of Bubas' assistants who was on his way to replace Bob Cousy as head coach at Boston College.

"He was in a dither because assistant coaches spent most of their time on the road all the time, and he said, 'I don't know hardly anything at all about basketball, I don't know X's and O's,'" Young said. "He said, 'I went up to Boston College, they gave me a nice new office, but I'm scared to death.'"

When Fellows was formally fired after the ACC tournament, Young thought he had a legitimate chance to coach the Terps. But things in College Park changed when Bill Colby, the athletic director, was fired himself shortly after firing Fellows.

Colby was replaced by track coach Jim Kehoe, who quickly fired football coach Bob Ward, a former Terp player and assistant, who came in the same year as Fellows and lost all nine games after 12 players flunked off the team before the season started. The Terps went 2–8 his second year.

When Kehoe hired Lefty Driesell, Young had a couple of options. He could have returned to Catholic as the coach and athletic director. He chose to go to American because it had the budget for Young to hire an assistant. Young brought Tom Davis, who had just finished his doctorate at Maryland, with him to American.

"I thought I had a better chance [to win] at American," Young said.

Taking over basically the same group that had finished 4–19 the year before, the Eagles built into a solid local power that eventually finished 21–6 and made the NIT four years later. He then went to Rutgers after calling the school's new athletic director, Fred Gruninger.

"Tom Davis and I were at the Final Four, we're shooting pool one afternoon, and he said, 'Why don't you call Rutgers?'" recalled Young. "I said, 'Why should I call Rutgers for?' We had a good team and some really good players."

Gruninger wasn't in, but Young left a message.

"A week or two later, I'm sitting in the office at AU and I get a call from Fred Gruninger and I go visit," Young said. "The AD at

AU, Bob Fraley, said that I'd never leave. He was a great AD. We had a great relationship. It wasn't easy leaving."

Young took the job, and three years later—with some of the players recruited by Bob Lloyd and an assistant coach named Dick Vitale—led the Scarlet Knights to an undefeated season before losing two games at the 1976 Final Four. Davis took over for Young at AU and hired a former Maryland point guard named Gary Williams as his assistant.

"It's funny how things work out," Young said.

90 Billy, Jimmy, and Gary's Coaching Tree

Many believe that Maryland's struggle to remain a national power after winning the championship in 2002 coincided with the departure of longtime assistant coaches Billy Hahn and Jimmy Patsos, both of whom became head coaches.

Hahn, who joined Williams for his first year in College Park after being a head coach at Ohio University, left to go to LaSalle in 2001, following Maryland's first trip to the Final Four. Patsos, who had started as a graduate assistant early in Williams' tenure, left in 2003 for Loyola (Maryland).

"Billy was good, especially early on, because we both went through all that," Williams said, referring to the probation imposed by the NCAA for violations committed by former coach Bob Wade. "He was a good addition because he had been a head coach and had been through tough times."

Hahn was a tireless recruiter and spent a lot of time going to high school games and AAU tournaments that became a vital part of recruiting. Patsos had similar DNA and took his talents as a bartender in Georgetown to convincing high school players to come to Maryland.

Hahn's head coaching career was derailed when LaSalle star Gary Neal was accused of sexual assault. Though both Neal and eventually Hahn were cleared of any wrongdoing, Hahn had a difficult time getting another job before landing at West Virginia as an assistant to Bob Huggins.

Patsos struggled for several years trying to rebuild the 1–27 Loyola team that he inherited, but eventually got the Greyhounds into the NCAA tournament for the second time in school history in 2013. He then left to become the head coach at Siena.

While Patsos appears on the brink of getting the Saints in the NCAA tournament, only two of the nine former Williams assistants who took head coaching jobs—Fran Dunphy and Rick Barnes—have had sustained success.

Dunphy, an assistant to Williams at American, was one of the most respected coaches in the Ivy League at Penn, winning a school-record 310 games and 10 league titles in 17 years.

After following the legendary John Chaney at Temple, Dunphy took the Owls to the NCAA tournament six times in the first seven years, has won 214 games, and has gone to the NCAA tournament seven times in 10 years.

Barnes, who was on the Ohio State staff for one year under Williams, is closing in on his mentor's coaching marks. In 29 years as a Division I coach—including 17 at Texas—Barnes has won 619 games as of 2016.

It didn't take long for Barnes to find work after getting fired in 2015, but his first season at Tennessee turned out to be his first losing season (15–19) in a career that has included 21 tournament appearances—with one Final Four, four Sweet 16s, and three Elite Eights.

Fran Fraschilla was an assistant under both Williams (at Ohio State) and Barnes (at Providence) before returning to his native New York as the head coach at both Manhattan and St. John's.

Fraschilla made his way West to New Mexico, where he coached four years before launching a successful career as a color analyst for ESPN, where he currently works.

Hahn spent 12 years with Williams in College Park—one fewer than Patsos—starting out with him there in Williams' first season in 1989 and going through the first Final Four team in 2001.

Hahn, who had been a head coach at Ohio for three seasons prior to returning to his alma mater like Williams, left to become the head coach at LaSalle for three seasons and has been an assistant under Huggins at West Virginia since 2007.

Dave Dickerson, who played at Maryland under both Lefty Driesell and Bob Wade, also returned to his alma mater and finished a six-year stint in 2005 under Williams to become the head coach at Tulane for five seasons before becoming the associate head coach at Ohio State.

Mike Lonergan first made his name as a head coach at Division III Catholic University, where he had played and later led the team to a national championship amid nine NCAA tournament invitations in a 12-year career.

After spending one year with Williams at Maryland, Lonergan got his first Division I head coach job at Vermont, where he took the Catamounts to one NCAA tournament in six years. Lonergan went to George Washington, where the Colonials have also gone to one NCAA tournament and won the NIT in 2016.

Williams even had a Driesell on his staff—Lefty's son Chuck, a former Terp point guard who, like Hahn and Dickerson, came back to College Park for a stint. Driesell spent four years there before becoming the head coach at The Citadel. He is now a high school coach in Washington, D.C.

91 The True Meaning of No. 3

Juan Dixon wore No. 12 at Calvert Hall because the team didn't have any single-digit jerseys. When he arrived at Maryland as a redshirt freshman, he took No. 5 because Terrell Stokes wore 12 and Laron Profit had the number he most wanted, No. 3.

"As soon as Profit graduated, I hopped right in it," Dixon said.

Dixon had always wanted to wear what became an iconic jersey in College Park because his older brother, Phil, had worn it and because his late mother, Juanita, had told Dixon that it represented the three levels of basketball: high school, college, and the NBA.

While it was well-chronicled that his parents both died of AIDS related to their drug addictions, Dixon said that his mother "always knew what my dreams were" and that she would tell him that he would someday play professionally.

"That No. 3 meant a lot to me because I wanted to follow in my brother's footsteps, and my mother knew what my dreams were," Dixon recalled in the spring of 2016. "It's more than just a number, it's a message. A lot of people don't know that."

Dixon also knows how a generation of Maryland fans grew up wearing his number.

One of them was my younger son, who finally retired it when he graduated college in 2015.

It's hard to say whether my son Jordan was Juan Dixon's biggest fan, though it's difficult to find anyone who was more dedicated to keeping what Dixon had done at Maryland on the back of a jersey as long as Jordan did.

It wasn't just for all the basketball teams he played on. No. 3 made it on his back for Little League baseball and JV lacrosse in high school. If he had played football and been a linebacker or offensive guard, he would have somehow talked the coach into giving him his beloved number.

There were other Maryland players he loved, too: from Joe Smith to Steve Francis to Steve Blake to Grevis Vasquez, but there was also something about No. 3. Even after Dixon stopped wearing his own number during a couple of NBA stops, Jordan kept up the tradition.

"It's more than just a number," Juan Dixon said, "it's a message. A lot of people don't know that." (Grant Halverson)

It will be interesting to see how long Maryland keeps No. 3 off limits. When Gary Williams was coaching, no one dared ask for such an iconic number. In Mark Turgeon's third year, incoming freshman Roddy Peters was first issued No. 3, but then changed to No. 2.

The only other number that hasn't been worn by a Maryland player after it was so identified with a former star was No. 34, worn by Len Bias. Considering the attention it would generate—and the pressure it might cause—it seems doubtful that it will be worn again.

92 Redemption in 1984

When the Terps hoisted the ACC tournament trophy at the Greensboro Coliseum for the first and only time during Lefty Driesell's 17 years, a lifetime of near-misses—and one horrendous call four years before—were suddenly wiped away.

In the aftermath of Maryland's 74–62 win over Duke, one fan said, "This was more than just a basketball game. Those North Carolina fans here don't realize that. This culminated 15 years [since Driesell arrived in College Park] of suffering."

Though he would downplay it at the time, as he had done with many big wins, the 74–62 victory over Duke was understandably important to Driesell, who had lost in his five previous final games.

After promising for years that if ever won the ACC tournament, he would attach the trophy to the hood of his car and drive around the state of North Carolina "for several days," Driesell backed off on such bravado.

"I don't think I'll do that now," he said that day. "I was much younger then. I'm 52 years old and I better go home and get some sleep…. It would be a little fun, but I'm flying back with the team."

Said athletic director Jim Kehoe, the man who had hired Driesell away from Davidson in 1969, "You don't know how much this win means to the man. He deserves every bit of attention he'll get now."

Keith Gatlin, then a freshman who had grown up in Greenville, North Carolina, recalled a different Lefty in the team's locker room.

"He was very pumped up," said Gatlin, who was the team's point guard. "For so many years the ACC championship was eluding him. Obviously, he was happy, and there was a sense of pride that he was the person who brought it back to College Park after a long, long time."

Gatlin was all too familiar with a couple of the famous ACC tournament finals where the Terps had nearly won. But this time there would be no otherworldly performance by an opponent—as there had been by Tom Burleson in 1974—and no controversial call.

Make no mistake: there were many Maryland fans in the building that day and possibly one tall baldheaded coach who believed that the victory against the Blue Devils in 1984 was payback for when Buck Williams was undercut by Kenny Dennard going for an easy putback to win in 1980.

This one was simply a basketball game, and the Terps might have benefited from the fact that Duke had played a closely contested game against archrival North Carolina in the semis. Though Maryland had also won a close semifinal against Wake Forest, there was not the same emotion involved.

Gatlin called the 1984 game "a tale of two halves" in that Duke's Johnny Dawkins dominated the first half and Len Bias dominated the second half. The two sophomores were the league's rising stars and were ready to take over as the ACC's top player after Michael Jordan departed Chapel Hill.

"Johnny Dawkins couldn't miss in the first half, he was having his way with us," Gatlin said. "We went to a zone in the second half and we got a couple of stops and we got some momentum and Lenny went crazy. Everybody played well, but Lenny just took off in the second half. You couldn't stop him."

Bias wound up scoring 16 of his 26 points in the second half, including 10 during a 24–3 Maryland run that erased what became a 42–34 lead to help put the game away.

Gatlin said that Bias benefited from the fact that he didn't have to bang inside because Ben Coleman was "doing the grunt work" inside and Herman Veal "was a junkyard dog, and Lenny could roam, hit the glass, and just concentrate on scoring."

It meant a lot to Gatlin, who grew up an N.C. State fan hating both Duke and North Carolina.

"It was sweet because anytime you could win an ACC Championship in Greensboro, that was big, because it was a Carolina-based tournament and a Carolina-based league," Gatlin said.

Gatlin had committed to the Wolfpack as a junior in high school; during Gatlin's senior year, N.C. State won the national championship and both Jim Valvano and his top recruiter, Tommy Abatemarco, had told Gatlin that he would take over after Sidney Lowe and Dereck Whittenburg graduated.

During the summer after his junior year, Gatlin won the award for the best playmaker at the Five-Star camp, and "it just took off from there." Among those who wanted the lanky point guard with the accurate set shot was Driesell.

"I told State I was coming and then I went on my visit and fell in love with Maryland," Gatlin said. "It was very hard to leave the state of North Carolina, but Maryland had a great track record with

Eastern North Carolina guys—Buck Williams, Charles Pittman, John Lucas."

There was a story circulating around the campus after Gatlin committed to Maryland that the reason he chose the Terps was that he had made a bet with a secretary in Driesell's office over a tennis game. She said that if she beat him, he'd have to choose Maryland.

"She did beat me, but that's not the reason I came to Maryland," Gatlin said with a laugh. "It's funny, all the times I played her after I came to Maryland, she never won once."

93 Bison Dele, RIP

When the news came of former NBA player Bison Dele's death in July of 2002, there was barely a ripple of recognition that this was the same person who Maryland fans cheered loudly—though briefly—as Brian Williams during his one season in College Park.

Though not nearly as shocking as when Len Bias had died 16 years before from a cocaine overdose, it was just as tragic. Dele, who had played eight years in the NBA before retiring suddenly after signing a big contract with the Detroit Pistons, was 33.

The circumstances of Dele's death were murky.

Police believe Dele and his girlfriend were killed by Dele's brother, who authorities surmise dumped the bodies while the three were aboard a 57-foot sailboat in the Pacific, somewhere off the coast of Tahiti.

Dele's brother, Kevin Williams, who had changed his name to Miles Dabord, later overdosed on insulin.

Of all the players who had passed through Maryland during the basketball team's modern era, Brian Williams was one of the most intriguing. He stayed only a season playing for Bob Wade in 1987–88 before transferring to Arizona, but he left his mark.

Williams had not only played a significant role in Wade's demise as a college coach—saying that he didn't think he'd improve his game had he stayed—but he had played a big role in one of Wade's most significant victories.

It came during Wade's second year at Duke when Williams, a freshman, scored three times on Maryland's first four possessions and set the tone for a 72–69 upset of the seventh-ranked Blue Devils at Cameron Indoor Stadium.

An hour before the game, the laconic Wiliams strode onto the court, the only Terp, and smiled at his surroundings. The smile grew larger when Duke fans started chanting "Overrated...overrated" at a player whom many considered one of the best young big men in the country.

From a corner of the gym, Duke coach Mike Krzyzewski watched.

"He just kind of soaked in the atmosphere," Krzyzewski said a few days later. "He got a feel for what it was going to be like. Once the game started, he wasn't intimidated. He sparked them at the beginning of the game.... A lot of seniors wouldn't do that [come out by himself]."

Though not nearly as spectacular as the 41-point performance Bias had as a senior at Cameron, Williams finished with 14 points, seven rebounds, and the ultimate respect for the Maryland freshman. Williams liked it so much that he called Krzyzewski when he was considering transferring.

Williams simply summed up the experience as "interesting," which is how many who knew the 6'9" forward summed up Williams.

The son of Gene Williams, a musician and one of the original Platters, Brian Williams spent much of his childhood in Las Vegas before his parents got divorced and he moved with his mother, Patricia Phillips, and his brother to the Los Angeles suburbs.

Though he could have played for any college team in the country, he chose the Terps.

Though some thought it was a prearranged marriage made by recruiting powerbroker Sonny Vaccaro after Wade had lost Alonzo Mourning to Georgetown the previous year, Williams likened his decision to play for a program still reeling from the death of Len Bias two years before to investing in the stock market.

"It's like buying a blue-chip stock when it's down," Williams said.

On the only winning team Wade had in his three years in College Park, Williams averaged 12.3 points and six rebounds, shooting a little better than 61 percent from the field.

Williams might have been the biggest beneficiary of Buzzy Braman's short-lived role as the team's free throw shooting guru. Shooting around 40 percent before Braman arrived unannounced one day at practice, Williams finished the season shooting 60 percent from the line.

By the time he was done with his freshman year, Williams had become one of the leaders on Wade's only NCAA tournament team, one that finished 18–13 with a second-round loss to Kentucky in Cincinnati. He was expected to be the centerpiece of the program going forward.

When word got out that he was thinking about leaving, Maryland students staged a rally in front of his dorm and put together a petition pleading that he stay. Wade and Perkins went as far as to fly out to California to talk with Williams and his mother.

It didn't help. By late May he had made his decision and by July he was on his way to Arizona. After sitting out the next season and playing two years for Lute Olson, Williams was the 10th overall pick of the Orlando Magic after his redshirt junior year in 1991.

Williams was known more for his weirdly well-rounded nature—including the name change and teaching himself how to play several musical instruments—than for anything he had done on the court in the NBA.

His high school coach in California said it best when Williams was a freshman at Maryland.

"Brian is a very sensitive kid," said Saint Monica High School coach Leo Klemm. "Somewhat eclectic, he fit in with a lot of different kids here, not just athletes. Maybe because of his background, he doesn't get all excited from the bright lights."

Far from those bright lights, somewhere in the Pacific near Tahiti, Bison Dele died.

Back in Maryland, barely anyone noticed or remembered that he was once Brian Williams.

94 The Turgeonites

Mark Turgeon was in his first season, struggling to find a rotation with the players who remained after the retirement of Gary Williams. Alex Len, an incoming seven-foot freshman from Ukraine, had been suspended for his first 10 games by the NCAA after accepting per diem from a pro team.

There was little excitement about the team during games at the Comcast Center, and sophomore students Jamie Morris and Cory Frontin wanted to do something to get the few fans that showed up pumped to see the Terps.

"We really admired Turgeon, we really liked the person and the coach," recalled Morris. "We got the sense that he left Texas A&M because he wanted to come to a program with a rich basketball tradition and we didn't think people were giving him the love he deserved."

One night at dinner in the South Campus dining hall right before winter break, Frontin mentioned that he had bought a new suit and suggested that he and Morris should wear suits to the first game after finals, against Cornell, and try to look and act like the new coach.

"The real problem was how people are going to know we're not just frat guys dressing up in suits, part of a [fraternity] rush," Morris said. "We came up with the idea that we would put some chalk in our hair. It didn't work very well so we switched to baby powder."

Morris and Frontin recruited a number of their friends, including a couple of female students, to join them. Steve Ernst became a regular and helped choreograph some of the dance moves the group made.

Justin Sawyer, Morris' cousin, took part, even though he was still attending a local junior college and had to sneak into the student section.

"We didn't think it had any staying power, we figured we'd do it two or three times, and the message would get across," Morris said. "We did it intermittently toward the end of the non-conference season and people told us, 'We like what you're doing, do it for some conference games.'"

The group got some air time on national television for a home game against North Carolina. ESPN color analyst and Maryland alum Len Elmore had been tipped off about the coach's look-alikes and called them "The Turgeonites."

"We did not take it seriously enough to give ourselves a name, but he thought it was pretty funny," Morris said. "We never wanted the attention to be about us, we just wanted people to be excited about Maryland basketball and about the Terps."

A tradition was born.

Ann Turgeon, whose seats were a couple of rows in front of the student section, told them she loved the act, especially the gray spots in their hair.

"She informed us that he [Turgeon] was getting a little self-conscious, that it was getting a little too gray," Morris said.

Turgeon's two sons, Will and Leo, eventually dressed up for a game and joined the Turgeonites.

The only problem is that the original Turgeonites would eventually graduate, turning the act over to Sawyer and others. Sawyer's two years at Maryland were memorable as a Turgeonite, since they coincided with the team's return to the NCAA tournament in 2015.

Sawyer admits that things got a little dicey when the Terps fell back to 17–15 in 2013–14, and Turgeon was on the hot seat after five players with remaining eligibility left.

"We thought, *We love doing this and we still love the coach and everything, but we're not sure if he's still going to be around*," Sawyer recalled. "We kept it going, and eventually things turned around and everything. It was kind of cool to be there during an interesting time."

If there was a positive about being a Turgeonite when the team wasn't as good, it was securing prominent seats right behind the bench did not take a lot of work. Sawyer has passed on the leadership to another friend currently in grad school.

"We're trying to keep it going, passing it down the line," Sawyer said. "It was kind of a nice thing to do throughout college, but we're content to pass it on to a new generation of Terp fans. It kind of exceeded our wildest expectations."

95 Will The Big Ten Ever Feel Like Home?

Of all the moves made throughout the country in the rapidly changing world of big-time college sports, Maryland's decision to leave the ACC after 60 years for the Big Ten seemed to make the most sense and elicit the most emotional response from its fans.

While many of the school's longtime boosters and former athletes were basically kept in the dark as university president Wallace D. Loh and Big Ten commissioner Jim Delany negotiated quickly and quietly behind closed doors, the bottom line made total sense.

The payout—more than double the ACC's $17 million television package per school at the time with the potential of it getting up to $45 million annually—seemed to placate many. The reality that the ACC no longer looked anything like the league the Terps joined in 1953 also took some of the edge off the decision.

Not that Delany was oblivious to the angst of many in leaving the ACC.

"I know there's some ambivalence and maybe some anger," Delany said in addressing Maryland fans. "But I hope that over time, we can embrace each other and realize that we can be better together than we were apart."

More than two years into the marriage, most have forgotten what they were so upset about. The ACC, with the addition of Louisville and Syracuse, looks nothing like the league Maryland was a part of for so many years.

"We went from one nice neighborhood to another great neighborhood," men's soccer coach Sasho Cirovski said on the one-year anniversary in 2014. "I can tell you nobody has been talking about the ACC around here for a while. You look at the success across the board, and it was just fantastic. Right now, everyone is extremely excited about the Big Ten."

Winning more titles (seven) than any school in its first year also helped defuse the situation for coaches and other critics who didn't like the move, but couldn't say so publicly. Former basketball star Tom McMillen, who was outspoken against the move when it was announced, had started to change his mind.

"As I look back on it, this has been a positive decision," McMillen said during the summer of 2014. "The revenue side is so compelling, I think if they would have showed us in a little greater deliberation, I think it would have put away a lot of concerns right away."

Three years after eliminating seven sports to reduce a reported $21 million deficit, $15 million in first-year ticket sales spurred by a 14 percent rise in attendance helped the once financially strapped athletic program "meet our projections," according to athletic director Kevin Anderson.

As for Mark Turgeon's program, the first two years brought success on the court and a continued uptick in recruiting. Turgeon acknowledged that the team's signing of Diamond Stone, who had long been considered a lock to stay in state at Wisconsin, was the result of the Big Ten's draw.

After being picked 10th going into the first season, 2014–15, Maryland finished a surprising second with a 14–4 record and beat Wisconsin, the league's regular season and tournament champion, in its only meeting that inaugural season.

Picked to finish first going into its second year, Maryland finishing a disappointing tied for third at 12–6 after a late-season slump. But as the two years unfolded, rivalries started to develop that would soon make Terp fans not harp on the loss of Duke and North Carolina.

"The only rival we had [in the ACC] was Duke and Carolina, and we weren't their rival," Gary Williams said. "That's sentimental and it's all nice, but as you get older, those are very important to you. But at the same time, the Big Ten in what they're doing with the TV network and things like that, it's where it is right now.

"To be in a league like the Big Ten is very exciting for the students now in school who started when the Big Ten started. That's going to be fine. They're going to have their rivalries. There's going to be opportunities to feel like it's a Duke game or a Carolina game was for us."

Instead of the Blue Devils and Coach K, there were the Michigan State Spartans and Coach I. Instead of the Tar Heels and the Dean Dome, there were the Indiana Hoosiers and trips to Assembly Hall. Instead of visits to outposts like Blackburg and Tallahassee, there were equally long jaunts to Lincoln and Iowa City.

Gary Williams, who coached in the Big Ten at Ohio State before coming to Maryland in 1989, said that the "old fans will never look on the Big Ten the same [as the ACC], that's just the way it is…you've got to watch being provincial.

"It's okay for the ACC to bring in eight Big East teams, but it's not okay for Maryland to go to the Big Ten? When I say that, people say, 'You might be right about that. Who was our football rival when we were in the ACC? We never had a football rival.'"

96 Maryland's First African American Player

Two years before Texas Western made college basketball history at Cole Field House, Billy Jones made his own history in College Park, becoming the first black men's basketball player at Maryland as well as in the ACC.

Jones, who grew up outside of Baltimore and led Towson High to a state championship at Cole Field House, joined a team that included a sophomore point guard named Gary Williams. While Pete Johnson, another African American, was recruited with Jones, he wound up being held out because of academics.

"Billy fit in from Day One," said Williams. "I don't remember an awkward situation with the players. The tough part was that Billy always had to be on his guard. I'm sure there were things said by people around campus that really bothered him, but he never showed it and, by doing so, he paved the way for other [ACC] schools to recruit black players."

Jones said he was accepted by his teammates on a campus where he was one of around 200 black students, including a football player, Darryl Hill, who had arrived in 1963.

"Society on the College Park campus was no different than anywhere else," Jones said. "As much as possible, we did things together, but Gary Williams and the rest of the guys were welcome in places where I was not. You're captain of the basketball team as a senior, and you get no offers to join a fraternity? I understood. I wasn't even irritated."

Not that there weren't moments when Jim Crow reared its ugly head.

"One night we were to take a late train home from Durham [North Carolina] after a game at Duke," Williams recalled. "We all piled into the snack bar to eat before boarding. But when they wouldn't serve Billy, we all left."

There were also times when Jones was made to feel proud for what he was doing.

"We were sitting in a hotel restaurant in New Orleans when a black chef came out of the kitchen, shook my hand without saying a word, and walked away," he said. "Or I'd be walking through the Charlotte [North Carolina] airport with the team when a bellhop tapped me on the shoulder and gave me a wink as if to say, 'Hey, black guy, keep doin' what you're doin.'"

Gary Williams said that he and the other players on the team got a taste of what Jones and later Johnson went through when Jones took a group of teammates to a concert in Washington, D.C.

"There was a big rumor that the Temptations were going to be there," Williams recalled for a 2002 book *Tales from Cole Field House*. "The Temps didn't show, but there were eight other acts. You never thought about Billy's situation, 'What's it like to be the only black guy on the team?' But when you walked into that theatre, you looked around [being the only white people] and you said, 'Wow.'"

What's interesting were two games less than a month apart at the end of Jones' sophomore year.

The first was one Jones played in for the Terps, in the ACC tournament in Raleigh, North Carolina. In the same state where four black men known as "The Greensboro Four" staged a sit-in at a local Woolworth department store, Jones suited up against the Tar Heels.

Jones said he received a fairly warm reception from some of the fans.

"Some basketball people appreciated what I was doing," Jones said.

Except for hearing a South Carolina fan using a racial epithet during a game in Columbia earlier that season, Jones said that he received "better treatment" in the ACC than he did back home in Baltimore during high school, where he was once hit with a stick in the groin during a lacrosse game and had a team bus rocked after a basketball game.

One of the things Jones did with his teammates was sneak in through the back door of Cole Field House to watch the 1966 NCAA championship game between Texas Western, which featured the first black starting lineup and lily-white Kentucky.

That game opened a lot of eyes across the country, even Jones'.

"From a historical perspective, I didn't realize what I was watching when Kentucky played Texas Western," Jones said. "I can remember Texas Western reminding me of how we played back home. It was the city game. There was a sense of pride in watching those guys play. They reminded me of the guys back home."

Jones would later become a Division I head coach at Maryland-Baltimore County, leading the Retrievers to five winning seasons in 10 years before going into private business. For years, Jones said he would receive letters from college students asking him to reflect on being a groundbreaker.

"As one who took on a challenge and didn't back down," he said. "I went to college, did as asked, got my degree, and moved on. I made a positive impact and—if you understand the time we were in—you know the complexities that were involved…. I tell the kids, 'Be selfless. Do things that have social impact. Leave a mark that people will remember.'"

97 The Probation Years

Two of the better coaching jobs Gary Williams thought he did during his 22-year career at Maryland came with the Terps in the throes of an unfairly harsh probation handed to the program in the aftermath of Bob Wade's firing.

With NCAA investigators on campus for much of the 1989–90 season, Maryland finished a respectable 19–14, including a 6–8 ACC record that saw the Terps sweep North Carolina. If not for the expected probation, Williams thought his team deserved an NCAA tournament bid.

Perhaps the best coaching job Williams ever did in his Hall of Fame career came the second year, after leading scorer Jerrod Mustaf left for the NBA and starting point guard Teyon McCoy transferred to Texas when the probation was announced.

Unable to bring in high school stars who wanted to play in the NCAA tournament—not to mention on television, which the Terps were not allowed to do for the first season of a three-year probation—Williams had to make do.

Led by Walt Williams, whose decision to remain in College Park has long been credited by Gary Williams as the reason the program didn't disappear into oblivion, the Terps got off to a respectable 8–4 start that included winning the ECAC Holiday Festival over No. 12 South Carolina.

"For a guy to make his decision not to transfer, after his sophomore year, that's incredible. That wouldn't happen today, guys would go," Gary Williams recalled a quarter-century later.

Even when Williams missed a large chunk of the ACC schedule with a broken leg, the Terps remained fairly competitive. Maryland won seven of the 13 games they played without their leading scorer, largely due to the heroics of transfer Matt Roe and former walk-on Vince Broadnax.

"I've always felt they've not gotten the credit," Williams said. "A lot of things got lost with Joe Smith and Keith Booth [arriving in 1995]. Those two guys changed the program, but all those guys did a great job the first couple of years."

Gary Williams recalled after his first losing season in 1991–92 when the Terps finished 14–15 how appreciative he was of his team, which was led by Walt Williams, the ACC's top scorer, but also by the likes of defensive ace Cedric Lewis, the younger brother of former defensive ace Derrick Lewis.

After finishing the 1992-93 season with a 36-point loss to top-ranked North Carolina in the ACC tournament, Gary Williams recalled a reporter telling him in the locker room, "Now that the sanctions are off for next year, you guys will really play hard."

Williams, knowing what the program had been through, nearly exploded.

"I said to him, 'Are you kidding me? Did you watch the game?'" Williams told him. "These guys were playing for the love of the game, that's all they played for, that's all they had. There was no NIT. No nothing. This was it. And yet they played as hard as any team I ever coached."

98 The Fuel That Drove Dixon

When he showed up on the Maryland campus in the spring of 1997, nobody paid much attention to Juan Dixon. He looked more like a high jumper than a basketball player, a 145-pounder on a 6'3" body.

"I was a tough 145," he said.

Dixon joined a team that was a mix of veterans like fellow Baltimorean Rodney Elliott and Lithuanian Sarunas Jasikeviscious, as well as up-and-coming standouts such as Terrell Stokes, Laron Profit, and Obinna Ekezie.

"I felt like a little kid being around grown men," Dixon recalled.

Yet inside, Dixon had the same confidence he had at Calvert Hall, where he became the school's all-time leading scorer.

"I was very confident," Dixon said. "I knew coming into Maryland that I had a lot of doubters, wondering what Coach Williams and his staff were doing offering me a scholarship. I always believed in myself and my ability to contribute at Maryland."

While Dixon can't recall a particular practice his redshirt freshman year that gave a glimpse of what was in store, he could tell that "Coach was excited that he had a kid who could put the ball in the hole in a variety of ways—behind the three-point line, mid-range, or get in the paint."

As part of the scout team, Dixon liked replicating certain teams. Ironically, one of his favorite to imitate was the hated Duke Blue Devils.

"Duke played at a fast pace, up and down, shot threes," Dixon said. "There was probably a practice or two where I went off and made shots at a high level. I didn't back down. There were times when I would play pickup, I didn't back down to anyone. I wanted to show those guys I belonged."

The confidence had been a part of Dixon's game ever since he was 15 or 16 years old.

"It started with my big brother and, of course, I wanted to follow in his footsteps," said Dixon. "Watching him play basketball through the city of Baltimore, seeing who he competed against. I remember the first time I beat him one-on-one, he never took it easy. I just went nuts, I left the court, screaming and yelling. My confidence took off from there."

During the summer before his junior year at Calvert Hall, Dixon had to remain in Baltimore to go to summer school while his AAU team was playing in tournaments outside the city. In a summer league game against older college players, Dixon scored 55 points.

"My coach at the time, his name was 'Baseline,' and he just let me go, let me play," Dixon said. "From there, I knew I was capable of playing basketball at a high level. I felt like if I wanted to score, I could score on anyone. That's when it started."

Dixon didn't have any delusions of grandeur when he got to Maryland.

"I didn't go into the record books and see who's the leading scorer, who was the leading three-point shooter," Dixon said. "I loved the game so much and I was just so passionate about winning. I just wanted to do my job, whatever it was, to help this team win games. Everything else worked itself out."

Playing behind Stokes and Francis as a freshman, Dixon said that whatever time he got he earned.

"I worked my ass off," he said. "I wanted to prove I belonged. Me breaking scoring records and three-point records, that wasn't on my agenda. I knew that I wanted to perform well. I knew I wanted to prove all the naysayers wrong. I wanted to prove Coach Williams right. He put his neck on the line for me and I felt I had to do the same in return."

99 Memories of Len Bias

Thirty years tends to dull the memory for many about most things in their lives.

For those who played with, coached, or even followed Len Bias during his career at Maryland, the three decades since his tragic death in June of 1986 do little to erase those snapshots from his remarkable career in College Park.

Dave Dickerson was a freshman when Bias was a senior, a quiet country boy from Beaufort, South Carolina, who was admittedly a little intimidated being on the same court—and playing the same position—as Bias.

"There was something about Lenny that I had never seen in a person and a basketball player—he had 'it,' whatever that 'it' is, he had it," said Dickerson, who returned to his alma mater as an assistant under Gary Williams and is now associate head coach at Ohio State.

"He had the flair, he had the charisma. Most importantly the two things I saw in him that I haven't seen in a player to this day is the work ethic and toughness and his competitiveness. It's the best I have seen to this day.

"He was the toughest person at the University of Maryland, he was the toughest basketball player in the country; there was nobody tougher. He was tougher than Armon Gilliam at UNLV, he was tougher than Olden Polynice at Virginia, he was tougher than any player that I have seen. It was on display every day and he made it look easy.

"In the preseason he won every race. He outlifted everybody on the team. He outshot everybody on the team. And those things he took pride in. He won every sprint [at practice]. He won every shooting drill. He won every rebounding drill. He won every defensive drill. This was back in the day when the ACC was real. Everybody had a great player, and he was the best of all the great players in the best league in college basketball."

Lefty Driesell, who for years couldn't bring himself to even talk about Bias, said that he saw Bias evolve from a temperamental high school player at nearby Northwestern High to a player who worked harder than any he ever coached in his 17 years in College Park.

"He used to play one-on-one full court in the off-season and the summers, and that's why he was in such great shape," Driesell recalled. "I think I told him Michael Jordan used to do that. He was the only one—football or basketball—that could bench 300 pounds at that time."

Driesell said he also gave Bias a tip that Driesell had used during his own college career at Duke.

"I told him to jump as high as he could on his jump shot, and nobody could block him," Driesell said. "That's what I tried to teach all my players, but he jumped really high on his jump shot.

That's why he could always get it off, even when he had his back to the basket.... He didn't take bad shots."

Driesell said that Bias never got his due on the defensive end.

"He was a great defensive player," Driesell said. "When we beat North Carolina down there at the Dean Dome, I think we were one ahead, and he made the block on Brad Daugherty's shot. Then he dunked it back over his head. He was a great rebounder, too."

Recruited by only a handful of schools and seriously courted by only two other programs, North Carolina State and Oregon, Bias picked the Terps because of their proximity to his family's home and the relationship he had established with Driesell after attending summer camp at Cole Field House.

"He lived about five blocks from the school, he was one of the easier ones to recruit," Driesell said. "The only one I thought I had to beat to get him was [Jim] Valvano."

Dickerson said that Bias had a tremendous influence on him.

"From a personal standpoint, I became a better basketball player and a better teammate from being around him for one year because I got a great tutorial in what it took to be a great player," Dickerson said. "I appreciated what it took to be a Terrapin. I took away from him the pride of the university and for the basketball program."

What Dickerson uses to this day was what he noticed in Bias' relationship with Driesell.

"You need to have a relationship with your head coach," Dickerson said. "From what I observed, Coach Driesell and Lenny had a great relationship. And if you're going to be as good as he was, you need to have a collaborative partnership effort, and Lenny had that with Coach Driesell. I saw Juan Dixon had that with Gary Williams and I've seen Jared Sullinger had that with Thad Matta."

Karl Anthony-Towns, who won NBA Rookie of the Year in 2016, lists Bias as the player he would most like to emulate.

Dickerson relayed the story: "When he signed [with the Minnesota Timberwolves], somebody asked him who his favorite athlete of all time was, and he said, 'Leonard Bias.' The guy who was asking said, 'Leonard Bias? He was deceased 20 years before you were born.' He said that he had one of his jerseys. Where he got that, I don't know."

Driesell still gets upset when he hears those who believe that Bias' drug overdose brought irreversible shame to Maryland.

"It bothers me that people say that Leonard Bias hurt the University of Maryland.... Guys like Walt Williams and Tony Massenburg came to Maryland because of Len Bias," Driesell said. "A lot of guys did.... Leonard Bias is one of the greatest things that ever happened to Maryland. He's still getting Maryland publicity, you know what I mean?"

100 My Career in College Park

My 30-plus years around the Maryland basketball team didn't get off to a stellar start.

In Denver to cover the 1985 PGA Championship, I had to call Lefty Driesell to get his reaction to a story in a Norfolk, Virginia, newspaper that said there was a "50–50 chance" that he would leave Maryland and return to his hometown to coach Old Dominion.

The phone rang at his beach house in Delaware and I introduced myself as the team's new beat writer for the *Baltimore Sun*.

"I'm on vacation," Driesell growled in a drawl that would become very familiar to me.

That was followed by a distinct click, a sound that this generation doesn't understand.

I tried again.

He didn't wait to hear who was calling, though this was before caller ID.

"I told you, son, I'm on vacation," he said.

Another click.

A couple of weeks later, I was on campus to interview athletic director Dick Dull. Dull's secretary told me he'd be right out of a meeting, and when his door opened, Driesell was with him. Dull had not heard about our encounter earlier on the phone.

"Coach, this is our new beat writer for the *Baltimore Sun*," Dull said.

I tried to break the ice by saying that we had, uh, talked.

"I'm sorry, you know I was on vacation, you know I didn't mean anything by it," Driesell said.

It was the start of a great relationship that lasted one year professionally and continues to this day.

My relationship with Driesell took some interesting twists and turns that first year, including going on a recruiting trip to my hometown, Brooklyn, New York.

The team had lost the night before for its fifth straight loss to start the ACC season, and there I was sitting next to him the next morning on a bumpy flight to New York.

"I guess this is fitting," Driesell cracked, giving me my lead to a story I was writing about the coach.

One of the more interesting moments that first season came after a practice, and I was taking shots with a walk-on from Baltimore named Mitch Kasoff. At the time, I was 32 and had not played basketball in a couple of years.

"You want to play one on one?" Kasoff asked.

We did, and after I hit a couple of early shots, some of Kasoff's teammates stayed to watch. There was a point late in a game to 11 where things were tight, and I had the ball in the low post, pump faked Kasoff into the air, and hit the shot after he came down.

"Where did you learn that?" Kasoff asked.

"The streets, Mitch, the streets," I joked.

Knowing that his teammates would have given him a very hard time had he lost to an aging sportswriter and having gotten my point across to those watching, including Len Bias, that I knew a little about the sport I was covering, I relaxed a little and Kasoff won.

That first year was an interesting one in terms of covering one of the most memorable personalities in my career—Driesell. Though the Terps recovered from their slow start, they were still on the NCAA tournament bubble going into their last home game against Virginia.

After calling Virginia athletic director Dick Schultz, the head of the NCAA tournament selection committee, to ask about Maryland's chances, I then informed Driesell that Schultz had told me the Terps had to beat the Cavaliers the next day at Cole Field House.

"Dick Schultz, he's the Virginia AD, what does he know?" Driesell barked.

Reminding Driesell that he was also in charge of the selection committee, I got perhaps the best quote ever given to any sportswriter.

"If we don't get in, it'll be the biggest rip-off since the Louisiana Purchase," Driesell said.

That professional relationship as coach–beat reporter didn't last. Three months after the season ended with a second-round NCAA tournament defeat to UNLV in Long Beach, California, Bias was dead. Four months after that, Driesell walked sadly out of Cole Field House with his wife and daughter to close his 17-year career at Maryland.

But my association with Maryland went on, through Bob Wade and Gary Williams and now with Mark Turgeon.

One of my favorite memories of Maryland's championship weekend in 2002 was my seven-year-old son, Jordan, getting every player on the team to autograph his hat. But there was one missing—Williams. "He's only the coach," Jordan said.

A few years later, Jordan sheepishly asked Williams to autograph his hat.

As sad as it was to see Driesell leave in 1986, it was equally emotional to watch Williams at his retirement press conference in the spring of 2011, choking on his words but walking out of Comcast Center with one last fist pump.

Now, in the spring of 2016, it will be interesting to see where the Terps will go under Turgeon. It took him four years to get Maryland back in the NCAA tournament and five to get the Terps into the Sweet 16 for the first time since 2003.

Just as I got to watch Bias play his senior year, and Joe Smith play two and Keith Booth go all four, it was fun to see the development of Dez Wells—both on and off the court—during his three seasons in College Park and see Melo Trimble come back with what Turgeon said will be a "chip on his shoulder" for his junior year.

Will there be another dynasty at Maryland? Will it be like the one that was left a little unfulfilled in the era of McMillen, Lucas, and Elmore or the one that wasn't with Dixon, Baxter, and Blake?

Cole Field House will become an indoor football practice facility in the near future, and Xfinity Center might have a few more name changes in years to come. But Maryland will remain a basketball school, especially given the dynamics of the Big Ten.

Fear the Turtle.

Sources

Baltimore Sun, Friday, August 8, 2014, "G. Williams still emotional about return to UM Basketball Hall of Fame." Author: Don Markus

Baltimore Sun, November 30, 1993, "Freshman Smith bursts on Terps scene, soaring above Williams' fears." Author: Don Markus

Baltimore Sun, November 17, 2015, "Star recalls his shining debut, Joe Smith's big first game as a Terp in background as Hoyas visit to renew rivalry." Author: Don Markus

Baltimore Sun, Friday, October 18, 2013, "Memories, fans rush back at Cole Field House Former home of Terps will house a sellout crowd as Maryland Madness returns."

Baltimore Sun, October 19, 2013, "Like old times Driesell, Williams, ex-players join raucous celebration of new teams." Author: Don Markus

Baltimore Sun, Friday, August 8, 2014, "G. Williams still emotional about return to UM, Basketball Hall of Fame." Author: Don Markus

Baltimore Sun Magazine, 1980, "Maryland Red, White and Amen." Author: Kent Baker

SI.com "How Maryland started Midnight Madness with a midnight run in 1971." Oct. 14, 2014

Baltimore Sun, Nov. 30, 2006, "UM Meets Challenge, Vasquez foils Illini with Ibekwe out." Author: Heather Dinich

Baltimore Sun, March 4, 2002, "Cheers, tears, victory bring down the house Finale: Maryland ends the Cole Field House era with a win against Virginia and a celebration of 47 years of teams, players and fans." Authors: Paul McMullen and Don Markus

Baltimore Sun, Oct. 13, 2013, "Like old times, Driesell, Williams, ex-players join raucous celebration of new teams" Author: Don Markus

Baltimore Sun, May 6, 2011, "Retirement stuns coach's friends, No hint came at booster function this week." Author: Don Markus

Baltimore Sun, August 9, 2014, "G. Williams reflects on enshrinement, 22-year Terps coach's peers and players sing his praises at Naismith Hall of Fame." Author: Don Markus

Baltimore Sun, June 18, 2006, "A hole unfilled, The once-storied Celtics have been unable to recapture their magic since Len Bias' death, Len Bias: 20 years later." Author: Don Markus

Baltimore Sun, January 28, 2001, "Late Duke rally stuns UM, 10-point deficit erased in final :54 of 2nd half; Devils win in OT, 98–96" Author: Gary Lambrecht

Baltimore Sun, May 10, 2011, "A new era Terps tap Texas A&M's Turgeon as next coach." Author: Jeff Barker

Baltimore Sun, October 4, 2014, "'Bias' induction into Athletics Hall of Fame 'way overdue' Nearly two decades after death, former Terps star among eight honorees. Author: Matt Zenitz

Baltimore Sun, July 17, 2014, "UM to induct Bias into its Hall of Fame, Overdose death of Terps basketball star in 1986 threw program into turmoil. Author: Don Markus

ESPN, Grantland, March 13, 2013, "JJ Redick on playing JJ Redick". Author: Robert Mays

Baltimore Sun, April 8, 2007, "Tamir Goodman hasn't lived up to the hype, but he is true to his beliefs 'Jewish Jordan' still keeping the faith." Author: John Murphy

Baltimore Sun, September 11, 1999, "Goodman picks up dribble, tells Terps he isn't coming; Friction over Sabbath miffs Jewish recruit." Authors: Paul McMullen and Ken Rosenthal

Arizona Republic, May 6, 2016, "Alex Len Saves A Friend From Drowning in the Dominican Republic." Author: Paul Caro

Baltimore Sun, Tuesday, April 2, 2002, "UM front line pulls inside job on Indiana, Baxter, Wilcox, Holden too tough for Hoosiers to handle down stretch" Author: Ken Murray

Baltimore Sun, March 2, 1995, "Smith put-back helps Maryland put down Duke." Author: Don Markus

Baltimore Sun, March 3, 1995, "Terps' Hahn wins attention in fill-in role RAVE REVIEW." Author: Don Markus

Baltimore Sun, March 17, 1999, "Baxter handles heavier burden; Maryland: Since Obinna Ekezie went down, low-key freshman Lonny Baxter has muscled up, providing the Terps with solid play at the center position." Author: Paul McMullen

Baltimore Sun, February 6, 2002, "Man behind muscle finds fitting career, Terps' strength coach excels at conditioning" Author: Gary Lambrecht

Baltimore Sun, March 30, 2002, Saturday, March 30, 2002 "TOP TERP, Juan Dixon: A close examination of his career reveals a strong argument for the senior guard as Maryland's all-time best player." Author: Paul McMullen

Testudo Times, March 3, 2016, "Maryland has a student ticket problem." Author: Alex Kirschner

Baltimore Sun, Jan. 24, 1988, "No Mere Freshman: Terps' Williams Shows Maturity on and Off the Court." Author: Don Markus

Baltimore Sun, April 4, 2014, "Towson's Jones Reflects On Being Maryland's First African American in Basketball." Author: Mike Klingaman

Baltimore Sun, December 10, 1999, "History in black, white and gray; College basketball: The Wildcats' 1966 NCAA title game loss to Texas Western in College Park ranks as one of the sport's most important games, but those touched by the event place it in the context of the times. KENTUCKY RETURNS TO COLE." Author: Paul McMullen